BREAKFAST EPIPHANIES

Sara and Toby live in Sussex.

BREAKFAST EPIPHANIES

*How we planned our modern marriage
and stayed true to ourselves*

Sara Hulse and Toby Starbuck

ATLANTIC BOOKS
LONDON

For everyone we love.

Published in Great Britatin in paperback in 2006 by Atlantic Books.
Atlantic Books is an imprint of Grove Atlantic Ltd.

9 8 7 6 5 4 3 2 1

A CIP catalogue record for this book is available from the British Library

ISBN 1 84354 246 3

Designed by Nicky Barneby
Set in 11/14pt Sabon by Barneby Ltd, London
Printed in Great Britain by Mackays of Chatham plc, Chatham, Kent

Atlantic Books
An imprint of Grove Atlantic Ltd
Ormond House
26–27 Boswell Street
London WC1N 3JZ

www.groveatlantic.co.uk

CONTENTS

AUTHOR'S NOTE

This book is a record of our personal journey; a whistle-stop tour of world faiths and philosophies. It is by no means comprehensive in its exploration of humanity's myriad belief systems.

Notably absent are two of the world's 'great' faiths, Judaism and Islam. Countless lesser religions, cults and sects also go unmentioned.

We would like to take this opportunity to apologize to any gods or goddesses whom we may have offended by their omission, as well as to their faithful followers everywhere.

Each step on our travels grew out of the last, with little time to plan and less to ponder where our path might lead. Countless lifetimes have been spent in search of spiritual truth. We had a year, and deadlines, and stuff . . . So, sorry if we missed you out and please don't smite us.

Sara and Toby

FIANCÉ'S INTRODUCTION

This story has a happy ending.

I'm sorry if that's something you'd rather have learned towards the end of the book, but I think it's important to be upfront. Not that I want you to worry about what you're getting into. No natural disasters survived here, or massacres witnessed, or mountains scaled with prosthetic limbs. But there is loss of a sort, as well as love. And a pain from which I would have protected Sara, had I known how.

At the end of our long journey together, I find myself changed. As Sara sought answers to questions I never thought to ask, I tagged along and carried the bags, until some of her insatiable curiosity rubbed off. A year ago, if you'd asked me about God, or the soul, or life after death, or pretty much anything that wasn't filed under 'fact' in my personal encyclopedia, I could have laid out my stall and sold you the truth – as I saw it – with all the confidence of a showroom salesman. Essentially, although I never used the term myself, I was an atheist. Now, though, I'm not so sure. I mean, I've got my theories . . . but those I will leave to the end.

For the moment, I want to introduce the old me, before I found myself playing Watson to Sara's soul-searching Sherlock. In her story I am as much an obstacle as an aid to progress. This, in a nutshell is why:

I was a naughty child. I honed my satanic skills tormenting my little sister, Emily, a sensitive, bunny-loving blonde moppet. By the time I'd finished with her, she was a bed-wetting, snarling psychopath. In my tireless schedule of pre-teen terrorism, any surplus mischief was vented on my parents. I suspect that I never quite got over the arrival of my baby sister. It certainly took her a good few years to get over me.

By my mid-teens, a destructive cocktail of emerging hormones held despotic sway over my emotions and brought me to the verge of all-out war with my menopausal mother. I turned the tricks I'd picked up teasing Emily on my long-suffering mum with all the self-obsessed zeal of the adolescent male, raging against everything and nothing. My family suffered and stood by me. They have my eternal respect and unconditional love.

Throughout my troubled youth, a charge frequently levelled against me by one despairing parent or the other, was that I was a 'godless child'. What they really meant, of course, was that I was a right little fucker, and in that sense they were spot on. But they were right in another way, too. I *was* godless. I am. I always have been. And while I might have got there on my own eventually, Mum and Dad had a lot to do with that. They raised me without faith. In retrospect, maybe that's why I caused so much trouble for them as I grew up. They never did put the fear of God into me.

By my twenties, the big issues – illness and death, those ugly universals that the faithful would say are sent to test us – had stained my life and tempered my outlook. A generation of family elders disappeared in the space of half a decade. That was tough. Then my indomitable mother proved domitable after all, succumbing to a cancer that robbed her of at least a score of her biblically allotted years. That was almost unbearable.

The fog of grief thinned with time, of course, and I began to see a brighter future. But even in the dark days of farewells and funerals, my philosophy, such as it was, never shifted. When things were bad, I never dropped to my knees, or turned to the east. I never 'believed' and I never needed to.

My parents' iconoclastic tendencies, their cool rejection of religion's easy answers, also held fast. There was no hastily adopted dogma in Mum's final months of life. She had a bit of reiki. That was about it.

When a Starbuck died, none of us expected to see them again, white-robed and haloed or otherwise. We just got on with missing them.

Early in our relationship, Sara used to teasingly accuse me of being 'closed-minded'. I think she was missing the point. I was never closed to the possibility of the supernatural. Nor was I bold enough entirely to dismiss the notion of 'divine' or superhuman intervention in the creation of universe. Thus, I shied away from the label 'atheist'. I was, however, at least as open to the possibility that the entire universe was utterly, uncompromisingly, hopelessly random and pointless.

Fundamentally, I was opposed to the intervention of man in matters of faith. I rejected all religious texts, maintaining that the only meaningful relationship with 'God' was one-to-one. Judgement had no place in my personal theology. Eternal damnation and heavenly reward were human inventions, tools of political and sexual repression. An eternity in Hell for covetousness? Grounds for appeal, surely.

I can't speak for the rest of my family, but I suspect that they always shared my secret assumption that adherence to religious doctrine is a sign of massive intellectual failure. Have faith, sure. Just don't organize it. And never let anyone tell you that *they* are closer to God than *you*. No matter how pointy their hat is.

'Faith,' the 25-year-old me would have told you over the top of his Jack Daniels and Coke, 'of the official, church-going variety, is just inherited belief. A complete set of largely groundless assertions about the world that our children are lumbered with even before they squeeze their way into it. It's a very peculiar thing, if you think about it. I mean, consider the reaction if you were to point at a newborn and confidently declare, "That boy is a Tory", or "What a pretty little Humanist". But a kid is Catholic or Jewish, Muslim or Hindu from birth.'

'Mmm,' you mumble, stirring your drink with a straw and scanning the bar for an escape route.

'Yeah, and in my opinion, that kind of hothouse brainwashing is a form of self-perpetuating child abuse. It's not a birthright, it's a ball and chain around your baby's neck from day one. An inbred obstacle to intellectual advancement, and the progenitor of social apartheid.'

We've all got our pet theories about faith and religion, of course, to which all too many ill-judged dinner party conversation openers attest. But when yours is as finite and unbending as my mine was, the chat dries up pretty quickly. 'Isn't that right, you at the bar?'

Oh. He's gone.

Even with my heels dug in, mind you, I was all for tolerance.

If the Ruskies couldn't knock God out of their loyal citizens in the gulags of Siberia, there seemed little point in trying to criminalize worship. I did my best to actively discourage it, though. There were so many more interesting ways to use your brain on a Sunday . . . Friday . . . whenever.

So, I had never known God. Which wasn't to say that I didn't know what the inside of a church looked like. I was packed off to Sunday school, presumably to give Mum and Dad an hour's peace every seventh day. Pressed on the subject, my dad will mumble something about moral grounding and the importance of shared cultural heritage, but I suspect that at the time the prospect of a shag was the principle factor in my introduction to Christianity.

They drew the line at dipping my head. Resisting pressure from their own parents and the parish press gang, Mum and Dad reasoned that I should be free to choose my own path when I was of an age to do so. Of course, having survived my first decade without the benefit of a strong godfather figure to steer me down the path of righteousness, I chose the way of Sunday morning lie-ins and sniffy scepticism. My little sister, Emily, found her own path to agnostic apathy and, to date, has shown no sign of spiritual awakening or religious conversion. Essentially, my whole family's been off God's radar for two generations.

So that was the man that Sara met: a sceptic and a secularist, suspicious of believers and truth pedlars. What on earth did she ever see in me?

Well, the Big Bearded One isn't the only human concept where faith comes into play. There is another force in the universe, as intangible and influential as the Prime Mover. Its followers are countless, its writings endless. It has all the best

5

hymns and the communion rites beat anything church has to offer by a country mile. It's called love.

This, then, is my family's, and my, saving grace; we Starbucks are hopeless romantics. Mum and Dad married in the summer of love and dragged it out for thirty-odd years before death did them part, somewhat ahead of the expected schedule. My sister and I might have missed out on the Disney holidays and gift-giving arms race of a middle-class divorce, but our parents' unfashionable insistence on staying together left Emily and me with an unshakeable belief in love ever-lasting. It's a trait that has got both of us into trouble over the years, but I know neither of us would change a thing. It's working out for me. It will for Em. You've just got to have ... what's the word?

Love, of the puppy variety, came into my life at the age of fifteen, in the fabulously perky shape of Charlotte Gilliland. I weathered a surge of aggression from many of my classmates, who couldn't get their mullet-cut heads around the fact that I had attracted the attention of the highly desirable, heavily hair-sprayed Charlotte. They forgot their anger as soon as Charlotte forgot me. I tried everything to stop her turning her back on our three weeks of happiness. I took my brace out. I bought her chips. I drew a tearful frog in the back of her German exercise book. Nothing worked. I typed out the lyrics of 'Heaven Knows I'm Miserable Now' by The Smiths, let the postman carry them the half-mile to Charlotte's house, and swore off love for ever.

Girl number two was a big one, my honest-to-goodness 'first love'. Rachel was the archetypical English rose, a pale-skinned, pink-cheeked beauty who actually read all the books I just pretended to, and was fast becoming the Kate Winslet of

the school drama department. I wowed her with my sophisticated sixth-form charm and for the remainder of my school
career, we became one of those teen couples who have the
space between their names replaced with an ampersand.

There was a lot of romance in my relationship with Rachel.
Of course there was; we were teenagers. There were poems and
quotations, cribbed from the classics and the indie singles
chart. There were moonlit, mistletoe kisses and hoarded souvenirs of every new experience. But with the benefit of hindsight, and the peaceful perspective of a reformed criminal, I
have to admit that the defining characteristic of my five years
with Rach was my red-faced, clumsy, fruitless and frustrating
quest to get into her still VAT-free knickers. With fifteen years
to my seventeen, Rachel held out till she reached legal age, by
which time I was heading off for a gap year in the States. There,
I squandered countless opportunities to work the Hugh Grant
angle, returning a year later into the arms of my equally faithful
girlfriend. We finally 'did it' that summer. 'It' was, naturally,
rubbish. Nor did it ever get particularly spectacular. A combination of mutual body awareness issues and basic sexual
incompatibility put the dampeners on 'Rachel&Toby' the
moment we moved from childhood sweethearts to adult lovers.
I was a complete twat, of course. A self-obsessed, insensitive
student knob-head with one eye out for the next opportunity.
Complacency and force of habit kept us together until Rachel's
first term at Cambridge. She dumped me. By post. It hurt a lot,
but thanks, Rach. God knows when I would have got around
to it.

Girl number three was a rebound shag that somehow got
dragged out into four years of almost uninterrupted misery.
Maybe I was punishing myself subconsciously for the sins of

neglect and disinterest in my previous relationship. I've thought a lot about why two people as patently unhappy as Katherine and I would stay together for so long, without children or debt to bind them. The strongest theory requires me to admit a character failing that is common to many young men. I didn't know how to dump.

I don't mean that I didn't know how to dump someone without causing a scene or hurting their feelings; I simply didn't know how to do it at all. Until well into my twenties, when a relationship had runs its course, I would become more and more of an arsehole, until my unfortunate girlfriends found themselves wondering why on Earth they were with me at all, and resolved not to be. Hey presto! Bachelorhood regained, with the added bonus of self-pity and an excuse to drown your sorrows by going on the pull with your mates. This wasn't a conscious policy for break-ups; it just worked out that way. Partly because I was a sucker for crying women, and would foolishly promise to 'try harder' at the first sign of tears, when what I should have said was, 'Look, this just isn't working. You're sucking my will to live.' Besides, it seemed like bad manners to turn away a girl who actually wanted to have sex with me. Better to shatter her illusions with a series of small disappointments, leading to an uncomfortable, loveless farewell.

In Katherine, however, I met my match: she was a woman whose capacity to absorb disappointment was apparently infinite, and whose natural state was a dangerous blend of blind optimism and depressed resignation. The omens of lifelong relationship Hell were water off a duck's back to Katherine. In four years, we never once saw a movie we both enjoyed, never went on holiday, never shared a friend. I was suspicious of the number of guitars and youth groups that figured in her family's Christian lifestyle and, although Katherine herself was the agnostic black sheep of the family, I couldn't help but feel alienated.

We rowed a lot. We made up a lot, in bed. We had no money and spent night after night shut up in a dingy East End cell, drinking cheap white wine, fighting and shagging. If hadn't been for the cat – a highly significant factor in the misguided longevity of our affair – whom neither of us wanted to upset, we might very well have fought to the death in that flat. And no amount of make-up sex is going to revive a corpse. Remember that.

The end for Katherine and I was drunken, sudden and bitter. The decision was mutual after one of our trademark fights went too far. I left the cat, half my CDs and good deal of self-respect behind me. Katherine left London for a teaching post in Cheltenham. We met for lunch in Soho six months later. It was a strange encounter. Separation had done wonders for both of us. With half a year cushioning us from the devastating events of our break-up – and neither of us looking to turn back the clock – we were finally able to communicate. We discussed our faults like shrinks swapping case notes. What kept us from the realms of mud-slinging was a detached acknowledgment of mutual fault. We'd brought out the worst in each other from the start, and four years of complacency and misguided loyalty had turned dissatisfaction into full-blown bitterness. Whatever we had, it was never love, but, by the end of our epic axe-burying session, we were able to part company as friends. The kind of friend you think about every now and again, but don't have to talk to often – or at all – to know that they're still your friend. The kind of friend you never, ever see again.

There followed the only period of prolonged bachelorhood in my adult life. I learned to dump. I'm not saying I did it with any panache, and I hated the fact that I would be leaving as the bad guy, but my newfound ability to acknowledge incompatibility early on saved me from an emerging pattern of lengthy, monogamous, power struggles. The next time I committed to someone, I decided, she would be someone on my wavelength. Someone from a slightly less happy-clappy home, who shared my politics, my philosophy, my taste in movies.

Then along came Sara. Five foot, one and a half inches of concentrated joie de vivre with a dancer's body, a wicked sense of humour and a smile like an invitation to a party. I fancied her from first contact, and when we started dating, I was keen to keep my head. No more hasty affairs.

My play-it-cool resolve lasted about three weeks. Ironically, Sara had settled an argument that Katherine and I had never managed to put to bed. Always more eager to push things forward, Katherine had frequently ridiculed my objection to marriage on principle. Time and again, when she teased me about weddings and babies, I wheeled out tired old arguments about 'outdated institutions' and 'meaningless contracts'. Katherine would smile on one side of her mouth and chide me playfully, 'You just haven't met anyone you want to marry, yet.' She was right, of course. Three months after meeting Sara, I would have wed her in an instant. I threw caution to the wind on Primrose Hill, and told her as much.

It took Sara a year to take me seriously. I dropped to my knees and dirtied my best trousers on a warm September evening. We moved in together at about the same time, and then, as our engagement entered its third year, we hit a snag

... or maybe it was a rut. Our whirlwind romance was beginning to look decidedly long-winded.

So what was stopping us? It hurts me to say this, but when Sara and I got together, there was another man in her life. An older man, with power and influence. Not too flash, the goody-goody type. Does a lot of charity work. Walks on water ...

Sara's a Catholic. She'll tell you different some of the time, but she is. I've seen her filling out hospital forms. When she gets to the box marked 'religion' she hovers for a moment, then scribbles it in quickly – guiltily, you might say. The thing with Catholicism is they get you young. And if I got the old fairy switcheroo, then Sara is a papist changeling. At some point in her delicate development, as ideas of self and society whirled in her head, Sara was spirited away in the night by the Holy Catholic Church and replaced by a little girl full of fears and glories, demons and angels.

She's not a churchgoer, regular or otherwise. If Sara were seized by the urge to confess, she'd have to Hail Mary her arse off when the priest heard how long it's been since the last time. In fact, Sara's dream-catching, spell-casting, reiki-healing, tarot-reading view of the world was always somewhat at odds with the official RC-approved version of events. Nevertheless, when we met, the faith in which she was schooled and raised still held sway over her heart.

Therein lay our dilemma, once my ring was on her finger. While Sara could no longer claim to be an active participant, she still felt the ties. So when it came to our wedding day, one thing was always certain: it had to be Catholic.

At first, I acquiesced, reasoning that my beloved's positive conviction outweighed my mere lack of conviction. The religious aspect of our wedding would have no spiritual significance to me, but I was more than happy to join in the fun. After all, I could make the promises and mean them, with all my heart.

Unfortunately, there's no such thing as day membership in the Church of Rome; they expect you to join the club. And, while I'm comfortable with the idea of having and holding, in sickness and in health, I'm far less happy with the idea of swearing allegiance to the Holy Pontiff and buying into his particular brand of answers.

I never imagined that an issue of religion could impact my own life. However, the business of starting a family, the prospect of extending Catholic ritual in our lives to include possible christenings and confirmations later on, sparked months of fireside theological debate in the home we shared. 'Living in sin', I think her lot call it.

We got nowhere. I couldn't present Sara with an alternative that would cater for her spiritual needs. If it wasn't in church, she wouldn't feel married, said Sara. So, with nothing to add on the marriage front, I turned my attention to the God she knew.

Sara found herself living with the devil's advocate. I teased her about Bible stories and prophecy. I pointed out that it was the accident of adoption that placed her among the saved. I railed against fundamentalism and Puritanism. I went too far.

Sara's faith, she tells me, was rock solid until I started to chip away at it. But that's what I did, and I started a landslide that would see us squander our savings on a year-long spiritual odyssey.

When I thought about Sara's loss of faith, even in the midst of the crisis, I was divided. I know how desperately patronizing this sounds, yet foolishly I thought she was making progress. I couldn't abide blind faith, the unquestioning adherence to any of the big clubs that's usually dictated by accident of birth or geographical location. I rejected the idea of a 'chosen people' because it presupposed the inevitable damnation of, well, *everybody* else. So I preferred to see Sara's extraction from Catholicism as an introduction to a broader, humanist view of the world. I was acutely aware, though, that I hadn't given Sara anything to fill the Jesus-shaped hole in her life. After all, I didn't have any answers. That was the whole point; nobody did.

In retrospect, it was incredibly arrogant to suppose that by indulging Sara's soul-searching, I could steer her towards my way of thinking. It was also foolish to assume that no amount of exposure to new ideas would dent my cosy, who-cares approach to spirituality.

As I followed Sara from hilltop temples to city museums – meeting bishops and brahmins, scientists and soothsayers – the goalposts shifted for both of us. Did we find any answers? Well, at the very least, the questions changed, and we came home happier, if not holier.

So, as I said at the beginning, there is a fairy-tale ending. For starters, let me take you back to the morning that my tendency to tease tipped Sara over the edge, kick-starting our unlikely quest. Then, I'll leave you to Sara. After all, this is her story.

September 2003, Kilburn

It was a Saturday morning. The intercom chirruped. We flicked off the cartoons and buzzed our landlord's estate agents into the lobby of the building like foolhardy Transylvanians inviting in the vampires. Five flights up, a little black cloud followed them in through our front door and settled over Sara's head, where it would remain for the rest of the day.

'Look at that view,' said one Alpha male, striding past us and throwing open the balcony doors. 'I'll have to get a picture of that.'

He fired a volley of instamatic shots over the balcony wall, at the suburbs and city spread out below, then spun on his polished heels and stepped back inside. Sara, shivering theatrically, shut the balcony doors behind him and glared at his pinstriped back with a Paddington Bear stare.

'Do you want to look ar—' I began, but he was already off, scanning the walls with a device that looked for all the world like a Star Trek tricorder.

'Roomy,' nodded the agent. His tricorder bleeped in agreement.

Agent number two appeared by the stairs.

'What do you reckon, Malc? Two-hundred?'

Sara wobbled and grabbed the pocket of my jeans to steady herself.

'One-eighty, one-eighty-five, more like. The view'll sell it in no time, mind.'

Well, that was that, then. Bye-bye, Kilburn. If we'd toyed with the idea of putting in an offer, we'd been well and truly priced out of the market. Sara slumped on to the sofa as I saw out Dolittle and Dally.

'This is my home,' she sighed as I joined her. 'What now?'

'We could look around. We might find something we can afford,' I tried.

'Something tiny, or grotty, or in Lewisham again,' said Sara, shuddering.

'Maybe now's the time to move out, then,' I said. 'Escape to the country where we can actually afford to live ... within commutable distance.' The last comment to counter Sara's look of wide-eyed terror at the thought of dark nights and farm smells.

'It's doing my head in, Toby,' said Sara. 'I can't stand the insecurity. I need my nest. I'm a girl.'

'Well, there's nothing we can do today,' I said. 'We need financial advice and a proper plan. And it's Saturday, so I say fuck all that, let's go out and get pissed.'

'I don't really drink much, Toby,' said Sara.

'A-ha!' I said. 'Knew that. Just testing. What I meant to say was, let's go out to a museum, or a gallery or something ... and have a coffee afterwards, and take your mind off all of this crap. Hmm?'

I wriggled my eyebrows. Sara smiled.

'Can we go to the Natural History Museum?' she asked. 'There's a really good coffee shop there.'

'There's an exhibition at the Tate Modern I quite fancy,' I said.

'Does the Natural History Museum do cakes?'

'South Ken, it is. Bus or tube?'

In retrospect, we should have chosen the Tate. Or the V&A. Or anywhere other than London's great temple to Darwinism. Our trip to the Natural History Museum opened a can of vermes – that's worms to you – that have since wriggled their way into every corner of my life.

'Best exhibit?' I said. We had done the rounds from aardvark to zebra and were leaning over the balcony at the top of the great hall.

'Um,' said Sara. 'The fish. The cola-can.'

'Coelocanth.'

'Him. Yes,' said Sara. 'I think it's fantastic that everyone thought he was dead – extinct dead – and he was really just lurking. Lying low. Clever boy, your cola-can, when you consider what we do to the fishies that let themselves be seen.'

'Oh, so you care about fish now, do you? Are you going to cut them out of your diet and become a proper vegetarian?

'I *am* a vegetarian,' said Sara indignantly.

'What kind of vegetable is cod, then?'

We watched the visitors below in silence for a moment.

'What was your best exhibit?' Sara asked, eventually.

I rolled my eyes in mock disbelief. 'Hello? Animatronic T-rex?' I mimed the gnashing teeth and, frankly, poofy forelegs of the giant carnivore.

Sara's smile broadened and became a chuckle, which was what I'd been aiming for. I curled an arm around her narrow shoulders and breathed the smell of her hair.

'What about those bears, though, eh? I've always loved bears. It's a Milne thing, I think. Or an Ernest Shepherd thing, rather. Not Pooh, though, it's the bears in *Now We Are Six* that I love. The ones that jump out and eat you when you step on the cracks in the pavement. I was twenty-five before I could walk a straight line on flagstones.'

'They do look fierce,' agreed Sara. 'Even stuffed bears look fierce.'

'Fierce and hungry,' I said. 'Although I suspect that's the look they went for in Victorian taxidermy circles.'

Sara was definitely looking sunnier. I was on a roll.

'Amazing predators, mind you,' I began. 'I tell you what, if your Noah had a couple of polar bears on board when he opened his cruise business, he'd have had to take forty penguins just to keep 'em in lunch. That's on top of the breeders.' I was getting into my stride. 'You can't fit a food chain into two-hundred square cubits. That's where it falls apart.'

I waited for the laugh. Sara had fallen quiet again. I brushed her hair from her face and was surprised to see tears in her grey-green eyes.

'Babe?' I asked, dabbing her cheeks with my sleeve.

'Why did you have to say that?' she asked, seriously. 'You know what I've been going through.'

'But I didn't think ... It was only a joke. I mean, you were never a literalist, were you? They're just stories, surely?'

'Of course they're just stories. I'm not stupid,' Sara snapped. 'But when you have faith, there are some stories you just don't question. That's the whole point. They might not make sense, they might be strange or miraculous, but the usual rules don't apply. You just believe them, because they're part of the story of your faith.' Sara was crying freely now. 'Obviously the ark wasn't real. Otherwise, where did Noah manage to pick up his, his kangaroos, or his arctic foxes, or his, his ...'

'Naked mole rats?' I suggested.

'His naked mole rats, yes.' Sara sighed and turned her back on the great hall. Her eyes fell on the enormous cross-section of a giant redwood, mounted against the wall. Its rings were labelled with dates from history: the Industrial Revolution, the Roman occupation of Britain, the birth of Christ. This ancient tree was felled in 1869, but seeded long before. Before Christians or the man who inspired them ever walked the Earth. It was whole and alive for longer than the mighty

Church of Rome has so far managed. Granted, the Pope's lot are gaining ground, but if you chainsawed the Vatican and counted the rings tomorrow, the tree would still romp home. I pointed this out to Sara, who in turn pointed out that I wasn't helping.

'Can we just go home?' she sniffed.

'No coffee?' I asked.

'Coffee at home,' she ruled.

We followed the winding stairs to ground level and left the museum in silence. Sara's rain cloud met us at the door, like a belligerent but faithful terrier, and followed us to the bus stop, grumbling ominously.

An hour and a half later, we sat in the window of a West Hampstead greasy spoon, nursing overpriced all day breakfasts. (Of course, this being Jamie Oliver's neighbourhood, the grease on the spoon was actually extra virgin olive oil and the bacon butties were maple-cured.) I was on my second organically reared sausage, lost in the Everyman Crossword, when I registered Sara's growing restlessness. Looking up from 1 down, I pushed her long fringe out of her eyes and asked her what was up.

Can open. Twelve months later, I would still be finding worms in my trouser turn-ups.

'It's this whole museum episode,' said Sara, her brow furrowed. 'It's left me reeling.'

'Go on,' I urged, folding my paper and tucking it under seat.

Sara sighed and nodded. 'OK,' she began. 'Of course I always knew that the Noah story wasn't literally true, right? I'm not mental. I'm not some kind of Tennessee creationist. I mean, if you stop and think about it for a moment, the whole idea's potty. Two of everything on a big barge for the rainy season? And one old man to get 'em all into boxes and on-board without eating each other? It's ridiculous.'

'I read a creationist magazine once,' I chimed in, 'that said Noah took dinosaurs on the ark with him. But after the flood, there wasn't much food to be had, so we ate them.' Sara stared at me blankly. 'Thus, no dinosaurs.'

'Fascinating. Not helpful.'

'So what's changed?' I asked, trying to keep Sara talking before she retreated inwards with her existential angst.

'I dunno,' she admitted, reluctantly. 'Something's shifting inside me. I'm stuck in this spiral of negative thoughts and I can't shake out of it. I feel like I've been walking around with my skirt tucked into my knickers for thirty years.'

It took me a while to get my head around what Sara was telling me. She was a Catholic. Sure. Whatever. I think I'd always reacted to that fact the same way I would to her being, say, French or an Arsenal fan. These weren't things you chose, they were things that happened to you. As such, they weren't necessarily indicative of any personal preference or philosophy. It had barely occurred to me that Sara's being Catholic meant that she actually believed in God. She was an intelligent, introspective woman, after all. Surely she'd consigned religion to the nursery like ... well, like I had. It staggered me that Sara could get to thirty years old without ever taking a detached, intellectual look at the myth and moral teaching that sat at the heart of her religious upbringing. I shuddered at the power of a myth that had gripped Sara so tightly as a child, that it had simply never occurred to her to question it in adult-hood. Until that moment in the museum, Sara had taken her

SARA HULSE & TOBY STARBUCK

deeply buried faith for granted. But with one, flippant comment, I had helped it to the surface and shat all over it.

Her knife and fork were clattering on the plate, a rogue tear was threatening to make a break for it. Sara's faith was drifting away from her as I watched, as powerless as the unicorns that Noah left behind.

'I'm not sure that I believe in God any more,' she blurted over the lip of her coffee cup, 'I've been feeling like this for a while, but now . . . Oh, I just don't get it any more.'

She flinched, as if she expected the lightening bolt of a vengeful God to spear her like the stick through a toffee apple. When nothing happened, she relaxed her shoulders and carried on.

'*And* I really don't think I want to get married in church any more,' she mumbled, shoving soggy toast aside. 'It should mean something, that sort of thing. If the ceremony's not spiritually significant, we might as well ordain a mate and tie the knot in a nightclub.'

I tried to make the right sympathetic noises at this point, though I suspect a small smile might have escaped as the chance of ducking out of the big church wedding blinked into existence.

'And you can wipe that grin off your face,' said Sara. 'I'm not about to turn my back on the supernatural, I'm far too much of a hippy.' A look of determination was spreading across her troubled face. 'This calls for drastic spiritual action. Maybe another religion will make more sense.' Determination was giving way to panic. It was going to be a long day. 'Something friendlier. Buddhism . . . Baha'i ?'

'Maybe you don't need a religion.' I suggested.

Sara sat up and narrowed her eyes as she thought aloud.

'Could I be married without God?' she pondered. 'Is love really enough?'

'Hello?' I tugged at her sleeve. 'Fiancé. Right here.'

'Oh, sorry,' said Sara, shaking herself back to the present. 'It's just that they seem such silly little words for such hugely important things. Love. God. They've always been synonymous in my mind. If I'm losing one, how do I know I won't lose the other?' She closed her eyes. 'Tobe, what am I going to do?'

We left the café and picked our way through the traffic outside, gridlocked by roadworks a mile away. I took Sara's hand as we crossed the road, but she slipped out of my grasp and quickened her pace. The invisible force-field of spiritual funk kept me at arm's length for the rest of the walk home.

Back at the flat, we passed on our deceptively uncomfortable rented sofa, and climbed back into bed together. I, propped up on pillows, channel-hopped with the volume down and did my best to lip-read *Columbo*. While Sara sat beside me, grumbling quietly.

'Are you listening?' I suddenly registered. I nodded.

Sara sighed dramatically and flopped back against her pillow. I waited for her to carry on.

'I know you didn't mean to go stirring up trouble, Tobe,' she started, 'You're just not that well-equipped for sympathetic listening when it comes to a crisis of faith. I mean, God's like the Tooth Fairy for you, or Batman. He's childhood fantasy. You've got the emotional detachment of a prison psychologist where my faith's concerned.'

A sharp nudge hit me in the ribs.

'*Are* you even listening to me?' Sara demanded.

'Of course I am, darling.'

'What was I saying, then?'

'Which bit?'

'Just now. What was I saying?'

'Um ...'

Of course, I had been listening, in a multitasking sort of way, but the delay in ordering my thoughts about her half-heard woes gave Sara a window of opportunity to attack.

'I knew it!' She batted me with one of her many pillows. 'You don't even care,' she protested. 'You think this is all some stupid phase. That I'll come out the other side of this all calm and reasonable and bloody sciency! Well, what if I don't, eh?' I shrugged pathetically, taken back by the force of Sara's protest. 'What if I never feel happy and loved and – and – *meaningful* again? Because if there is no meaning, and no love, there's just hormones. And no point doing anything at all except enjoying yourself and hoping for a swift exit ... and that's shit.'

'And what do you expect me to do about it?' I asked. A poor choice of response in retrospect. The pillow bounced off my head and onto the floor. I left it out of harm's way; she only had three shots left.

'I expect you to listen instead of pretending to listen, and show me some support, instead of nodding and grunting like you're bloody bored,' said Sara, glowering. 'Even if you are.' She snatched the telly remote and hit the off-button. 'I'm thirty, Toby. I want to have children, you know? Soon.'

'Me, too,' I replied, sincerely. 'We could do that tomorrow. We don't have to wait for you to resolve this – your – this thing.'

'I want to get married first, you know that. I don't want bastards.'

'*You're* a bastard. Born out of wedlock and all that.'

'And you're a wanker, nevertheless I do want to marry you, and *then* have your babies.'

'In which case,' I tried, helpfully, 'you'd better get cracking and find God while all your bits are in order. Plus, we need a place to live, and somewhere to do it, you know? No more fucking about. Let's get married.'

'But—'

'No buts. No more sitting around. We work better with a deadline, so let's set one. A year to find your faith again, or something to fill the gap that doesn't leave you feeling pointless and unmotivated. A year to sort out the wedding itself, whatever form it takes. We'll need to move faster on a place to live.'

Sara sighed and stared wistfully at the view from our bedroom window.

'What if we don't make it?' she asked. 'What if the year's up and I'm still swimming around in a big, black sea of guilt and uncertainty?'

'Guilt promotes goodness. Uncertainty promotes tolerance.'

'And you promote a load of old bollocks,' Sara added, smiling for the first time in hours. 'Seriously. What if we run out of time?'

An ultimatum can be a dangerous thing and, although we had both become increasingly keen to make good on our promise of three years, the pressure of a time limit could prove counterproductive. I thought for a moment and found a compromise.

'We need to play it like heads or tails. Heads – you find your perfect spiritual solution, this in turn leads to the perfect wedding. I'll go along for the ride, whatever makes you happy at this point. Then we breed like bunnies. Tails – if we can't find any answers in a year, we do it quickly and painlessly and have the party of our lives with all our friends and family, and we move on. And then, hopefully, we breed like bunnies.'

OK, so I'd done nothing, ultimately, but shelve Sara's problems for later. Nevertheless, the suggestion that we get proactive on the faith issue prompted a remarkable change in Kilburn's emotional weather-front. Looking positively chipper, she gathered up pens and paper and disappeared into the spare room 'to make a start on things'.

Determined not to lose the initiative, or any potential brownie points, I dug out paper and a pen to help plan Sara's path to enlightenment. I mean, I wasn't looking to kick-start her conversion from one world view to another, but I could see the benefit of broadening her horizons.

Of course, we should start by looking into a formal religion or two – probably get her lot out of the way – before trying something a bit more exotic. Something Eastern, for contrast, Hinduism, perhaps. And what about atheism as a valid philosophy in itself. I added it to my list. Then I scrumpled my sheet of notes and lobbed it in the general direction of the wastepaper basket.

For the next two hours, every effort I made to catalogue potential points of interest along Sara's soul-searching route came to nothing. The problem, essentially, was that with so many faiths and world views to choose from – all noisily proclaiming that they were right and everyone else was wrong – it stood to reason that we could not hope to experience them all. Where to make the cuts?

Limited to one lifetime – and with a bit of luck, con-siderably less – Sara's spiritual odyssey would have to start out on a different tack. We would look for truths within the faiths we encountered, and aspects of each way of life that appealed to us personally. Sara might have other ideas, of course, and if I had to get used to the idea of a revitalized religious streak in my partner, I was sure I could handle it. Anything would be better than this impenetrable, metaphysical fog.

I stared down at my latest, and so far uncrumpled, sheet of notes. It looked more like a GCSE revision spider diagram than the ordered itinerary I had planned, but at least I'd managed a few pointers.

First and foremost, Sara had unfinished business with the Church of Rome. On paper, Catholicism is a uniquely passive and generous faith, built on the promise of unconditional love, infinite forgiveness and profound sacrifice. Historically, however, it has often been used as an excuse for appalling oppression and, as anyone who's ever seen the Inquisition's tools of the trade will testify, some imaginative violence. I worry about the whole concept of Armageddon, for that matter. Putting a full stop on history in your holy book naturally encourages a certain sort of fatalism. Has man ever enjoyed an 'age' without considering the end of days? And might the inevitable short-termism of our apocalyptic leanings have slowed our cultural and intellectual progress?

On a more mundane level, the exclusivity of Christianity, in common with many religions, could be said to encourage man's ugliest tribal tendencies. Nowhere is this more apparent than in Northern Ireland, where doctrine has turned communities with similar belief systems into warring factions.

In pockets of conservative Christian society, and particularly in Republican America, a failure to recognize the place of myth in religion has led to a fundamentalist strain of

Christianity that is growing in popularity. A new kind of Puritanism threatens the arts through funding boycotts and noisy protests, while Creationism has been allowed to sneak in the back door of faith-focused high schools. Indeed, the President of the United States, George Bush Jr., has publicly shown his reluctance to entertain Darwin's theory of evolution; perhaps because to do so would enrage so many hardline Christian voters.

My personal problem with Christianity was that it seemed to have been hijacked by so many self-righteous bores over the years. I doubted whether a faith riddled with contradiction, hypocrisy and absolute morality would have the subtlety to help relieve Sara of her turmoil. I couldn't imagine that a quick chat with the parish priest was going to answer any of the questions that had rocked her faith in the first place. But it was right that we start there, right that they had their say, and imperative that I conquered the sense of pompous indignation that rose in me every time I even thought about religion.

Then what? 'Head East,' my notes said. The suggestion felt trite; it was the sort of thing posh kids did after college so that they had something more than 'Secretary – Beer Soc.' to put on their CVs. Did anyone really discover themselves in the pantheistic heartlands of India, or the mountains of Buddhist Tibet? If oriental travel is such a life-changing experience, why does Anita Roddick still run a soap shop? And shouldn't Richard Gere be worried that he might come back as a gerbil?

That said, the Eastern faiths would provide the perfect counterpoint to linear, literalist, Western Christianity. Hinduism, for instance, neatly shows how two staggeringly different ideas about the workings of the world – one monotheistic, one pantheistic; one apocalyptic, one cyclical – can come to the same basic conclusion: that we should all try being nice to people if we expect the same in return. In particular, I hoped Sara might be interested in reincarnation, the most widely shared afterlife alternative to the Heaven and Hell system of reward and punishment. At least if we ended up back at square one, none the wiser, I might be able to convince her that we'd have better luck next time round.

Of course, I had my own ideas about what would work best for Sara. And living with my big-mouthed brand of human-ism, I'm sure, had hardly primed her to see positivity in the godless universe. We'd need to find a humanist authority; someone with a scientific eye and a moralistic heart to show that we don't have to abandon Utopia when we let go of God.

What else, Islam? Who was I kidding? I hadn't the strength, nor Sara the stomach, for Islam's rigid moral code and sexual division. Judaism? A closed shop, living in the shadow of its Nazarene splinter group. Paganism? Yesterday's nudes.

Clearly, this wouldn't be the sort of journey we could map out in advance. We'd go where we needed to, follow our noses as new questions or contacts arose. Of course, we may have been about to waste our time and money chasing rainbows, but with some journeys, it's not the arriving that counts. It's the getting there.

Sara reappeared at sunset, with a neatly printed 'To Do' list, which she stuck to the fridge door with a fistful of crumpled Sellotape.

'We have magnets,' I pointed out, spotting her handiwork.

'Too temporary,' she replied. 'Sellotape means business. These are our ten commandments for the year to come.'

I glanced at the list. 'There are only two of them, and they're more like goals.'

'Well then, they should be easy enough not to wheedle out of, shouldn't they?' She read aloud:

TO DO
1. Find God and/or inner peace
2. Plan and execute wedding

'The first one's a doozy,' I said. 'People spend their lives searching for inner peace. I'm not sure it's something you can do on sabbatical, but I've been having some thoughts in that direction myself. Number two I can get behind. Not sure about 'execute', though. It's a bit of a harsh term for a wedding, isn't it?'

Sara drew a fat black marker across item two on her list so that it read: 'Plan and — wed—'

Then she crossed out the beginning, to leave simply 'wed'.

'To the point,' I said. 'Anything else? When's the contract up on this place?'

'Three months,' Sara groaned. 'Better add "Find flat". There's no point renting when we've got the deposit sitting in my savings account,' she said firmly, adding a third item to her list.

TO DO
1. Find God and/or inner peace
2. Plan and execute wedding
3. Buy house

'If you're serious about this soul-searching business,' I asked, 'how are you going to go about it?'

'I've thought about that,' said Sara, 'I know soul-searching is an inward sort of thing, I've just always been an outward sort of girl. I miss travelling, Tobe. If we're really going to have babies and put down roots, I want to see a little bit more of the world first. While I can still cope with cheap hotels and spicy food. I suppose I could lock myself up in a library, but I'm not really the booky type.'

'You're in publishing!' I protested. 'You work for a literary agency. You read for a living!'

'Well, obviously I'm a bit booky,' she admitted. 'But I learn better when I do things first-hand. All these questions I've got; they're the perfect excuse for a bit of last-minute globe-trotting before we offer ourselves into slavery for our unborn children, don't you think?'

'That's exactly what they are,' I agreed, fingering my notes, behind my back. 'An excuse. So how do we fund your jet-setting journey of discovery?'

'We've got emergency savings,' she said. 'This is an emergency. I've done the sums. We cut our working weeks to three days. Then we travel in short hops; stay for long weekends. If it's Britain, we take the Skoda. If it's abroad, we fly no frills. While we're at home, we live cheap and scour the papers for a place outside London – commutable distance – that won't cripple us mortgage-wise. If we get lucky on the house-buying front, we should be able to keep hold of enough cash for a modest round-part-of-the-world-trip.'

'And if a year gets you nowhere in particular?'

'We go back to work and save enough for a lavish funeral, because I can't live with this bloody turmoil.'

Sara grinned and strode across the room, flopping down next to me with a sigh.

'And you can deal with the general skintness?' I asked. 'The no new clothes, the buses and packed lunches?'

'Toby,' she pouted, evidently quite put out, 'this is me. I've lived in squats. I've nicked toilet rolls from pubs and eaten out of bins.'

'All right, all right,' I conceded. 'I'm up for it. We travel around, we talk to the enlightened and the opinionated. We – and I can't help wondering whether you've set your sights a little bit high on this one – reach a state of spiritual equilibrium and contentment, while flirting with the terrifying reality of near bankruptcy. And at the end of it all, we get happy, hopeful, confident, optimistic Sara back again, instead of fucked-up, fatalistic, angry, disillusioned Sara. Right?'

'That's the idea,' said Sara. 'Thanks for doing this with me.'

'For cutting down to a three-day week and seeing the world? I asked. 'Are you kidding?' I grinned. 'Actually,' I began, proudly revealing my scribbled notes, 'I've been thinking about this soul-searching business already. Wondering where we might go.'

'One step ahead of you, babe,' said Sara, presenting me with a bigger pile of neatly typed notes, 'You didn't think it took me three hours to produce that poxy list and count our savings, did you? I've been doing some research. I've booked us three days at Lourdes.'

'You don't even like cricket.'

'Not Lords, Lourdes. Like Madonna's kid; Lor-dezz. In France? St Bernadette, the Virgin Mary, miracles?' Sara leaned in and hugged me around the shoulders. 'We,' she said, breaking our embrace and grinning like a ten-year-old with tickets to Disneyland, 'are going on a pilgrimage.'

SARA'S PRAYER

Pussy said to the owl 'You elegant fowl!'
How charmingly sweet you sing!
O let us be married! Too long have we tarried:
But what shall we do for a ring?
    Edward Lear – *The Owl & The Pussy Cat*

Dear God,

Where have you gone? I've been looking for you every-where. You're not lodged down the back of my sofa – or my soul come to think of it. All I found was half a packet of pickled onion Monster Munch and some guilt. Where are you?

Amen.

I'm feeling bitter. I seem to have lost God and I'm not quite sure how. I've put in the time over the years: church, First Holy Communion, confirmation classes, religious retreats, and some serious praying. In fact, I worked out that on average, factoring in days off and occasional overtime, that I have prayed approximately 21,600 times in my life – 21,600 times I have dropped to my knees, bowed my head and clasped my hands together to commune, worship and broadcast my latest wish-list. And now I'm wondering why. Of course, none of this would be such an issue if I wasn't in a rush, but the fact is I have a deadline. I'm getting married. That means almost one year to reassess my ravaged relationship with God and decide whether or not to put him on the guest list.

It feels weird, at the outset of the twenty-first century, to be in an otherwise healthy relationship that's hampered by religious concerns. And yet, while mixed-faith couples no longer need to worry about burning at the stake, the issues that complicate their union are as vital as ever. Even when one half of a couple has no faith of their own, the believer of the pair can stir up all manner of trouble keeping parents and preachers happy for their own contentment. What ever happened to just falling in love and living happily ever after? And besides, why get married at all?

The week after Toby dropped to one knee to ask for my hand, I read that the London Marriage Guidance Council had changed its name to Relationship Council, as only 40 per cent of its clients were married. Apparently couples in the capital are more likely to settle for cohabitation than to take a stroll down the aisle. Marriage is always en vogue, as a glance at the glossy pages of *Heat* and *Hello!* reveals, but the compulsion to marry or face scandal and stigma is all just a memory in secular Britain. And yet, there I was, a Modern Millie with a monster marital dilemma.

The whole Natural History Museum revelation really had left me a wreck. Of course I knew that Noah's tale wasn't real.

A pick 'n' mix of every animal two by two on a wooden boat? Come on, it would be a groaning, splintering, animal ark porn-fest. No, my angst wasn't from a startling new discovery, rather, it was as if something at the very heart of me had shifted slightly.

I'd never really thought about my faith that much before. I took it for granted, like breathing. Of course, my God and my beliefs were a direct result of a geographical lucky dip and pietistic parents, but one could argue that this was God's plan, if one believed in God. The reminder that Noah didn't run the first mobile zoo, coupled together with Toby's enthusiastic atheistic reasoning, came at a delicate moment. A silly point of theology perhaps, but for me it was the straw that broke the Holy Ghost's back. And as I had sat there, faced with congealing breakfast foods at that West Hampstead café, it had felt as if a lifelong reserve of unshakeable, supportive faith was draining away like sand through a sieve. I had wanted to weep into my veggie bangers and beans as I considered my options because that day I had denied the existence of a very important someone. Him. It was like shunning your grandpa, your dad, your headmaster and your husband in one fell swoop. That's the problem with Catholicism; the renowned sense of guilt is as omnipresent as God is meant to be. The Catholic Church might as well personify guilt and slip him in alongside the Father, Son and Holy Spirit. If the Holy Trinity was the Beatles, Guilt would be Stuart Sutcliffe.

Toby had made all the right sounds as I had panicked and mourned. Unfortunately, the topic was too mammoth for a life-long agnostic and that little café. And as I had sat there, slack-jawed and pondering, I had begun to wonder for the first time if I could ever be married, *feel* properly married even, without

God? Could love *really* be enough? It seemed such a silly little word for an omnipotent force. Love, God and marriage were all too tangled in my psyche to comb into separate strands. I'd begun to wonder if rather than devoting another 20,000 prayers odd to Mr Invisible, I could spend the time loving other humans instead. But when I paused there for a moment, in that godless world, spreading my love among the people as we waited for oblivion, I realized that the thought was utterly terrifying: ride without stabilizers? I'd skin my knees in no time. It felt like the spiritual equivalent of cutting off my life support. I clearly wasn't ready to join the ever-swelling ranks of the secular army. I didn't know if I would ever be. And despite my new-found cynicism I still felt as if there was something bigger than us, curling up the corners, watching.

The realization that I had been liberated from everything I had been taught was as paralysing as it was emancipating. While God seemed to have vanished in a puff of smoke, I couldn't shake the legacy of Sunday School cautionary tales. It felt as if every second I might spend away from the fold was a step towards fiery torment in the hereafter. I simply hadn't realized how significant my faith had been.

It was all so ironic. Throughout my life I'd been spiritually settled but romantically screwed – now it was the other way around and driving me insane. I wanted to 'believe' because life was better that way, easier even. There was an explanation for senseless horrors, a safety net to catch me, a companion through loneliness and a promise that there was a scheme despite the chaos. And now I felt nothing except loss. Had I really wasted 21,600 prayers?

*

Before Toby came on the scene things were very different. Always the romantic, I peddled my eager heart to the wrong men hoping to find a great love. However, the often dubious assortment of Romeos with 'issues' and criminal records left me disenchanted and confused. I had three great loves and a might-have-been that never quite was, yet still found myself staring soulfully at the moon alone. Love became the complete embodiment of hope for my poor, self-tortured soul. Like Maurice Maeterlinck's fairy tale *L'Oiseau Bleu*, where a brother and sister seek the mystical bluebird of happiness, I had my very own metaphoric bluebird to find. One, I hoped, with a job.

By the time I finally did meet Toby I had all but given up hope that I'd ever settle down and get married. In retrospect I can see how a series of unfortunate events, however unpopular at the time, actually readied me for everything that was to come.

It all began in America ...

Fulton County Courthouse, Atlanta Georgia, 11 September 1996

I stood where my mother had so often predicted I'd end up – in the dock, sweating it out in a fifty-cent thrift store suit bought for the occasion of my first criminal trial. It was still summer for the Deep South and the court room was as hot and wet as a flask of soup in a Turkish steam room. Beside me stood my partners in crime, a motley crew in the classic rock style, their 'fuck-you' tattoos hidden for the day under ill-fitting polyester. The judge, a grizzled, dangerously handsome Charles Bronson type, frowned over the paperwork on his desk, glancing up at us inquisitively between sentences. Ours was the last case of the day, though we'd been there for hours already. We'd sat through the preliminary hearings for a murder, a triple murder, two rapes and an armed robbery, the convicted guilty uncomfortably near. Now it was our turn.

Judge Bronson sighed, swatted a hornet away and glanced once more at our arrest citation. My knees buckled. Six months ago I was a love-struck rock chick on the road to fame and fortune. Now, I was standing in the court of a Georgian courthouse about to make the move from rock band to chain gang, desperately trying to figure out how in the world I had got there.

Somewhere in Cornwall, seven months earlier

'Now, darling, don't drop the flaming torch in the corn field,' said my producer and boss, John, grinning up at me. He lowered his voice to a hiss. 'And hold on tight, we're not insured.'

I peered down at him, shielding my eyes from the glare of his shiny bald scalp. 'There's nothing to hold on to,' I told him.

John took a swig from his hip flask and mopped his sweaty face with a Starbucks napkin. 'Like riding a horse,' he replied breezily as he jogged backwards to rejoin the camera crew. 'Use your thighs.'

I was perched astride the gun barrel of a Challenger Tank, twelve foot from the ground, wearing a rubber bra, microscopic shorts, thigh-high PVC boots and a bondage mask, which kept slipping over my eyes as it was designed for a male gimp. A dozen or so people milled about below me smoking and sipping skinny lattes, biked in from the nearest town. John whistled and waved us into action. The tank roared into life and a runner stood on tiptoes to light my paraffin-soaked torch. We lurched forward, and my heartbeat skipped like a Morris dancer on slippery tiles, one slip and I'd be squished. I squeezed tight with my thighs and prayed for a quick death as we rumbled over the vast sun-charred cornfield. The camera crew, all dressed in black despite the heat of the midday sun, looked like the cheerleaders at the world mime championships. The wind whipped my hair over my eyes as I held the torch aloft and tried hard to look like a latter-day Boudicca. Against the odds, my grip on the gun barrel seemed to be holding. I began to get into character, feeling proud and capable. This was my dream, my first step on the road to fame, fortune and international adventure. Then I noticed the burning sensation in my right hand. My torch had dripped burning fuel down my arm. I was on fire. But I couldn't let go. It would ruin the shot and probably put an end to the cornfield. So the tank kept rolling and the torch kept blazing and I gritted my teeth and wondered how bad the scarring would be. As we reached the wall of camera crew I could hold on no longer and let go with a howl of pain. The ground immediately started smoking beneath me, there was a moment of surreal hesitation, then everyone started jumping about like Navahos on campfire night. I could see David, our principle investor, tearing a strip out of John in the background. David, a millionaire Brit and the heir to a high street photography chain, had never wanted me as the presenter for John's Cyber Punk Documentary. He had a stated preference for oriental girls, the younger the better it seemed. I was a green-eyed Irish girl, the wrong side of

to see this at the time, and stuck by John in his self-destructive spiral. Damned if he didn't almost take me down, too. He dressed me up as an S&M puppet, and paraded me around the sex industry in a thinly veiled attempt to pimp me for a production budget. The penny finally dropped on the night of a scantily clothed photo shoot when, after one whispered direction from John, the photographer dragged me out of the house and warned me I should never return.

So, faced with the abrupt cessation of my showbiz dreams and a lack of direction, I did what many girls do. I threw myself into a misguided relationship with a handsome, pleasant but mismatched new love, Keith, and ran away to America with his band. I was running again, all rational thoughts scattered like dandelion seeds in a draft. Two things kept me sane: my family and my faith.

You see, growing up, for me, wasn't just the assault course of shifting puppy-fat, incongruous crushes and red-cheeked experimentation. As a Catholic I lived under the spectres of a judging Heaven and a Milton Hell. But it was all very comforting really. Weekends were spent with the huge Irish family all crammed merrily into a Lambeth council flat surrounded by Bleeding Heart holograms, vats of holy water, royal family themed paraphernalia and nun-smuggled poteen. We ate potatoes of every variety, drank Irish coffee with very little coffee in it and fought each other for the comfy chair. If anyone was worried about anything – a rattle on a motorbike or a stiff knee – we just had it blessed. Simple. I was never alone, even when I wanted to be, because He was omnipresent. So I simply got on with it in the knowledge that no matter what I did, or looked like, my divine soulmate would never leave me or let me down. OK, maybe I was a bit of a flirt, as

He wasn't the only God in my life. I embraced other religions, cast spells under a full moon and had a go at meditation in a vain attempt to achieve Buddhist enlightenment. But at the root of my polytheistic comprehension and Native American Indian dream-catchers sat Catholicism, the reason for my existence and inevitably to be my conclusion. I wanted to go to Heaven when I died, after all, that is what living is all about for a Catholic. We live through the misery, pain and lessons so that we can die, because apparently that's when life gets really good. And while I had people rooting for me in Heaven and on earth there was a point to everything – no matter how bad things got, I was loved.

Back in Atlanta, 11 September 1996

The band and I had arrived in Georgia intending to blaze an indelible trail. Before leaving England we'd scratched out our names on a bench somewhere in an Essex village hoping desperately to return and see them in neon lights instead. But while the boys' battered Richenbackers were still stashed in the overhead lockers of our 747, things had started to go wrong. Customs had us pegged as troublemakers. The latex gloves were warmed, lubed and ready for use.

In retrospect, I should have never worn that leopardskin top; it marked us out from the sensible travellers. One glance at my Rod Stewart tribute outfit and bony fingers were beckoning us into the shabby, secret rooms of Immigration and Deportation. We were escorted by armed guards away from the law-abiding decent folk and split up. Our inter-rogators decided that I was a prostitute – the leopardskin top, I'm telling you – there to fund the boys with my shagging skills. Had John phoned ahead? We were bullied, tormented and teased before finally being released without charge.

Our freedom, however, was to be short-lived. The very next day we were back in the slammer, unaware of an Atlanta by-law that made the public consumption of alcohol a crime. We were picked up in the car park of the first American bar we set foot in, for having the audacity to drink beer in the open, without the decency to cover our cans with a brown paper bag. Guns were waved about, we were stretched out on the bonnet of a police cruiser, and our newly reinstated passports were promptly taken off us again, pending a court appearance the following week.

When we finally got our hearing, in the sweltering, steamy afternoon heat, it was very quickly apparent where Judge Bronson's sympathies lay. He called the rotund little Hitler who had booked us in the car park to the stand. Officer Robertson removed his hat, smoothed his buzz cut and followed his snout-like nose to the bench. I wiped sweaty palms on my itchy second-hand suit and glanced down the row of bandmates. Court veteran and bass guitarist Stuart shot me a relaxed wink; everyone else looked as nervous as I felt.

'Officer Robertson,' said the judge, sprawled over his desk with lazy authority.

'Y'r Honour?' said Robertson, worrying his hat brim with fat fingers.

'I see that there are four bodies on the bench there. Would you concur?'

Officer Robertson followed the line of Judge Bronson's hammer then passed along the line. He silently mouthed the numbers as he counted us.

'Yessir.'

'And yet,' said the judge, brandishing Robertson's report, 'only three names appear on your report. I wonder,' this he addressed to us, 'whether one of you kids is superfluous to requirements? Is one of y'all tagging along because you don't want to be the only one of your friends without a fine?'

We said nothing.

'What do you think, Officer Robertson? Is it three and one here for moral support, or were all four there on the night?

Officer Robertson stuttered and puffed. 'Well, sir, see—'

'Case dismissed.' Bronson banged the hammer, making Robertson jump.

'You kids can get out of here. Robertson, you time-wasting fool, there are times when you might consider cutting the tourists a little slack. I believe it's illegal *not* to drink on the streets of London, isn't that so, friends?'

We laughed and prayed thanks for the coolest courthouse in the Confederacy.

'I'm afraid I'm gonna have to hit you with the court costs, kids. $25 apiece. Robertson, if it were up to me I'd have your badge. Get out of here. I'm sure there's a jaywalking grandma out there just waiting for the long arm of the law.'

We left the courthouse elated, if slightly poorer, but the whole affair had been pretty stressful. As Keith and I picked the events apart in the bar later that evening, what began as a playful post-mortem soon turned into a drunken argument, then a bitter, accusing, all-out fight. It was a pattern that recurred throughout our relationship – bicker, fight, fuck, repeat – and an inauspicious start to our time in the States; time that continued with months of living in a roach-infested warehouse with a heroin-addled Confederate lunatic and a colony of hissing geckos; the slow, depressing conversion of the band from next big thing to also-ran; my personal failure to provide my generation's answer to *On the Road*; and a series of suspected infidelities. When we finally cut our losses and headed back to Southend-on-Sea, it didn't take too long for us to realize that Keith and I didn't need or want each other any more. Single again, I decided I'd had my fill of dubious men, and even more dubious bosses. I wanted a quiet life and a proper job, one where I didn't have to wear rubber. I wanted to stop running for good. And no bloke was going to shag things up for me either. I toughened up post-Keith and resolved to shield myself from Cupid's arrow. Love was for sissies anyway. Never again would I have so much as a drawer in a boyfriend's flat. Never.

338 Euston Road, London, 1998

I liked the look of Toby the first time I saw him, on the fifteenth floor of a London publishing house. It was the very first day of my new job and brand-new, hotpant-free, existence. Toby arrived – traditionally late, as I was to discover – for an in-house marketing meeting. He slung a powder-blue jacket on the back of his chair and grinned at me. That was it really; I was smitten. And from the moment we shared our first drunken snog by the piss-soaked staircase of Charing Cross station a year or so later, I had a feeling we had a future.

Toby finally proposed to me on a very sticky Soho night, a fingernail moon slung low in neon-lit darkness. He'd taken me for a romantic, expensive dinner where we held hands over the condiments and gazed lovingly at each other until we went boss-eyed. It was that sort of place. As we left I saw him

43

fumbling in his pocket and assumed he had pinched an ashtray. How wrong I was. Instead, Toby dropped to his knees in the middle of Lexington Street and popped the question. The Green Cross Code man would have turned blue if he'd seen us, but love doesn't look both ways. A small crowd of rowdy revellers and a tramp with his penis out saw what was happening and for a moment a hush fell. The tramp tucked his mouse back in its house and craned his head to catch my answer. It was the most romantic moment of my life. I had finally found the man that I wanted to grow old and hopefully not too wrinkly with. I was going to be Mrs Starbuck.

For weeks I waggled my diamond-festooned finger at delighted friends and family. And then we hit the snag. A very big one. How and where, exactly, were an agnostic and a Catholic-in-crisis ever going to get hitched?

I had always expected a Catholic church wedding. My proud father was going to sweep me down the bridal runway. There would be incense, towers of star-gazer lilies, a kindly parish priest and a semi-deaf OAP belting out 'Here Comes the Bride' on a clapped-out organ. It was what I had always dreamed of – except the brief phase where I wanted to get hitched in white DMs at a local indie club in Essex. But I was no longer so sure if I needed a priest's say-so, in which case I had no intention of dragging my poor fiancé through a ceremony that neither of us believed in. And anyway, despite my gnawing disillusionment, I still respected the Church too much to stand up and lie to it.

One way or another I needed to settle things; unfortunately B&Q doesn't do spiritual poly-filler, it's not that easy to find. I even asked Jeeves on the web, but he only provided Catholic dating agencies. I'm not naive enough to think that one can ever settle the God question for good – not on this side of the veil at least – but before I tied myself to Toby, body and soul, I needed to find a way of dealing with my own changing beliefs that would alleviate the nagging fear of damnation.

GROTTO BOUND

In Tibet there is a snow-laden pyramid of rock that reaches high into the heavens. This is the mighty Mount Kailash. Hindu mythology recognizes this sleeping giant as the only residence of the gods that can be visited by man in his mortal body. It is one of the highest, most desolate and remote places on earth. Hindus, Buddhists and others besides believe that spiritual brownie points can be earned by following the 53km pathway that circles it. A single circuit is said to eradicate a lifetime of sin. After 108 circuits you're in Nirvana. The truly pious travel on their knees, performing a succession of outstretched prostrations, rubbing their humble garb to tatters and pushing their bodies to the limit of endurance.

We made it to Lourdes, Catholicism's Pyrennean hot spot in two and a half hours, sitting down. There wasn't an in-flight movie, but we did get sandwiches.

Toby will tell you that I'm playing it cool with the flying part. OK, so we didn't get to France by walking on our knees

– we had a schedule to keep – stress-wise, our hop across the Channel was a little like the road to Mount Doom. Don't get me wrong, I love to travel – I'm inexhaustibly keen when it comes to digging around in strange places and have that same naively fearless quality of a Victorian missionary – but when it comes to the actual travelling, I'm a nightmare. You'd never suspect it from the number of stamps in my dog-eared passport, but I have a dread of flying. Or, more specifically, of suddenly not flying any more at altitudes where 'not flying' is a terminally bad idea. It hasn't stopped me getting about, however. In my hardcore traveller days, I simply steeled myself for the miracle of modern aviation with a cocktail of black market Valium and hard liquor. Toby's weaned me off the hooch these days but the fear remains. It shortens my temper like a bushido blade shortens samurai warriors and leads to pre-flight tiffage with laughable predictability.

Twenty-four flights in three years. Eight international airports. Six leading airlines. Four really shitty ones. We have never been involved in a near miss, never had engine trouble or hit bad weather. We've never been hijacked, or shot at, or had to perform an emergency landing on water. We've never started a holiday without a good bout of anxiety-fuelled bickering in the airport lounge, either. And yet, however sound the vessel, I feel closer to death every time we set foot on a plane together.

The drive to the airport was surprisingly peaceful. Although we reached our pre-booked parking space with enough time to pop home for a snack before we checked in, I was eager to catch the shuttle bus to the terminal as soon as possible, in case we hit heavy car park traffic.

Five minutes later, with only five hours to go before we boarded, we were tucking into the 'full-Irish' at a shamrock-festooned theme pub. Toby commented that he thought I was being 'suspiciously well-behaved'.

'Are you OK?' he asked.

'I'm fine.'

'Not panicky?'

'Fine. Morning, Sister.'

I sat up straight and smiled brightly as an elderly nun with a tartan carry-all brushed past our table. I couldn't help peering after her as she joined a group of wimple-wearing friends in the non-smoking area. I let out a small sigh and turned back to my breakfast. Toby looked as if dots were being joined in his head. He turned in his chair to survey our fellow diners. There were a lot of grey cardigans, a lot of flat shoes, and an awful lot of little, silver, dead men on strings visible. Toby glanced surreptitiously at me.

'There's enough dog collars in this room to kit out Crufts,' he whispered.

I was too busy scanning the patrons of the pre-fab pub to reply. I sat with my back straight and my shoulders back, nibbling a grilled tomato daintily. The assembled clergy seemed to be eliciting a sort of papist Pavlovian, convent-schooled response in me. I was on my best behaviour.

'My God,' said my fiancé, 'what did they do to you at that girls' school?'

'What?'

'They must have whipped you into shape pretty ruthlessly,' he suggested. 'You've been as quiet as a church mouse since you spotted your first cassock. You didn't even squeak on take-off.'

'You have no idea what a Catholic girls' school was like, so don't make assumptions,' I replied.

'I've seen pictures.'

'I've seen your pictures,' I told him, 'and, for the record, it was a very loving, supportive academic environment ... With no naked gymnastics and no spanking.'

'Careful, babe.' Toby pressed a finger to my lips. 'They might hear you.'

I sank back into my seat.

My reversion to well-mannered Catholic schoolgirl lasted all the way to Lourdes. The presence of so many nuns and priests had a sort of sedative effect that kept my mind off flying and on looking holy for the black and white brigade that made up about 20 per cent of our fellow travellers.

On the far side of the eerily unmanned customs hall stood Ray, our pilgrimage rep, holding a clipboard with the tour company's Holy Mary logo emblazoned across its back. He ticked off names as the ill, the elderly and the ordained filed past him and on to the hotel shuttle bus. Not for the first time that day, Toby and I were greeted with a look of ill-disguised surprise. We were too young and too scruffy for the Lourdes crowd.

'At least you've got the advantage of being an insider,' Toby whispered.

'What do you mean?' I asked him.

He shrugged. 'Well, you can cross yourself convincingly and know when to stand, sit or kneel. I'm beginning to feel like an imposter.'

'This is your Lourdes survival kit,' beamed Ray, suddenly

beside us and handing us both a scarlet nylon tote bag; big on logo, light on contents. Inside were a handful of leaflets about the town's many miracle-themed attractions and a copy of the pilgrims' punishing schedule of mass, confession, Mass and communion, with an optional trip to the funicular railway on Sunday afternoon – before Mass.

'We will be seeing you for the six a.m. Mass, won't we?' asked Ray softly.

Toby looked at me. I'm sure my eyes gave away the fact that the prospect of dawn worship was no more appealing to me.

'Erm. Not sure about that,' Toby squirmed. 'Busy day ahead of us, might help to get a little more rest.'

'Ah.' Ray made a tick on his clipboard notepad. 'Well, we'll be seeing you for international Mass in the underground basilica at nine, then?'

Toby stuttered and turned beseechingly at me.

'Don't think we can make it tomorrow, I'm afraid. We've got an appointment with Father Liam, the English-speaking priest in the Domaine,' I replied.

'Oh,' nodded Ray, satisfied. He smiled again and moved silently down the aisle of the bus.

'Nice one, darling,' Toby said, stuffing our survival kit into the overhead rack. 'Classic avoidance white lie; simple, and convincing. The name was dangerous, mind you. What would you have done if there really was a Father Liam, eh?'

'There is,' I grinned. 'We're going to see him at nine o'clock tomorrow morning.'

He checked my 'poker face' for signs and the grin dropped. 'Oh.'

'What did you think we were here for? The bars?'

'Well, no,' he began, 'although there might be bars. We are in France.'

'Sorry, babe,' I said, 'the only spirit you're getting close to this weekend is the heavenly kind.'

'Wine?'

'No doubt you will.'

I'd been to Lourdes twice before. The first time I was three and mostly into wearing a potty on my head and bashing people's kneecaps with baguettes, so my visit didn't have much impact. My mother was fighting breast cancer and had come for a dip in the famous baths. That trip holds powerful, magical memories for her. To this day she believes that the power from this holy place and the healing waters might have contributed to her recovery.

Pilgrimage number two was a nun-run school trip. I was among the saved back then, but still more interested in buying rabbit-tail key rings and sparkly rosary beads. Father Dorricott, Sister Colombanus and the team bravely chaperoned an army of teenagers with training bras and warbly voices to foreign lands. We were bursting at the seams with holiness and hormones. I was an ardent believer and despite all the youthful shenanigans, the place affected me deeply. In between performing impromptu Mel and Kim dance routines for the boys with my best friend Deirdra, I worked hard and I prayed hard. I waved my candle furiously in the evening procession of light and marvelled at the abandoned crutches of the cured fixed to the walls of the grotto, visible evidence that God listened to and answered the prayers of the truly faithful. I remembered the deep impact those healing baths had on me.

Like my mother, I had trusted their powers without question. I believed that I had emerged from the water not just healed but magically dry, and shared this conviction with my equally devout classmates. Now I was returning, a Catholic bad apple with a cynical new outlook.

One of the things I missed most about my faith was the feeling of community that going to church gave me. It's the sense of belonging, of being missed when you're not there. These days, people drift about rather anonymously. But the religious stick together, congregations congregate. At Lourdes I felt emotionally overwhelmed; angry that I had lost my place in this world, but full of hope for the first time in ages. I wondered if there was any chance of a miracle for me on my third visit to this little mountain town.

The winding streets of Lourdes were bursting with life and we were swept through the narrow streets on a tide of pilgrims towards the Domaine, the spiritual centre of the town, where St Bernadette saw Mary among the rocks of a small grotto. The tightly packed crowd was a welcome defence against the bitterly cold, cloudless evening. That night, with the pilgrimage season in full swing, the grotto was heaving with worshippers. Tens of thousands of the faithful and the hopeful were ambling through the modest mountain town and towards the grotto; the streets of Lourdes were crammed with human traffic. The crowds flowed south in tight procession, until they crossed the River Gave and burst outwards to fill the broader paths of the Domaine, a magnificent pontifical playground of grey stone basilicas and rolling green pastures. Voices, united in song, soared towards us, growing stronger and clearer with every step. As we approached, I felt exhilarated and scared. Here I had known God. Would I find him waiting for me?

Toby held out a packet of chocolate pebbles. 'Want one?'

'I thought we bought those for your Aunt Jean?' I sighed, stirring from my reverie. He raised an eyebrow and jiggled the pack at me.

'Ah, well I thought we'd buy her the next pack. Want one?'

I shook my head. 'Nope, I feel too nervy to eat.'

'Why? Are you sure this isn't just because you polished off a bowl of ice cream and half of my croissant?'

I shrugged and glanced around uncomfortably. 'To be honest, I'm feeling like a fraud, surrounded by all these believers. We should be taking it more seriously.'

'We are, aren't we?'

'Well, yes.'

He shoved the sweets back in his pocket and looked confused. 'If anyone should be feeling like a fraud it's me.' He lowered his voice as we stood back to watch an assortment of priests glide serenely past in procession. 'I haven't even been christened.'

'Are we welcome, do you think? After all, you don't believe and I'm not so sure any more.'

'It's not members only, is it? The whole point is that anyone can come here, whether they believe or not. The very fact that you are here at all automatically works in your favour surely, because it shows you at least have an open mind.'

'I suppose so.'

'And anyway, if it wasn't for cynics poking about,' Toby continued, 'how would we ever learn what's true and what's not? If a belief system is solid, it should be able to take a little examination.'

We walked on, past a huge statue of Mary surrounded by brightly coloured roses. Toby gave my hand a little squeeze.

'We're as welcome as anyone. Let's catch the show.'

The light had faded and hundreds of candles were flickering in the twilight. We found a spot with a good view and let the space fill up around us. To the right of the grotto stood an illuminated statue of the Virgin Mary. A young man knelt in a pool of light and managed to lay a single red rose at her feet before what looked like a bouncer emerged from the shadows to move him on.

'It's the actual grotto,' I whispered to Toby in a trance. 'This is it.'

As I watched the faithful stream past Bernadette's grotto, kissing the wet stone walls, conflicting emotions coursed around me. The wooden crutches that had once lined the hollowed cavern had rotted or been removed, yet the queue of believers still snaked endlessly around the grotto just as I recalled. They shuffled slowly, quietly, touching the cool, smooth rocks, worn down where thousands of hands had touched before, and filling containers of the special water. It was like a prayer-camp wet-T-shirt competition. I emptied out my Evian bottle and went to fill it from a tap.

'Why don't you fill yours?' I said to Toby.

He shook his head. 'Nah, it's OK. It's only water.'

'Not only water, *Lourdes* water.' I reminded him. 'Miracle water.'

'Hmm.'

He was being careful. He was surrounded, after all. But while I filled my bottle to the brim I spotted him slapping a little on his face, like aftershave. Eager to join in and probably also scared that they'd rumble him, I'd also caught him practising earlier how to make the Christian sign of the cross, murmuring something about 'Spectacles, testicles, wallet and watch', and it had made me grin. It wasn't that I was trying to convert him, mind you, after all I needed re-conversion myself. I downed a couple of pints of the good stuff and we headed for our hotel, so I could be near to the loo when the miracle worked its way through me.

Like me, Toby loves France. He likes the French and their booze and their breakfast foods. While Lourdes had both of these in abundance, it was clear he was unsettled by the town's one-trick tourist trade. This was France deep down, you could tell by the fresh bread and stinky cheese, but first and foremost, thanks to a flash of light 150 years ago, Lourdes is Pays de Bernadette Soubirous.

Bernadette was the first of nine children born to François and Louise Soubirous. Her father was a miller who found the daily grind did not cover the rent on his property, and the family were plunged into poverty. In 1855, Bernadette fell prey to an outbreak of cholera. She survived the epidemic only to develop chronic asthma and also tuberculosis, conditions that were to remain with her for the rest of her life.

On Thursday, 11 February 1858, little Bernadette was gathering firewood with her sister, Toinette, and a friend, Jeanne, near the grotto of Massabielle. While her companions splashed through a stream, Bernadette, wise to the dangers of catching cold, stopped to remove her stockings. She heard a rustling in the trees behind her and turned to look. The trees and the wind were still. She turned back to the grotto and was blinded by a brilliant light. When her vision cleared, she saw a beautiful lady in a white dress with a blue sash. Following the lady's lead, Bernadette made the sign of the cross and prayed the

SARA HULSE & TOBY STARBUCK

rosary. Then the lady vanished. (Toinette and Jeanne missed the lot.)

Over the next five months, Bernadette saw the lady on seventeen further occasions, with a growing audience of onlookers who gathered to hear this poor young girl relay messages from an invisible spirit. 'Pray for the conversion of sinners,' said the mystery lady – which Bernadette did – and instructed her to 'drink of the water of the grotto and wash your face'. This was a slightly stranger request, but Bernadette got down on her hands and knees in the mud of the Massabielle grotto and drank the dirty water for the Mayor and all his dignitaries to see. By vision number fifteen, the crowd had grown to 7,000. At vision sixteen, the spectral lady announced herself, through her corporeal representative, Bernadette, to be 'the immaculate conception'.

These days, this extraordinary St Bernadette story – she was beatified in 1925 – is bread and butter for the townspeople of Lourdes. The old town is dominated by gift shops selling identical collections of rosary beads, holographic icons and little, white Mary mints in oval tins. The Domaine itself looks for all the world like the religious equivalent of the Glastonbury Festival, albeit with less littering and better toilets. Instead of the Pyramid and NME stages, you've got the Upper and Rosary Basilicas; instead of the Dance tent, there is the echoing, subterranean sound-system of Pierre Vago's 1958 Underground Basilica of St Pius X, with its capacity of 20,000. Smaller chapels and tents dot the landscape and groups of Spanish and Italian youths, awol from school trips, gather to smoke under the trees.

About that rustling. Let me play devil's advocate for a moment, and advance Toby's cynical take on the legend.

Bernadatte Soubirous, wheezing, sickly and underfed, has in the last three years survived cholera, asthma and the tuberculosis that will eventually do for her, aged thirty-five, in 1879. She is poor and ill-educated but devout, and her devotion carries her through the trials of subsistence as she gathers what little wood she can find near the scrubby grotto, to fuel the stove at her family's one-room lodgings, in what was once the town jail. Tired and hungry, her immune system battered by years of attack, Bernadette succumbs to an epileptic seizure. It's not unlikely. Even today, epilepsy is the second most common neurological condition after migraine. (Apparently 30 per cent of people will suffer an epileptic seizure at some point in their lives.) Stress, tiredness, malnourishment and illness can all be benefactors in the build-up to a seizure. When a seizure comes, it can be presaged by any number of 'warning signs'. Some speak of a wave of calm overcoming their body. Some talk of blinding lights, violent headaches or burning visions. Some hear the rushing of the ocean . . . or the rustling of leaves.

So, what if Bernadette had, not a vision of Mary, but an epileptic seizure? There's no need to suggest wilful deception from the outset on Bernadette's part; she may well have interpreted her experience in religious rather than medical terms. However, what if in relating her experience to siblings and friends, then parents and townspeople, Bernadette set in motion a chain of events that overwhelmed her completely, and left her with no choice but to play for the crowd or lose her new-found celebrity status and the three square meals a day that came with it. As Hippocrates said even before the birth of Christ: 'People believe that this disease is sacred simply because they don't know what causes it. But some day I believe they will, and the moment they figure out why people have epilepsy, it will cease to be considered divine.'

It wouldn't matter to the truly faithful though, I suppose. The distinction between a vision and an hallucination is a modern one. But what really troubled Toby, he told me as we wandered through the crowds, is the industry that has grown up around Bernadette. The miracle industry.

There have been sixty-six Vatican-approved, honest-to-goodness miracles connected to Lourdes, and specifically to the 'healing' spring water, since 1862. Today, the muddy puddle has been transformed. A 20,000 gallon reservoir of grotto spring water is piped around the Domaine to row upon row of gleaming chrome taps. An endless stream of pilgrims wait in line to drink, wash or fill flasks and bottles from the 'h$_2$oly' spring.

At the heart of the grotto-plex are the baths, a twentieth-century addition to the St Bernadette experience. Total immersion in the icy spring water is by no means compulsory for the Lourdes pilgrim – Bernadette herself was instructed by the virgin only to drink a little and wash her face – but it's the ride with the biggest queues. And if we can believe the glossy periodical that passes for a parish paper in this neck of the woods, it gets results, too.

The next morning I dragged my bleary-eyed fiancé through the bustling streets back to the Domaine. He was a little put out as the group trip to the mountains, our only non-religious activity, had been knocked off the schedule and replaced with a 5 a.m. mass.

An icy wind blustered around tight corners and we dug our hands deeply into the depths of our pockets and shivered. I'd made contact with Father Liam Griffin before we left England, and he'd been happy to meet up with us. He was charming and friendly on the phone but with every step towards his office the nerves and nausea grew within me. I hadn't explained the full significance of this particular appointment to Toby. The whole Lourdes thing, the meeting with a Catholic priest right in the heart of where I had once felt close to God, was so that I could try to move forward. I wanted Father Liam to tell me that whatever I decided it would be all right, that God would be there for me even if I wasn't for him, that I was free to choose where I married, even if it wasn't in the family fold. I was hoping for a lot, but then a lot depended on it.

We found Father Liam's office on the second floor of a neo-gothic building in the Domaine's resource centre. He welcomed us at the door and ushered us into a sunlit room with a bird's eye view of the milling pilgrims in the courtyard outside. Father Liam was a tall, smiley type with greying, black hair and an air of calm. We sat at a low coffee table, waved away his offer of tea and biscuits and fell into an easy chat. After swapping small talk I briefed him on our business in Lourdes and worked up to one of the questions that had been bothering me.

I shuffled to the edge of my chair. 'I have lost my faith, Father.'

Father Liam formed an igloo with his hands to perch his chin on and nodded for me to carry on.

'And I'm not sure where this journey will take me.'

'Of course,' he agreed. 'And doubting is progress.'

I smiled at him; he really was a very nice man.

'Will I always be welcome back if I do decide the God I have always known is the right one?' I asked.

'Yes,' Father Liam confirmed. 'You will always be welcome back.'

'Am I welcome if I don't believe?'

'Ah.' He paused for a moment to gaze out on the swelling crowd of believers below. 'But why would you want to be welcome if you don't believe?'

'Because I'm not sure,' I explained. 'I'm not sure if I ever will be. Although while I say that I don't believe, there is still a nagging part of me that tells me I'm wrong. I know that the religion says we should believe without seeing. Surely God would give us *some* proof to stop us all bickering if he truly existed.'

Father Liam indicated to the thousands of people outside. 'Some people would say he has – you just need to look out there for that.'

I sighed. 'I have such a void without God and nothing to fill it. I could kid myself that I do believe and carry on as before, but that's not enough. You must know that.'

'Of course,' he agreed. 'God is everything and in everything. After you have finished searching you might come to a better understanding of it all, and have a stronger belief in Him. Then you will have discovered everything for yourself rather than simply being told what is right.'

'But what happens if I don't find it again?' I asked.

He shook his head slowly. 'I don't think that will happen.'

I met his gaze. 'But you can't guarantee that, can you? I might not. And in this quest for spiritual stuffing, what happens if I conclude that my God, or rather your God, isn't the right one?

'Go on,' Father Liam encouraged warmly.

I flopped back in my chair and explained how I thought that

religion was born from varying cultures trying to harness and understand the same inexplicable thing and that doctrine was simply the paperwork. I apologized for blasphemy and told him I believed that all religions contain the same or at least similar positive message and that surely it shouldn't matter what people believed as long as they were essentially good people.

'It's crazy that if there really is one God he'd have us all warring over him,' I ranted. 'People are prepared to die for their faith. How can every religious group be the one true faith? Surely the very existence of each one cancels the others out? And it might even be,' I continued, 'that at the end of all this I conclude I don't need a God after all, and love for humanity is enough.' I sat back in my chair. 'I might go secular.'

Father Liam smiled and began to explain my situation. As he did I simply couldn't control the steady flow of minor blasphemies that escaped my lips. 'God.' I gasped in response to every new point. 'Jesus!' Toby nudged me in the ribs several times but nothing could stop my automatic profanity. It had been too long since my last confession, I'd forgotten the etiquette.

Apostasy, that's my problem. Once a Catholic always a Catholic. It seems that thanks to a family tradition to sign me up in infancy, I'm locked into the Church of Rome, whether I like it or not, for all my dying days – and quite possibly beyond. Any change of heart on my part means automatic damnation. I've read *Paradise Lost*, so I've some idea what to expect. It's not an enticing prospect. Father Liam, however, explained Heaven as 'being with God', and Hell as 'having missed the opportunity'.

Toby, who has never been among the saved, neatly side-steps

the problem of apostasy. He gets to stay on the list of heavenly potentials, while I wait for my tent to become available at Camp Lucifer. Of course, if I'm really on the road to total rejection of my former beliefs, I shouldn't let a little thing like the myth of eternal torment bother me, but surely, when Hell itself is on the cards, it's worth hedging your bets a little. Was Father Liam trying to scare me gently back towards the Jesus?

'What about the short-term?' I said, changing the subject. 'In your mind, and from a religious perspective, what is love?'

I watched while Father Liam absorbed my query. It was such a vast question, with so many possible answers.

'Well,' he began gently, 'first it's an emotion. But it's the easing of others primarily.' He paused thoughtfully. 'If I had to give you a definition I'd say that it was putting others before you. And of putting God before anyone.'

'So we have to put God first, then others, then us last?' I asked.

He shook his head. 'It's more about loving God in other people.'

'OK, then, back to our dilemma.' I said. 'What about marriage, Father? I can't lie at the altar. I don't want to have to. I'm not sure whether I believe or not and don't know if I ever will again. All I am certain of is that I want to be married. Surely a benevolent God would want his child to be happy?'

Father Liam smiled conspiratorially and winked at me. 'You'll be back,' he said.

He clearly wasn't getting the whole loss of faith thing. It was exactly this blind conviction that I was running from. I tried not to cry.

'What about an Anglican marriage?' I asked.

His eyes widened. 'Yes, you could do that if you got a

dispensation for the Pope.' He grinned. 'Are you close to him?'

'Jesus!' I slumped in my chair, biting my godless tongue.

Toby discreetly jabbed me in the arm again. It was all so ridiculous. To be honest though, I wasn't keen on getting married in an Anglican church anyway; it's just too close to the Roman Catholic model, despite the centuries of sectarian fighting that say otherwise; a case of 'meet the new boss, same as the old boss, but with married staff and less flash uniforms'. Anyway, it wasn't about God A versus God B; my problem was with religion in general. I drunk deeply from my hip-flask of grotto water and hoped Father Liam didn't get the wrong impression.

'What about a Catholic blessing? Could I have one of those, if I had a secular ceremony?'

The priest shook his head again. 'There's not really any such thing. If you're looking for a marriage that's 100 per cent—'

'Kosher?' said Toby.

'—approved,' continued Father Liam, 'it has to be a Catholic ceremony in a Catholic church. Sorry if that scuppers your plans.'

He could see I was getting desperate and smiled kindly.

'Let me ask you this. You are committed to marriage itself. Why? Could you not live without it? What is it that makes you want the ceremony?'

I thought for a moment. Why was I so set on marriage? I'd been happy cohabiting for years. What was it that made it so important? I didn't have an answer.

Guilt, of course, that's largely what it came down to. I couldn't disappoint my parents, who still believed, when it came to seeing me walk down the aisle. They had put up with a lot from me over the years, the least I could do was give them the wedding they wanted. And hadn't I dreamed of a good-old fashioned church wedding myself for thirty years? Despite all this, it just didn't feel right. It wasn't my fault I was bloody Catholic. As I was adopted, I could have ended up being brought up in any religion, or none at all. And to be honest, I wouldn't have cared what creed, gender or colour the family were, so long as they loved me. But I wonder what would have happened in terms of a self-developed religion if nobody had wanted me. Would a Catholic God have still recruited me somehow, even as an unwanted nipper in a children's home?

All these team colours were giving me a headache. In my mind, Toby was the perfect partner and a good moral person regardless of his godless upbringing. If we were lucky enough to have children I hoped that our family life would be based on love and mutual respect, with or without the weekly ritual of a Sunday service. Part of me felt damned, part didn't give a damn. Unless I could appease the former, or unleash the latter, I was beginning to wonder if I would ever feel properly married outside of the Catholic Church. Because it seemed, if it wasn't R-C, it was straight to H-E-L-L, for me at least. That's the crazy thing. In our multicultural world, the Church of Rome accepts the legitimacy of all marriages, regardless of faith, provided it's the faith you were born with. However, if you are born lucky – that is Catholic to the Catholics – and you marry a heathen, well, don't say they didn't warn you. The Catholic Church is like the Reader's Digest junk mail database; once you're on the books, there's no way back.

*

'I wasn't expecting that,' I said, as we left Father Liam's office and wove our way through the crowds in the esplanade.

'What were you expecting?' Toby asked.

'Answers,' I replied. 'Now I don't know what to think. He told me to embrace the process of soul-searching.'

'And?'

'And that's all well and good, but if all my soul-searching and free-thinking leads me anywhere except straight back to the bosom of Mother Mary, I get to rot in Hell for all eternity, while you . . . what does happen to you?'

'Dunno,' he shrugged. 'Limbo?'

'While you swan about in limbo with some limbo bimbo.'

'Only if the Christians are right,' he reminded me. 'And you shouldn't let a little thing like damnation get you down. Maybe you'll find a bigger God to protect you. One who knows kung fu. And anyway, I don't think limbo can be that attractive a prospect, Sara. I mean, why struggle for a first-class afterlife if there's an economy option that's perfectly acceptable once you get used to the food?'

'The point is, I'll always have that hanging over me,' I told him gravely. 'You'll never know how deeply rooted this stuff is even if you think you might have an inkling. Some people never quite manage to stop believing in Santa Claus, you know? The sort who witter on about "the spirit of Father Christmas" being real.'

'Well, it's the spirit of the thing that's important—'

'But say there was a chance, even a faint chance, that Father Christmas really did exist, imagine what you might be prepared to do on the off chance that he might slide down your chimney with a sackful of booty once a year and save you from seasonal money worries for good?'

'If only.'

'Quite. Well, imagine that the pay-off isn't a lifetime of board games and patterned socks, but an eternity of bliss in the presence of God. And the penalty for failing to leave out a sherry and a mince pie for Santa—'

'—And a carrot for the reindeer.'

'—is eternal pain and suffering on a level beyond all earthly woes. What would you do?'

'I might be tempted to put out the sherry and mince pies.'

'And the carrot,' I added.

'I've forgotten where this was going,' he admitted.

'I'm a Catholic,' I yelled, scattering a flock of pigeons at the foot of the Crowned Virgin statue. 'Don't you get it, Toby? They've still got me.'

The next morning we went for our head-to-toe spiritual sheep-dip in the heavy, grey concrete of the Lourdes bath-house. Passing the bowed heads of sobbing women, Toby and I were separated into single-sex groups. The nerves kicked in.

I bit my lip.

'What's wrong?' he asked.

'Oh, nothing, don't worry. It's fine.'

Fortunately Toby is well-versed on the complexity that is woman. He knows that 'nothing' generally means 'everything'.

'What's up?'

I admitted I was finding it difficult to get a sense of peace or perspective because of the copious hoards of pilgrims. There was suffering, pain and bravery as far as the eye could see. People had saved up and travelled from all over the world to be close to God and to hope for a better life. It was devastating not to share this conviction any more, like watching everything through a glass wall. And yet, I still couldn't help hoping, rather selfishly, that I might also find a cure.

A few years back I found out that I had temporal lobe epilepsy. I'd always been a bit odd: experiencing apocalyptic visions that came true about a week after I saw them; knowing when people died; sensing things. But the year prior to a nasty grand mal seizure it got out of hand. The NHS missed it, despite an EEG, a series of petit mal seizures, headaches, visions and uncontrollable mood swings. Being the hippy I was I assumed it signalled Armageddon. But then I found out what was wrong in a rather dramatic way. I almost died that night, choking on my own phlegm, and Toby saved my life.

No one really understood what it all meant. My mother and brother turned up with a sack of spuds and stodgy pastries; it was the Irish way. We were going to beat that pesky epilepsy with comfort food. My dad found out about the Mozart Effect, and told me that listening to the K448 piano sonata improved spatial reasoning and is also supposed to reduce epileptic seizures. It's all to do with it having a high degree of 'long-term periodicity'; in other words, wave forms repeated regularly, but not very close together, throughout the piece of music. So for the first few months I went everywhere clutching my Discman, playing Mozart on a loop. A neurologist was quick to confirm that I wasn't psychic or seeing angels at all. In fact, he told me authoritatively that my visions were nothing but petit mal seizures. My desperate need to write was labelled 'hypergraphia' and put down to a 'condition'. The bottom line was that I wasn't special. The spiritual, peculiar and magical world I had always known was quietened by medication. My head began to feel stuffed with cotton wool. I couldn't write. I couldn't feel. I began to lose God.

That's what I've been keeping quiet about this far. I mean, how many people have honest-to-goodness waking religious experiences to pin their faith to? When so much of my spiritual life had been written off as abnormal bursts of electrical activity, was it any wonder that I had gone on to question my beliefs on every level?

The poet Emily Dickinson, for whom the miracle of higher thought was ample proof of divine creation, once referred to the human brain as 'the weight of God'. Of course, these days she'd have to argue the toss with an army of medically minded cynics. In fact, as we learn more about the purpose and malfunctions of the human brain, we present God with perhaps his greatest threat: will medicine one day reduce God to the effects of misfiring neurones or chemical imbalances?

Hyperreligiosity – the excessive devotion to religion – is an acknowledged effect of temporal lobe epilepsy, so I'm not alone in my obsession with spiritual matters. But awareness of my medical predisposition for soul-searching does my head in. Am I sincere in my search for the truth, or simply seized by a misguided neurological compulsion?

It's been suggested by scientists that neurological disorders, such as temporal lobe epilepsy, may well have been an important factor in the origins of prophetic religions. Experiments in this field suggest that the temporal lobes are key in experiencing religious and spiritual belief, regardless of whether or not you're epileptic, and this means that our attitudes towards religion are based on biology. Some of us are simply more receptive to divine suggestion than others and our brains have the power to produce religious awareness with or without our help. Recent advances in 'neurotheology' – the study of the 'neurobiology' of religion and spirituality – have even prompted some scientists to claim they can conjure holy visions in people, even in ardent non-believers. For example, a few years ago Swiss neuroscientist Olaf Blanke and colleagues at Geneva University Hospital, found a shortcut to enlightenment by electrically stimulating an area of the temporal lobe – the angular gyrus in the right cortex – of a woman who had epilepsy, and induced the world's first scientifically stimulated out-of-body experience. It's worth noting here that Professor Blanke has commented that although OBEs often occur for epileptics and migraine sufferers and after cerebral strokes, they also appear in healthy subjects, too. Neurotheologists such as Professor Blanke are gradually gathering data in an attempt to figure out why it is that some of us are predisposed to profound religious experience, while for others spirituality is holy water off a duck's back.

Professor V. S. Ramachandran, MD, Ph.D., is professor and director of the Center for Brain and Cognition, University of California, San Diego, and is adjunct professor at the Salk Institute for Biological Studies, La Jolla, California. He is one of the world's foremost brain researchers and also one of the first to experiment in the field of neurotheology by carrying out an experiment comparing the brains of people with and without temporal lobe epilepsy. He showed his subjects a series of words – either neutral, or ethically or religiously loaded – and measured their responses by the level of their perspiration. Ramachandran discovered that when the test subjects with temporal lobe epilepsy were shown religious words they experienced a huge galvanic skin response. In other words, the involuntary activity in the subjects' neural circuitry seemed to suggest that certain people are automatically more prone to religious suggestion. Ramachandran et al have even gone on to suggest that that there is a 'God spot' in the left temporal lobe of the brain. They suspect that epileptic seizures can sometimes damage the pathways connecting the bit of the brain that deals with the senses to the part that triggers emotional significance. This damage causes those affected to see great spiritual meaning in everything.

Many scientists exploring this field maintain a belief or at least an open mind regarding the divine, and are content to believe they have simply located the chunk of brain from which we can observe it. Professor Ramachandran, for example, suggests that within our brain circuitry could be a sort of antenna, making us receptive to God. But he also seems comfortable with a physiological explanation of divinity, and seems pretty convinced that God lives in the temporal lobes. If that is proved to be so, he has said, then a surgeon removing precisely the right area of brain matter could reasonably be said to have performed a 'Godectomy'.

History is crammed full of charismatic religious figures having dizzy spells and holy visions, and for a while now scientists have been wondering whether the likes of Moses, St Paul, Joan of Arc, Mohammed and St Bernadette might have suffered from what has been termed 'the sacred disease'.

Of course, we can't confidently diagnose dead visionaries of centuries past, but there are more contemporary examples. Born in 1827 in a God-fearing, American Midwestern farming community, Ellen White suffered a brain injury at the age of nine that left her disfigured physically and mentally and also prompted more than two thousand powerful religious visions. Ellen's experiences, which she obsessively recorded in notebooks, led the locals to consider her a prophet. She married an Adventist minister and with him founded the Seventh Day Adventist Church, an offshoot of Methodism, which currently has some 12 million followers around the world.

It was Gregory Holmes MD, director of clinical neurophysiology and epilepsy at Boston Children's Hospital and also a professor of neurology at Harvard Medical School, who first suggested that Ellen White's many visions may have actually been epileptic seizures. Inevitably, the Seventh Day Adventist movement was less than thrilled by his diagnosis. Their spokesman, Dr Daniel Giang, also a neurologist, dismissed the claim, arguing that the pattern of her visions was unusual for seizures, lasting from fifteen minutes to three hours rather than the usual three to five minutes. But the faithful have a habit of coming to the rescue of their own cherished doctrine – I've done it myself. It's not that hard to find a doctor who'll testify that cigarettes are harmless or that seat belts kill. When the stakes are so much higher – salvation or damnation – can one really trust a Seventh Day Adventist?

Religions tend to be based on their founders' teachings, however, not solely on any visions they have. To link the source of all religion to the temporal lobes of the brain, we'd have to be able to prove that all the teachings and institutions were associated with the lobes, never mind the visions. The role of visions in religion are essentially inspirational. They are supposedly signs of divine intervention, causing visionaries to commit to God's work and motivating others to follow. Their messages are usually positive or an upgrade to a previous religion; Ellen White just gave Protestantism a fresh interpretation, with distinctive features such as emphasizing that we should all live healthily. The visionaries' messages are often in keeping with some existing religious tradition because it's what they understand. Did anybody before the advent of Christianity have Christian hallucinations, for example? And when was the last time Our Lady materialized to a Muslim?

Religious believers aren't at all surprised that a part of the brain is associated with religious experience and might argue that temporal lobe activity is stimulated by the presence of God. What if the temporal lobes really did provide a connection to the divine? Could contact with the next world really be just a matter of tuning the brain to the right frequency? The big question is: why do we have this 'God spot' in the first place?

On a day-to-day basis, we can all feel proud of our own sense of reality. It's a carefully managed mental construct that keeps us from crushing introspection and walking into walls. But consider reality in a wider sense, beyond one's immediate surroundings and what's for tea, and the subject becomes mind-boggling. It's easy to speculate that our early ancestors preferred the invention of external Gods and complicated – but controllable – myths to a cacophony of unanswerable questions.

Julian Jaynes caused controversy when he was a psychology professor at Princeton back in 1976 by publishing a theory concerning the emergence of the human mind, founding it from the perspective of psycho-cultural history. In *The Origin of Consciousness in the Breakdown of the Bicameral Mind*, he suggests that the thought processes of our ancestors, living around 3,500 years ago, were not subjectively conscious as we understand it today. In fact, he suggests that it might even have been similar to that of schizophrenics or epileptics. People didn't understand about introspection and interpreted the voices in their heads as directions from their bossy, demanding gods – in such a way epileptics and schizophrenics continue to receive instructions from beyond.

If Jaynes is right, ancient man had it easy. No questions, no conscience, no cares beyond the immediate business of surviving in the ancient world. Have we really made any progress in all these years and at what price?

For now it's up to the growing band of neurotheology pioneers to work out whether God really is just in the mind. The question to be asked is whether transcendental enlightenment through meditation or prayer is a taste of an absolute reality, or just the brain acknowledging its own activity? Although there is evidence to suggest that our brains are hardwired for religion, we can't just dismiss God as a phantom of our brain chemistry. Perhaps religion has evolved as a survival mechanism; after all, studies have shown that believers often live longer and cope better in stressful situations – both fuelled and calmed by the power of their given faiths. But despite evidence to suggest there is nothing 'out there', many of us are finding it hard to let go of the possibility that there might be, because so far there is nothing else to fill that gaping void.

Queuing for the baths at Lourdes is a little like waiting for the National Express at Victoria Coach Station. Several hundreds of people are crammed on to hard seating meant for only a few dozen. Everywhere, people are praying for an end to their suffering. Wedged between giggling Spaniards, near the back of a seated queue, I shuffled sideways along the wooden benches as dry people went in through the bath-house's blue and white curtained doorway, and wet people came out. Across the way, I could see the men's queue and spied Toby being beckoned in. Clearly, the ladies' progress through the bathhouse was much slower. No doubt they were taking the time to use conditioner.

He waved at me, I grimaced back, and an attendant tugged him by the elbow to his feet and ushered him through the curtain.

An hour later Toby re-appeared. I had advanced about two metres along the snaking benches. He caught my eye and gestured his intention to find a cup of coffee. Another forty minutes later and I was in.

I was shown to a seat in what looked a little like the ante-room to a Crimean War field hospital. More blue and white striped curtains divided the room into a series of hospital cubicles. Posters on the walls invited me to pray for the healing power of Christ in every language of the Catholic world. As a dripping woman left the cubicle in front of me, grinning and thanking the bath-house attendants, I was pulled gently to my feet and ushered forward to take her place.

'English?' asked the attendant. Was it my lack of white socks and sandals?

'*Oui*,' I answered, defiantly.

'Hang your clothes on ze 'ook,' she said, unimpressed by my linguistic skills. She handed me a wet robe, heavy with dripping bath water. 'And wrap this around you.'

'Thank you,' I squeaked.

The searing sobs from a nearby Japanese girl reached a peak before ebbing away to a sniffle. She sat huddled in sopping robes staring up at a statue of the Virgin Mary. I removed my clothes and tried to shove my bra in my boot. The attendant fished it out with a pencil and dangled it in front of me, shaking her head.

'*Non*, take it with you.'

'But I—'

She dropped my slutty Wonderbra into my hand and wrapped my fingers tightly around it. 'Take it.'

'OK.'

Maybe there was a bra thief in town and she was looking out for me? Or perhaps I was a dirty Jezebel?

I pulled back the curtain to find two more attendants standing either side of a deep, grey stone bath.

'*Bonjour*,' they said in unison. Hah! Not so easy to spot us when we're naked.

'*Bonjour*,' I answered.

'Ah, English. 'Ave you been 'ere before?'

I nodded and they smiled at me and guided me forward.

The icy plunge was arresting, but the attentive kindness of the bath-house volunteers was one of the warmest experiences I'd ever had. As I stepped out of the bath, flanked by the smiling, gentle French women I was almost brought to tears. I stood up to my knees in freezing water, holding my scarlet bra above my head, and knew I should have been praying, but was too shocked with cold and spiritually muddled to speak. I tipped my head back into the freezing water, wanting to submerge my damaged neurones and wash away the condition that had blighted my health and rattled my faith to the core. A gasp of alarm escaped from the nearest attendant.

'*Mon dieu, madame*. Please, what are you doing?'

The arms guiding me tensed and pulled me upright.

'*Pardon*,' I said, and that was the limit of my French. I pulled a face that I hoped expressed the need for cranial healing. They tapped their temples in agreement and shooed me back to the changing room. As I pulled my jeans over wet legs and squeezed my socks out on the floor, it hit me: there was no 'miracle dry' at the Lourdes bath-house like I had remembered. I was wet, I was cold and, after half a day of waiting in line, I was hungry. There's no way that I will ever know for sure whether or not the Lourdes water is truly miraculous, although I'm sure that there will always be a part of me that believes. But at that moment another little piece of childhood magic had been washed down the plughole.

We spent the afternoon in secular pursuits; shopping and sight-seeing. Predictably, I suppose, Lourdes isn't big on secular sights. There's a hilltop citadel that was once prison to Elgin, the Athens-to-London removals man ... but it was closed. As the shadows grew long, I dragged Toby back to the banks of the river and sat glaring accusingly at the grotto on the opposite side. I felt cheated – and guilty that I felt cheated. I watched the holy hoards swarm across to the grotto and wondered what everyone would do if I dropped to my knees and had a vision. I'd had a few in my time, after all. Would I be laughed at, arrested, believed even? The initial energizing slap of the baths had faded quickly and now I couldn't stop shivering. I felt nauseous and wasn't sure whether it was because I was feeling so unsettled, or because the hotel where we were staying kept feeding me boiled lettuce. France is tough when you don't eat meat. The sun had by now disappeared behind the craggy silhouette of the Pyrennees and inevitably the firefly light of candles began to flicker in the darkness. Toby let me sit there glaring in furious silence until I sidled up for a hug. We hadn't spoken much about our experiences at the baths.

'So how was it for you?'

He shrugged. 'They asked me to kiss the statue of Mary. Is that normal?'

I nodded. 'Oh, yes.'

'OK, good. Well, there was a lot of praying,' he paused and shivered, 'and when the freezing grotto water hit my own personal trinity I felt like I'd been sucker-punched by God.'

I slumped in disappointment. 'So didn't you get anything out of it at all?'

He thought for a few moments and slowly nodded. 'I s'pose I might have,' he admitted eventually. 'I like the group experience thing that you get with faith, but at Lourdes they use that crowd dynamic even better by slowly chipping away at the numbers until you're alone with God'.

'What do you mean?' I asked.

'Well, you start off in a proper throng, don't you,' Toby explained, 'near the grotto entrance. Then you're thinned to a mob on the bath-house benches, slimmed down futher to a modest group in the changing rooms. In the inner rooms it's just you and a couple of nudists, and finally it's just you, God (in triplicate, of course, this being Catholicism) His mum, and a couple of earthbound helpers.'

'Get to the point.' I interrupted.

'It did leave me wide awake and bouncing with energy; positively tickety-boo, in fact. And, for a while, I admit, I hoped it had miraculously cured the dead disc in my back. But I had been carried along with the anticipation of the crowd, forced into a bottleneck of introspection by the bath-house queuing system, rolled in the snow and sent skipping into the sunlight. My feeling of elation was just like the high of riding a roller-coaster with your mates – and it lasted about as long.'

'No miracle cure for your knackered back, then?'

'No. Of course, I hadn't really been expecting a miracle, but then I don't really presume I'm going to win the lottery when I buy a ticket.'

'So still as cynical as ever, then?'

He nodded. 'Sorry, but the whole experience left me cold in more than one sense. My spiritual swim may have been an invigorating experience, in a Swedish kind of way, but it left me as empty as a Texan trucker in a London steakhouse.'

'What about the miracles?' I asked. 'There have been sixty-six, you know.'

He scanned the dark, rippling river and shook his head. 'Simple. Cold water has beneficial effects on people, with or without it having special superpowers.'

He was right, as much as I didn't want to admit it. People have been shrivelling themselves in frosty waters for centuries in a bid to improve their health. The Romans used cold water as a cure for headaches and stomach conditions. It is believed to supercharge the system, improving breathing, muscle tone and in decreasing fatigue. Reports have also claimed that it improves thyroid function and is beneficial for ME sufferers as it boosts the hormonal immune system. Cold water also stimulates the hypothalamus in the brain and the release of endorphins, which produces a feel-good factor, which of course you immediately feel the benefit of when you step out of the Lourdes baths. By the Vatican's own admission, Lourdes water has no therapeutic qualities. Visitors are encouraged to embrace the symbolic importance of water in the Christian story as a way of reconnecting with their faith. But perhaps you needed to have a little bit of faith left before you could reconnect.

It seemed I had come to Lourdes like an ageing rocker visits Brighton, without any real hope of reviving the past, or even finding a parking space for my motorbike.

'So I take it that it wasn't the experience you were hoping for either?' Toby asked, a heavy arm slung over my damp shoulder.

I shook my head and glared at the heaving grotto again.

'It's just not how I remembered,' I mumbled.

'How do you mean?' Toby asked. 'I can't imagine that they put on a different show for every season.'

I frowned. 'It's not the place or the stuff you get up to – the baths and the candles – it's just a feeling. It's not the same. I mean, I came here with school, it all felt so important. So worthwhile. Now, I don't know.'

'Why exactly *are* we here?' Toby asked. 'I know we're here for you, I just don't know quite what you're here for.'

'We're here for *us*,' I told him emphatically. 'Look,' I sighed, 'I want to marry you, right? Because I love you. But what if I don't love you for ever?'

Toby was taken by surprise. 'Are you planning to stop loving me?'

'Look, the way I was brought up, love was a God thing. Love comes from God and the greatest love of all is the love that God has for you. Every other kind of love – between families, or friends, or men and women – is just an aspect of God's love.'

'So?'

'So if there's no God, what is love? An illusion? A conspiracy? A misinterpretation of breeding instincts? I don't want to live in a world without love.'

'Do I need to start hiding the sharp knives?' he asked.

'It's so easy for you,' I sighed. 'Coming at the subject with a clean slate. I suppose it's a bit like being blind. If you're blind from birth, you're going to face problems, but if you lose your sight later, there's the added bonus of crushing depression.'

'I'm sure there are plenty of depressed people who've been blind since birth,' he argued.

'I just mean, a taste of honey, you know? This trip has made me feel like I was lured into a false sense of security for thirty years, then hung out to dry. You, on the other hand, will never miss what you've never had.'

'The way you talk about it, my parents brought me up godless the same way yours brought you up Catholic,' he said, 'But it wasn't like that. They left me to make my own mind up.'

'But that's what I envy; the detachment of your perspective. If I wind up openly rejecting the faith I was born with, I'll disappoint everyone I love. You could shave your head and wear robes and nobody in your family would bat an eyelid. In fact,' I slapped a hand on the table top, emphatically, 'I bet there's not a single, solitary, God-fearing, church-going soul left in the lot of you.'

'Wrong,' he grinned. 'We've a handful of Methodists left in the Cumbrian borders. Mum's lot, moved up from Nottingham.'

'Blimey,' I replied. 'They must see you as the black sheep of the family.'

'They're Methodists, not Puritans.'

'So what's the method?'

'Not sure.'

We buttoned our jackets and stood to leave. Dark clouds

had gathered over the Pyrennean foothills and the wind was gathering.

'This is exciting news,' I continued, shoving a hand into the back pocket of Toby's jeans to warm it up. 'Now that I know you've got a religious heritage of your own, I think it's time we got a little taste of it. We're going to have to take a trip oop north.'

'If we do,' he pleaded, 'don't try the accent. And before you condemn me to a six-hour drive, let's tackle one journey at a time. We're flying tomorrow, remember? Let's pray for good weather.'

'Bastard,' I hissed through chattering teeth, and we squelched off to our hotel to pack, our trainers soggy with grotto water.

THE LAST OF THE FAITHFUL

'We must have gone too far up the M6,' I said, squinting through the snow outside our car. 'Because, unless I'm very much mistaken, this is Norway.'

'We're five minutes away, otherwise I'd stop,' Toby replied confidently, slipping into second as the road dipped and turned ahead of us. 'Besides, the Skoda's in its element.' He gave Grandad's Eastern Bloc iron donkey which I'd inherited an encouraging pat on the dash. 'Built for sub-zero temperatures. Sit tight, we're nearly there.'

'How on earth do you know?' I asked him, peering out at the endless white. 'I can't see past the bonnet.'

'Did you forget your booster cushion?' he teased. 'I recognized the turn by the telephone box at that last village.'

'What telephone box?'

'The one obscured by driving snow, opposite the pub.'

'But you haven't been here for ten years.'

'Thirteen,' he corrected me. 'I've got a good memory for places.'

'And a good set of directions, thank God,' I said, waving his uncle's comprehensive instructions.

'What's the last bit?'

'Right at brow of hill on to dirt track. This is so country.'

'If they've still got goats, I'm going to make you get up at six to milk them.'

I couldn't hide my look of terror.

The back roads of Cumbria are a bad place to be in a blizzard. The range-warmed farmhouse kitchen at the heart of Uncle Peter and Aunty Jane's hilltop home was the perfect antidote. We sat around the table drinking sugary tea and breathing promising smells from the stove.

'No goats, then?' Toby asked, a mite disappointed.

'Not these days,' said Aunty Jane, chopping herbs into a steaming casserole. 'Just a pig and a parrot.'

'Hiya!' said the parrot on cue, bouncing back and forth along her perch in the corner of the kitchen.

'Wibbly's in the barn. She's a pet, not an eater,' said Jane. 'You can meet her tomorrow, if you like, but she's a bit shy of strangers, unlike Connie, there.'

'Hiya!'

'Hello,' I said cautiously.

'Clever Connie!' said Connie, and launched into an ear-piercing telephone ring.

Jane, Toby's mother's cousin, and her husband Peter, live in the borderlands of northern Britain. It's a forbidding landscape that bristles with the ghosts of Armstrongs and Grahams, the great raiding names of England's brutal frontier. The Walmsleys, Toby's lot, added their name to the parish rolls twenty years ago. Or rather, they didn't. The local vicar was quick to call; six potential parishioners, kids included, would have swelled his congregation nicely. But he was dismayed to learn, upon enquiry, that the incomers were Methodists. On the other hand, the local Methody folk were delighted to see their numbers almost double with the Walmsleys' arrival. The discovery that Peter and Jane's oldest daughter was an organist and chorister of considerable talent apparently went down a treat, too.

As they settled into life at Hilltop Farm, the village Methodist chapel became the heart of the family's social life. Sunday services, musical evenings and almost nightly suppers kept everyone busy, and formed bonds of friendship and community that proved invaluable as the children grew. They were, until the turn of the century, the last active representatives of Toby's rightful religious heritage, the liberal Methodist movement of Victorian Nottingham. Peter and Jane were the last bona fide churchgoers in his family. But he had brought me all the way to the snow-swept fields at the foot of Hadrian's Wall to find out why they too had ultimately joined their Midlands kin in apostasy.

'So when did you stop going to church?' Toby asked, eyeing Connie the parrot suspiciously.

'Oh, a few years ago,' said Peter, stroking a fine, red beard, shot through with white. 'It wasn't a cataclysmic decision. We just drifted apart.'

'I was wondering whether your mother's death had anything to do with it,' Toby admitted, Jane and family apparently having born the lion's share of burden following the rapid onset of Alzheimer's in his great-aunt Isobel. 'Was there a moment when you rejected your faith entirely?'

'Not at all,' Jane smiled, 'I'll be honest with you. We were never all that into the God stuff. Methodists are good people. They have a highly tuned sense of morality. We wanted our children to grow up around people who do the right thing, simply because it's the right thing to do. It's a decision we don't regret for a moment, and we still have friendships from the Walton Chapel. But with the kids all grown up, we started to long for our Sunday mornings again.'

'It's a big commitment, being part of a Methodist congregation,' explained Peter. 'In the Church of England, there's a central body that owns and controls everything, but Methodists are completely democratic, and each congregation effectively owns their own chapel and is responsible for its upkeep.'

'That sounds very idealistic,' I said.

'Yeah, well, it's far from ideal if you're the only carpenter in a congregation of twelve, with a Victorian property to maintain.'

'Fair point,' I conceded.

'A lot was expected of us,' said Jane, dishing up the veg.

'But the worst thing was having to sing and pray and stand there every Sunday feeling like a fraud. Not believing. So, we gradually just stopped going '

'Didn't anybody notice?' Toby asked.

'Oh yes,' said Jane. 'When we left, I'm afraid a number of hymn sheets were permanently retired. The reaction was one of sadness, mostly, and confusion.'

'It was heart-breaking, really,' said Peter.

So, the last God-fearing Christians in Toby's clan weren't God-fearing at all. They weren't even God-believing. He looked a little bit hard done by. He didn't come to Cumbria in search of salvation, but I had nuns, holy water and compulsive candle-lighting, and he was spiritually bankrupt. Instead of his religious roots, he found a couple of 'Undercover Humanists' who'd joined the club that came closest to their altruistic views. Their decision to tolerate or ignore the wilder tales of the club's sandal-clad founders was easy, as the benefits of membership outweighed the 'son of God' claims. Their kids grew up well-rounded, morally upright citizens. Then they handed in their badges and membership cards, and had a well-deserved lie-in.

'You know,' said Jane, lifting a huge casserole to the kitchen table and drawing up a chair, 'your grandparents never went to church.'

'But Grandpa Herbert signed the pledge,' Toby protested. His mum's father had gone tee-total for the Methodist cause. That required a leap of faith, surely?

'So did his brother, your Great-uncle George,' said Jane. 'But by the time we were kids, they just packed us off on a Sunday morning and had the house to themselves.'

'Maybe the war shook their faith out of them?' Toby suggested.

'Maybe,' agreed Jane. 'Herbert and George were both pacifists, like their father before them, but they weren't conscientious objectors. They signed up where they could use their skills. Herbert joined the Engineers, George to another regiment. Of course, it didn't keep them out of the conflict. Your grandpa was at Dunkirk. He must have seen enough to give him pause for thought, at the very least.'

Jane lifted the lid of the casserole. The mouth-watering aroma of coq-au-vin enveloped the kitchen. Toby looked over at me and scrunched up his face. I tried not to look panicked.

'You're going to tell me you're vegetarians, aren't you?' said Jane, eyeing us suspiciously.

'Sara is, I'm not!' Toby blurted out, ratting me out quicker than a seven-year-old in his big brother's headlock. 'Mmm. Smells lovely.'

I *had* asked him to tell them.

'No problem, plenty of veg,' said Jane with a grin.

'I'm so sorry. We forgot to tell you,' I said, staring pointedly at Toby.

'We didn't think,' Toby added. 'We're idiots.'

'Oh, for God's sake, don't grovel,' said Peter, laughing. 'More for the rest of us. Who wants spuds?'

Very Christian, I thought.

When the remains of dinner were scraped aside – optimistically prepared piles of sprouts consigned to Wibbly's leftovers bowl – it was time for me to learn more about what being a Methodist meant. Connie, meanwhile, was busy gnawing on Toby's hand.

'Nice Connie,' Toby hissed through gritted teeth.

Jane laughed. 'Oh dear, she doesn't like you, does she?' She flicked on the kettle. 'It's most unusual for her to take against someone like this.'

Connie sunk her beak further into his flesh. Blood tricked down the inside of Toby's hand.

'I think we should move her.' Peter carefully prised the bundle of agitated aquamarine feathers from Toby's finger and swivelled to face me. 'Want her?'

'What if she doesn't like me either?' I was apprehensive.

Connie was placed on my shoulder. She sat licking my hair

with her tiny black tongue and eyeing Toby suspiciously as he slapped Savlon on his ragged finger. I felt like a pirate.

'Is Methodism similar to the Church of England, then?' I began.

Jane nodded. 'Well it's an off-shoot. It's Protestant.'

'It started in the eighteenth century,' Peter added. 'A group of students, including the Wesleys, started a "Holy Club" in Oxford. I think they did it in an attempt to invigorate the Anglican church, which of course really rubbed the Anglicans up the wrong way.'

'A lot of it is basically Anglicanism, mind you,' Jane explained, 'but there are subtle differences. They don't have communion wine, for example, because you're not supposed to drink.'

Peter raised his glass of red wine. 'Cheers.'

'So what do you use in mass when you're meant to be drinking the blood of Christ? Vimto?'

'Close,' Jane replied. 'Ribena in individual shot glasses. I think the Methodists were pretty forward-thinking about germs, too. No chalice to pass around.' She picked up the brimming coffee pot. 'Anyone?'

Toby held out a mug. 'Me, please. I'll tell you a big difference. No tombolas at my junior school fête.' He looked bitter.

'Why?' I asked. 'What's wrong with a tombola?'

'Gambling,' he explained. 'My sister and I were forced to entertain ourselves buying back all the stuff Mum gave away for the jumble.'

'You little sod.' Jane laughed.

'She should've asked,' Toby replied. 'Just because you haven't seen a toy being played with doesn't mean it's no longer wanted. Children are hoarders too, you know.'

'Are you content now?' I butted in. 'I mean, without religion being so central in your lives? Do you miss the community?'

Peter licked the seam of his roll-up and shook his head. 'Spirituality doesn't need to be a group activity, does it?' He shrugged. 'It's meant to be personal, and in our case we have chosen to live without rigid beliefs about God, although with the discipline of religion.'

'Which is pretty much the exact opposite of most self-professed Christians,' said Toby.

'Sunday school was important when our children were young,' Jane chimed in. 'How else will kids get an understanding of religion? If you genuinely want to give your children an idea of it all, and a respect for other people's views, introduce them to a religion that you understand and let them farm their own ideas from that setting. It's important to open their minds to the possibility of something, but it shouldn't really matter what church you go to, or whether you go at all. But teaching a child to be cynical and sceptical and prepared for oblivion from day one – that's harsh.'

Peter stretched out his arm and Connie hopped gracefully from my head to his hand.

'I think parents often use church as an aid to morally grounding their children, but as they grow up, the act of going to church itself becomes irrelevant to them and they inevitably drift away,' he said.

'Do you think people use religion, then?' I asked. 'I sometimes wonder whether religions get more out of people than vice versa.'

Jane stretched out her bare feet on the cold stone floor. I shivered at the sight and wiggled my chilly toes encased in two pairs of socks.

'Sometimes, yes,' she replied. 'I'm deeply cynical about those Hollywood A-listers attaching themselves to Kabbala, or whatever it is they're into at the moment. Are they doing it just to make some sort of statement? Does giving away a percentage of their earnings alleviate the guilt that they're wealthy and pampered while others starve?'

'I suppose so,' I agreed, 'but what about love? If it isn't divine, what is it?' I looked from face to face. 'You see, it's this notion of a spirit, of spiritual love, that keeps me thinking that there must be something out there.'

'You're over-analysing,' warned Peter. 'You'll scrutinize the meaning of love away altogether if you're not careful.'

'So what is the meaning of love then?' I grinned.

He sat back in his chair and chewed on a thumb.

'Relationships,' replied Jane.

A knowing look passed between them.

'It's the simple things,' Peter added. Our aesthetic sense of the world is all tied up with our spirituality. Everything natural is beautiful, and love is a natural thing.'

Peter nodded, gazing thoughtfully out of the window. Something caught his attention and he squinted.

'Ok, everyone get up slowly and take a look.'

Chairs were scraped back disharmoniously.

'Shhh, we don't want to disturb it.'

We stared out on to the frosty landscape and Peter pointed towards a fence bejewelled with dozens of glittering icicles.

'No, there. It's moved. Just over there by the tractor.'

A roe deer was picking its way around the edge of the tree-bordered field, leaving a trail of delicate footprints behind it. It froze, sensing us, turned to stare right at us and then scampered into the trees.

'Beautiful,' I gasped. The only thing I've seen up so close in the wild is a dead badger. This is much nicer. It's just like *Watership Down*.'

'That's rabbits, you idiot,' Toby laughed.

'What's that rusty thing with wings?' I asked as we passed Gateshead on the journey home from Peter and Jane's farmhouse.

Toby glanced up at the dusty mound of land bordering the busy A1. 'It's the Angel of the North,' he told me. 'I thought we'd pass it, but I wasn't sure where.'

'Angel?' I asked, curling my lip. 'It looks like a giant bomber robot. It's a bit industrial, isn't it?'

'I think that's the point,' he said. 'Celebrates the area's industrial heritage and all that.'

We slowed with the traffic as we passed the giant structure on its hilltop site. Red like dying coals, the angel's vast wings spread wide to welcome travellers to Tyneside. Her feminine curves disguise the awesome strength of her weathered steel frame, rooted to the solid rock of the hill beneath her concrete plinth. From a slow-moving vehicle, she is difficult to ignore. The slow lane crawled forward as the other drivers on the road fell into the angel's embrace.

'It feels foolish to be leaving the north,' Toby murmured. 'I want to stay for a hug.'

'OK, that really is pretty amazing, up close,' I said, slightly choked.

'Like a sort of Fritz Lang wicker man,' Toby nodded. 'It must be 60 feet tall and, what, 150 across?'

'She's looks all warm and inviting,' I said, craning

backwards in my seat to watch the angel recede in our wake. I righted myself and frowned at the grey road ahead. 'I used to believe in angels,' I sighed.

'And now?' Toby asked.

'Now, I don't know,' I replied. 'I'd like to, and there have been times in my life when strangers have shown kindness at the most unlikely and vital moments. I like to believe some of them might have been angels. If I stop believing in God altogether, which is – let's be honest – the way things might be going here, surely I have to give up on everything that goes along with Him? Like ghosts and angels and fairies and mermaids?'

'Do you believe in mermaids?'

'Well, no. Maybe a bit. It's just nice to know that I have the option.'

'I'm not sure that follows,' Toby remarked. 'I've met plenty of Christians who'd hang you for a rainbow-painting, new age Satanist if they got wind of a soft spot for sea serpents.'

'Yeah, but I wasn't exactly your average Christian, either. Let's be honest about that as well, shall we? The Catholic Church provided me with a moral grounding, like Methodism did for the Walmsleys. It also gave me a set of rituals that are pretty hard-wired by now. When it comes to the actual faith part, I've always thought of that as a personal thing between me and God. The point is that there was a God. And angels.' I dropped the vanity mirror and peered into it, hoping for a glimpse of Gateshead's colossal guardian, but the angel had vanished behind us into a foggy Tyneside morning. 'It's just that if you lose God you lose so much more. Not just angels, but certainties about punishment and reward, and good and evil. Without God, you have to accept that all of the terrible things that happen in the world are our fault. They're not the Devil's deeds, or God working in mysterious ways, they're just the result of stupid people doing bloody stupid things. And horrible things. Evil things, by anyone's standards.'

'But horrific events occur all the time whether or not you believe Big Beardy's looking down from on high,' Toby protested. 'All that nastiness was going on when you had your faith.'

'That's what's so upsetting,' I said. 'I used to believe that no matter how rotten things got, it would all turn out all right in the end, that there was a master plan. Without the promise of salvation, it's down to people to sort their own mess out, which is terrifying because humanity's hardly chomping at the bit to build the world of tomorrow.'

'There's too much invested in destroying the world of today. Progress is petrol-driven.'

'Quite. Plus, I'm angry for allowing myself to be closeted in cosy absolutes for all these years. I was busy praying, safe in the knowledge that everything was coming up roses long term, when I could have faced up to the problems in the world and maybe done something constructive about them.'

'Don't beat yourself up,' Toby pleaded. 'You don't have to save the world one-handed.'

'If I don't, who will?' I shouted, hysterically. Then our eyes met and the giggles grabbed us.

'Driving,' Toby squeaked through gritted teeth, 'I'm driving. I can't get the giggles. Say something sad.'

'We are utterly alone in a meaningless universe,' I burbled.

'I know that,' he chuckled. 'Try something else.'

'Your dad's puppy will grow old and die, as do all puppies.'

'Good. Keep going.'

'And kittens, too.'

'That's got it.' He breathed deeply. 'Look, just because you're ready to dismiss the idea of a creator, you don't automatically have to give up on angels, or fairies, or trolls, or banshees, or mermaids for that matter ...'

I shrank into my sweater and peered over the top of its turtleneck at the road ahead.

'Where is this taking us?' I asked.

'York,' he reminded me, pointing at a sign as we whizzed past.

'Not the motorway, Tobe. The wedding talk, the stuff about faith and marriage and monogamy.'

'Go on.'

I sighed heavily. 'The Church can't give me my faith back, and no one's ever going to talk you into joining the throng. I went to Lourdes looking for closure, I think. I wanted to resign my membership of the Church, the way Peter and Jane left Methodism behind. And I wanted Father Liam to shake my hand and tell me everything was going to be OK. Of course, that was never going to happen. The reality of being damned by my own people is pretty stark, Tobe.' Hot tears pricked at my eyes. 'It means staring my decision in the face, really having the courage of new convictions, being able to let go of the mountain of guilt and live with the unshakeable suspicion that I'm setting myself up for a couple of miserable millennia in purgatory.'

'They got you young,' he joked, awkwardly. 'You're doing well.'

My bottom lip was practically resting in the footwell. 'I feel so cynical. I feel shit. And it's spilling all over my thoughts on love, too. Because having faith means automatically accepting the existence of miracles, magic, destiny, supernature. Romantic love is in the same category, so it needs a much greater effort to sustain a belief in love without confidence in supernatural design.'

'Love *is* a reality, with or without God.'

'Toby, why do you want to marry me?'

'Haven't we been here before?'

'I mean, why do you want to get married at all? We have unmarried friends who are raising children. We're in a stable, loving relationship. We're getting a mortgage together, which is pretty huge in commitment terms. Why do we want to waste all that money feeding a hundred people we never usually see, for the sake of a few photos in a leather-bound album?'

'Are you testing me?'

I shook my head. 'No.'

'I want to get married,' he began, 'because I believe in everlasting love. It's rare, but it happens, and I think I've found it with you. I want everyone I love – my family and friends – to devote one day of their busy lives to celebrating my good fortune and worshipping my beautiful new wife.'

My frown melted. 'So much of marriage is about practicalities – parental expectations and financial considerations. It takes the fun out of being in love, but that's not why we're doing it, is it?'

'No.'

But a sudden, overwhelming fear welled up in my stomach even so. My senses prickled with an ominous blast of what laid before us and all that I could taste was trouble. What if all this – my – soul-searching forced a space between us? Would Toby and I be strong enough to bridge the gap?

EASTWARD HO!

I glanced at the time on the ticket again. Perfect. If we left now we'd be there with plenty of time in hand – just in case . . .

Toby and I were leaving for a much-needed fortnight in the sun. After all the inevitable stresses and strains of moving home, we'd finally managed to relocate to West Sussex. Although I still mourned the loss of my beloved London it was nice to be able to see the stars at night. I'd even bought myself some wellies.

It was almost a year since we'd spotted an internet holiday bargain and booked our two weeks in Goa. Now, with soul-searching somewhat higher than sunbathing on my list of priorities, our cut-price Indian package holiday offered a taste of the mystical East. Would the ancient pantheon of Hindu gods be more welcoming to this wayward spirit than the doubt-and-you're-out damnation peddlers of my own faith?

'Are you sure we're not leaving too early? Did you check the ticket?' Toby was zipping up our suitcase and, as usual when we travel, being slightly grumpy.

'Of course,' I snapped back at him, 'About twenty times. Now, are *you* ready?'

He nodded and clicked the case shut as a cab honked its horn outside.

I think Toby can be forgiven for being pissed off about the seven and a half hours we subsequently spent in the Gatwick departure lounge.

My usual allowances for blocked motorways and train blazes accounted for the first three hours. My inability to read the twenty-four-hour clock accounted for the second three. Add a ninety-minute delay courtesy of Air 2000, named for the number of people they can cram on to an Airbus, and by the time we had stashed our baggage in the overhead lockers we'd been at each other's throats for the better part of a day.

Toby squeezed himself into place for the ten-hour flight to India and glanced sidelong at me. I sat, seething and tight-lipped, studying an article about anti-thrombosis aerobics in the in-flight magazine. As we taxied to the runway, Toby raised the white flag.

'Can we just try to enjoy ourselves?' he mumbled, squeezing my knee gently.

'Up yours,' I snapped. 'And that's my bad knee.'

Our Indian journey of love and spiritual discovery had begun.

Goa's one of those places that never gets cold, and once the monsoon's passed in September and October, the temperature quickly climbs into the eighties and nineties. There's no dashing around on fast-forward; unless you've got air-conditioning you're on the sloth trail. After making up, sleeping for twenty-four hours and eating some chips deep-fried in ghee, Toby and I were back in love and on track. Of course, back on track actually meant lying on a beach chewing pineapple chunks.

'We should be visiting temples, or something,' I told Toby, who was sprawled on a sunbed with his nose in one of those impossibly manly Joe R. Lansdale novels that he can't get enough of. 'I want to talk to someone important about religion and Hindu weddings.'

'No point rushing things,' he slurred, reaching for a bottle of the local brew. 'We're here for a fortnight. And can I remind you that this was our holiday, long before it was the eastern leg of your god-hopping world tour.'

Toby had settled into the Goan way of life quickly. Well, if you can't beat 'em. I slapped on some factor twenty-five and was leafing through Jackie Collins's latest to find my place, when a flash of orange caught my eye. I pushed myself up on my elbows and peered through my shades down the palm-fringed beach. A man dressed in a marigold *dhoti*, with a snow-white beard and eyes which shone blue even from a distance, was meandering along the shore, swinging a big, brass bowl in one hand and gazing out to sea. I nudged Toby, who had drifted off with his cowboy hat over his face.

'Who's the old guy?'

Toby rolled onto his front and followed my finger. 'That's a brahmin, Sara. He's the Hindu equivalent of a priest.'

Over the last four millennia or so, the Hindu tradition has evolved along several different lines and in the process given rise to a large number of varied sects. It's a bit like the division between Protestant and Catholic, and all the little off-shoots of each, only Hinduism got the jump on Christianity by a good few centuries, and has the benefit of multiple deities too.

Nevertheless, it all seems to hang together quite well and as India continues its relentless drive towards modernization, the ancient Hindu faith remains strong across the country.

'We should go and talk to him.'

'In a bikini? Is that appropriate?'

To be fair, I wasn't wearing much less than the brahmin. But then, I was wearing much, much less than I would have been happy with for an encounter with Father Dorricott, the much-respected and beloved parish priest from my childhood. I gazed at the retreating figure. He seemed to leave a snail-trail of silence and serenity through the hawkers and tourists. Then I looked at my ice-cold Diet Coke, half-buried in the sand under my sunbed. And at the half-finished bonkbuster on my towel.

'Tomorrow, then.'

Having resolved to track down a brahmin, we rose early the next day and padded through the hotel gardens to talk to the staff at the front desk. Their little office was a hive of activity. In India, it seems, anything remotely official or business-related automatically generates a phenomenal amount of paperwork. In the shady reception, we found two nimble, neatly attired women who were stamping and filing forms from a mountainous pile that lifted unnervingly at the corners with every arc of the room's electric wall fan. Toby coughed an 'excuse me' and the closest of the two sprung to attention behind the reception's polished boxwood counter. He explained what, or rather who, he was looking for. Her brow furrowed.

'Oh, I don't know. Rosa-Maria!' she called to her paper-shuffling colleague, 'do you know a brahmin?'

'Gosh, no,' said Rosa-Maria, joining us at the desk. 'Of

course, there are plenty to be found,' she smiled, 'but Ruth and I are Christians.'

'Ah.' Toby nodded at the little silver crucifixes that the ladies waggled under his nose. Thus the western-sounding names, the skirt and cardy combo in place of sari. Typical. We come all the way to India to dip our toes in the Mystical East, only to find that the Pope got here first.

'You'll find there are a lot of us in Goa,' said Ruth. 'You must have seen the cathedral as you drove in from the airport.'

'Sorry, no,' he admitted. We'd been shaking off a sulk and our fierce gazes had been fixed firmly on the floor of the bus as we rumbled past the state capital, Old Goa. 'But I'm sure we'll get there during our stay,' he added, diplomatically.

'You really should,' said Rosa-Maria, smiling. 'It is lovely on a hot day.'

Ruth curled the corner of her mouth, only slightly, but enough for her junior to pick up on the air of mild disapproval.

'And so good for the soul,' she added hastily.

'If you really want to find a brahmin,' said Ruth, ' start with the waiters. They wouldn't know a Bible from a telephone book.'

We thanked Ruth and left her at the counter, worrying her little silver cross between the finger and thumb of her right hand, and chuckling merrily at her own joke.

After centuries of toing and froing between Hindu and Muslim rule, the Portuguese arrived in Goa in 1510, with a big box of guns and a bigger box of Bibles. They converted or killed the Hindu population – with the backing of the Inquisition –

trashed the temples and plundered the stone for their Christian churches and cathedrals. Of course, the Vatican gradually revised its public relations policy and, in the years since nipple-scorching and fingernail removal left the list of priestly duties, the older faith has gradually reasserted itself in Goa.

Today, the population is about 60 per cent Hindu, 30 per cent Catholic, with a smattering of Sikhs, Muslims and Buddhists. This is a truly multicultural society. Religious tolerance is taken for granted, inter-faith marriages are not uncommon, and many festivals see members of different religions worshipping side by side in each other's temples and churches. The Goans' live-and-let-live attitude is a lesson to the wider world.

I had reservations about relying on catering staff to guide the latest stage of my spiritual journey but they came up trumps. Parminder was a Sikh barman in his early twenties who did not bear the trademark turban and beard – they'll come with his thirtieth birthday – but was proud of his 'fierce' Sikh gaze, which he liked to practise on nervous Scandinavian tourists. Sameer was quieter and a little younger. A local boy through and through, he worked the resorts during the holiday season and fished for red snapper in the river that ran past his home out of season. The affable pair smiled and shrugged when we explained our quest, no doubt confused as to why we'd want to spend our holiday in a temple.

'No problem,' Sameer said with a bemused smile. I almost curtsied.

We jumped in a cab and followed the dust-trail from Sameer's motorbike along winding, dirt roads, across the creek, past the salt pans and up into the hills and his village. We passed the usual carnival of waving, smiling Goans.

Women carrying mammoth objects on their heads, or parasols and babies in their arms. Labourers hacking at the roadside with pick-axes. Grubby-footed little girls in party dresses and dusty ribbons. A troop of sadus leading their painted elephant along the road.

The temple Sameer led us to was a concrete bungalow with rainbow walls and a ceiling hidden by fading, multicoloured tissue paper. A large, black hornet buzzed about the doorless entrance. We kicked off our sandals and followed him across the threshold and the cold stone floor to a painted concrete bench that grew out of the wall on one side. Maybe it was the anarchic colour scheme, the silence, or the break from the midday heat, but it was nice in there.

I was slightly nervous, as I was about to meet my first real holy man (priests don't count – too familiar). I was expecting someone in the Mr Myagi line. When our brahmin popped his head around the corner, I swear Toby did a little double-take. He looked about twelve; a slight, fair-skinned, doe-eyed youth, with fine black hair and eyelashes that could give the state's cow population a run for their money. I wanted to ask whether his dad was in.

Hinduism must be the least organized of all organized religions. There's no hierarchy in the priesthood. No man at the top. Instead, they have the caste system. Although in theory caste has no legal bearing these days, this ancient system of social organization permeates every level of Indian society, even in the permissive little outpost of Goa. It is widely believed that the brahmins, of Aryan descent, created the caste system themselves to maintain their dominance over a growing Dravidian population. If so, it was a funny way to go about it. Brahmins may be of the highest caste, but they are among the poorest, relying on donations and small fees from the performance of religious rituals. And I mean small. A board by the door proudly displayed the names of villagers who had donated more than 400 rupees – that's £6 – to help build the temple we sat in. One thing was for certain. If we plumped for a Hindu wedding, we'd save a bob or two.

Caste is for life. You're born a brahmin, you die a brahmin, whether you like it or not. That's not to say that you necessarily have to go into Godbiz these days – our personal brahmin had a brother who worked at a bank in Mapusa – as long as there is somebody to look after the family firm.

Our brahmin was, in fact, eighteen years old and had been learning his trade since the age of eight. He was to become a fully fledged holy man after he was married. Then he'd take over as the senior brahmin and perform duties like marrying people and being wise. At the moment he was a bit giggly, and his English was terrible, so Sameer kindly translated.

'They're interested in marriage,' he said in Konkani, then laughed at the young man's response.

'He says you can't get married today,' Sameer told us. 'You have to wait until Diwali finishes on Saturday.'

We explained ourselves and were treated to a run-down of the Hindu wedding ceremony. I had an vague idea that Hindu weddings went on for days and days, but it looks as though the modern world won't wait around quite that long, even in Goa. Now you can get through the ceremony in a couple of hours if you're pushed for time. But the traditional Hindu approach is much more fun, from a female perspective. Special day? Special week, more like.

A few days before the nuptials, a brahmin visits the bride's home to pray and to ask the gods to bless the coming marriage.

On the eve of the big day, the bride's parents welcome the groom's family with another short session of *puja*, or worship, and the giving of gifts. During this time, the bride and groom are forbidden from seeing each other. It's terribly bad luck. Also, it probably helps to prevent one half of an arranged marriage bolting for Bombay when they see who Mum and Dad have got lined up for them. But love matches are far more common these days. In fact, in Goa, they're the rule, not the exception.

There's still a page of wanted ads for brides in the local paper though, such as: Parents from Saligao, Goa, invite alliance for their 36-yr-old graduate spinster daughter (5′4″ – 45kgs) from God-fearing graduate bachelors up to 45 yrs.'

The colours and costumes for the big day itself – or rather, the big night as Hindu weddings traditionally take place after sun down – differ from state to state, as does the ceremony, but more often than not the bride will wear a red and white sari, embroidered with gold thread. The white signifies purity, the red abundance and fertility. The gold thread just looks pretty, and sets off her jewellery. The popular choice for the groom is a white *kafni*, a variation on the everyday *dhoti* – although I'm probably missing some subtle difference in the fabric folding.

Both bride and groom will be festooned with garlands of rose and marigold that hang almost to their knees. Beautiful.

The wedding ceremony takes place under a special four-poled canopy called a *mandap*. The bride is led under the *mandap* by her maternal uncle, who presents the couple with a cash gift. The groom, meanwhile, is ready and waiting, accompanied by his best man and a young girl, usually his sister. It's her job to keep him and the rest of the congregation awake through the ceremony by periodically shaking a small metal pot full of coins. Then come prayers for a harmonious marriage and invocations to Ganesha, the elephant God of prosperity and wisdom, and Vishnu's missus, Sataswati.

The bride's parents wash the couple's feet with milk and water to purify them in preparation for their new life together. Then the right hands of bride and groom are looped twenty-four times with a length of raw cotton to symbolize their bond (a temporary measure).

Then, a small fire is lit under the *mandap* and the bride and groom – clutching handfuls of rice, oats and leaves to signify the four blessings of wealth, good health, happiness and prosperity – are tied sari to *kafni* with a white cloth, and the bride's brothers lead them seven times around the fire.

There are many other various and wonderful traditions in the Hindu ceremony, which has remained virtually unchanged for the better part of 5,000 years. I like the flowers and the fire, but I'm not sure about the dress code. Toby doesn't look great in a skirt. And do we really want his sister to have to sit there rattling a charity box for three hours?

It's all sounds very romantic, I'll give you that, but tradition-ally, romance hasn't been the backbone of the Hindu marriage. Put yourself in the sandals of a reluctant bride, married off to some balding bachelor against her will. She's got to sit there and smile while her relatives literally tie her to a stranger. Earlier that morning Toby had showed me a story in the *Navhind Times* about a woman from an arranged marriage who had axed her husband repeatedly in the groin, then run off with her son-in-law. Call me an old softy, but I've always believed that love should be the message at the heart of mar-riage and that a wedding should be a public expression of a deep bond, not a chance to get to know your new spouse.

I also read about a 25-year old-man called Narayan Biswas, from the small village of Panchpara in Calcutta, who married his 85-year-old grandmother, Premodas. Fortunately under Hindu law it wasn't illegal for him to marry a blood relative. Narayan claims that their relationship is in no way incestuous; he simply wants to look after his gran in her old age and married her to show this commitment. He feels that years ago people cared about their local elderly community and nowadays this attention has diminished as life has changed and families aren't as united as they used to be. The upshot of this is that old people are often abandoned by their families and become homeless. Narayan couldn't bear that happening to Granny and, as he had no desire to have his own kids or be settled in an arranged marriage, he thought he'd pop the question to someone he truly loved. The couple managed to persuade a priest to marry them in a small Hindu ceremony, much to the shock of the neighbours and Narayan's parents. His father was especially cross that his mother was now his daughter-in-law. But in the end Narayan's honourable intentions were acknowledged and their marriage was accepted by the community. Narayan sacrificed his chance of a love match to ensure his adored grandmother was looked after.

I thought the Hindu wedding ceremony sounded wonderful. I thought the religion sounded wonderful. To round it up, everything was wonderful. But in fact the Hindu doctrine is just as ambiguous and inventive as Catholicism, despite being more tolerant of conflicting views, and the ceremony just a more colourful and lengthy version of a Christian one. Of course, the god or deities are called different names, and the doctrine is radically different, but the ways in which the individuals apply themselves to their faith are similar.

Toby and I wrapped things up with our junior brahmin, and his mum, who'd popped into the temple to check us out. Toby pushed a few folded notes through the slit on the collection box and pointed at the contributions board by the door.

The sun was setting when we got back to the hotel. We doused ourselves in mozzie cream and took a table on the terrace bar. A huge red kite pursued a brilliant blue kingfisher over the paddy fields. We watched as they tumbled through the sky, never more than two or three feet apart, looping and spinning, diving and climbing. It was a thrilling spectacle, but I was relieved when the little blue bird beat the odds and belted for the safety of the trees.

Sameer had told us that there was a Catholic seminary in Rachol, a couple of hours drive from Baga, over the Panaji and Sanvirdem Rivers. The next day we got up early enough to enjoy our hotel's complimentary breakfast of stale bread and weak coffee, and jumped in a cab for the long drive south. As such a large proportion of Goans were still Catholic we were curious to see how my religion was applied in India. And to see if they would also damn me if I turned my back on my faith for ever.

By ten thirty the sun was beating down on us as mercilessly as a playground bully. We stopped for petrol, Cokes and pistachio *kulfi* at a ramshackle gas station. Toby leaned against a wall and leafed through his Lonely Planet guide while I searched the dirt yard for a patch of shade.

'It's in the book, Sara. The seminary. They've got a collection of sixteenth-century apocalyptic art.'

'That's nice,' I replied, busy trying to stand in the shadow of the petrol pump while our driver filled up.

We eased ourselves back into the heat of the cab and drove on, leaving the highways, such as they were, for the byways and back roads to Rachol.

The seminary was a huge, white, Portuguese building with a long curving driveway and heavy arched doors. Inside, it was cool and dark, a common feature of churches worldwide. An Indian family – Mum, Dad, Granny and a blue-eyed boy of about four – were pottering about behind a long desk. On the wall above them, a peeling fresco showed the souls of the damned being tormented in imaginatively painful ways by a demonic host with a local flavour. Satanic elephants stacked bodies on their bloody tusks, while a many-armed cobra demon swallowed his victim whole. Toby wandered off to admire the art and returned to find me talking to Dad.

'But we've come a long way.'

'The Father does not allow guests to visit any more.'

'Could we just talk to him for a moment?'

'I will ask him.'

The little man disappeared down a gloomy corridor and we flopped on to a bench on the opposite. A moment later, the man reappeared.

'No,' he said with a shrug.

'He won't see us?' I asked, aghast.

'No, he won't see you,' said the man, and shrugged again.

'Is he busy?' Toby asked, slipping an arm around my waist.

'No.'

'Oh.'

I couldn't believe it. Turned away at the inn. Hadn't the

Church learned anything from that night in Bethlehem? Was damnation really that quick?

'Maybe he's had a bad experience with tourists? Maybe he's ill? Maybe . . . maybe his dog died?' I suggested optimistically.

'Maybe babe,' Toby replied, 'and maybe he just couldn't be arsed, I mean, we were there, he was there. I could have had a cheque for the lepers in my pocket. I might have been his next convert. You could have been on your way to jump off a cliff. Face it, he just couldn't be bothered.'

'And it's in the guide, too!' I complained. 'They can't just turn people away. I'm writing to Lonely Planet.'

'I'm writing to the Pope,' grumbled Toby.

As I sat on the back seat of our taxi-cum-oven, trying not to cry, I looked over at Toby. He was making a good show of being disappointed, shaking his head and sighing at all the right moments, but there was a glint in his eye that gave him away. He was secretly pleased!

'You smug bastard,' I muttered, slapping him on the arm with my sunhat.

He kissed me on the forehead and grinned. 'Strike three for the Church of Rome.'

'You patronizing git.'

'I love you.'

'Aargh!'

Back on Baga Beach, where we were staying, the mood had darkened. Rachol had been a downer for both of us. It was so, well, un-Christian not to spare a minute or two for anyone who'd dragged themselves into the Middle of Nowhere – which is actually part of Rachol Seminary's postal address

– looking for spiritual guidance. Despite my occasional suggestions that my fiancé is an Antichrist, he has actually never made it his business to attack my family's faith. He's got nothing against Catholics in particular, although he feels that their brand of earthly hierarchy and scriptural dogma neatly illustrates his problems with organized religion in general. On this mission of ours, he had admitted that he wanted to prove to me once and for all that he was as open-minded as the next person in spiritual matters. He was taking it seriously. And yet, despite all this, it was obvious he found the morning's events more than amusing.

I was determined to find a nice Catholic. Over a lunch of aloo gobi and steamed rice at a delightful family-run restaurant off the beach road, I got friendly with the owner, Stewart, and his toddling daughter.

'You need to see Father Mario,' said Stewart. 'He's famous. His family owns Sea View Cottages. I can't believe they wouldn't see you at Rachol. That's south Goa for you. You'll have better luck here.'

We settled our bill, said our goodbyes and followed Stewart's finger in the direction of Sea View Cottages.

Father Mario Pires is indeed something of a local celebrity. At seventy-seven, only his lack of teeth betrays him. He could pass for fifty with a good set of choppers. He has travelled the world from Europe to the United States and has a good friend in every port. Now retired, he uses his family's non-profit holiday home complex as a base for missionary work and a retreat for visiting priests and nuns, who can stay free for a month if they chip in with the Lord's work. He was also indirectly responsible for the birth of Goan tourism, and the hippy explosion of the late sixties. In 1968, a Swedish traveller and his Italian girlfriend found their way to the newly liberated state of Goa and washed up at Mario's door, looking for a place to stay. He hooked them up with a local family and thought no more of it. By next summer the word of the Paradise Priest had spread among the flower children of Europe. And the rest is hippy-story. Some 200 long-haired backpackers showed up that year. A few of them are still there.

Father Mario is one of the good ones. Any fool can tell that. He's devoted his life to helping others and spreading the word of his faith. And he's got that cuddly, guardian angel look, like a Goan version of Clarence from *It's a Wonderful Life*, and he single-handedly restored my faith in the goodness at the heart of Catholicism. This man would have put Mary and Joseph in the master bedroom and slept in the stable himself. It was truly heart-warming to meet him.

And, on the subject of his work, he'd be happy to marry us. I would have done it there and then if my parents had been handy. For once it seemed that doctrine, and going to church for six months and promising to bring up children in the church was all something we could think about down the line. Here was a Catholic who truly seemed to grasp that we just wanted to get married because we were in love, and that faith was organic and arrived naturally. That of course I might find God again, but there was no rush. Our previous experiences had us signing our souls away on the dotted line before stepping foot down the aisle. I know Toby warmed to Father Mario quickly too. While we leafed through Father Mario's scrapbook, thank you letters and donations, Toby pushed him on his pet subject, the members only nature of his church.

'Every Hindu we've spoken to says that a good Christian

can expect the same rewards in the next life as a good Hindu. Does that work in reverse? Will a good Hindu go to Heaven?'

'Well, yes.'

'So it doesn't matter if I'm a Christian or not. If I lead a good life, I'll get to Heaven.'

Father Mario had gone a bit quiet.

'Because the Church teaches that only those who accept Christ as their saviour will be saved.'

'Stop it, Toby. You're upsetting him,' I mumbled too quietly for anyone to hear.

'So wouldn't I go to Hell just for being a Hindu, no matter how good a person I was?'

Father Mario rolled his tongue over his lips and leaned forward on his elbows. 'Have you two had lunch?' he asked.

Father Mario impressed us both, despite his unwillingness to be pushed on points of papal doctrine. It was clear that his personal beliefs reflected the easy-going attitude that characterizes the Goan people. His gut response was inclusive. Of course a good Hindu would go to Christian Heaven; God rewards goodness, not mere obedience. However, Toby had put Father Mario in an uncomfortable position by asking him to admit that the teachings of his Church dictate that good people go to Hell. In the end, he fell back on that trusty Christian device, the vow of silence. Fair enough. Father Mario Pires is a loyal foot soldier for his faith. If Toby wanted a broader view of the battlefield, he'd have to hit the papal HQ, and that wasn't happening on our budget.

I felt warm and cosy as we pottered about in our hotel that night. Of course I'd reached no sort of conclusion but I felt more at peace with Catholicism. In truth, regardless of how isolated I felt from my given faith, I retain unshakeable respect for the people who still believe – after all, they're good people, well, most of them, and we need as many of those as we can get. I see a frail, old nun at Victoria Station most days. She stands there shaking her charity pot for a few pence. It's too cold there in the winter and too warm in the summer, aggressive commuters barge past ignoring her, but she smiles, nevertheless. Driven by an overwhelming belief in God and His message to promote love, she is trying to make a better world.

Toby and I had arranged to meet Sameer and his pal Parminder that night to say thank you for the brahmin visit. Parminder arrived at the bar first, Sammeer turned up a little later.

'Sorry I'm late,' he said. 'I had to marry a tree. It's a Diwali thing.'

We'd heard about this. The oldest bachelor of the house marries a tusil tree on the last night of Diwali. It assures good luck for the household and any weddings in the year to come. Sameer knew we were interested in weddings, even symbolic ones. Had he forgotten he was marrying a tree?

'I would have invited you if I thought you'd be interested,' he siad.

'Of course we're interested,' I said, linking arms with him as we walked to the taxi rank. 'Tell us all about it.'

'It was only a tree,' said Sameer.

We awoke with surprisingly clear heads on our last morning in Goa. We were determined to spend some quality time with our sunbeds before heading back to drizzly, cold London, so there was no mucking about. Showered and suncreamed, we headed for the beach.

'Have we got enough cash for breakfast?' I asked. We'd given up on the complimentary breakfast at our hotel. We couldn't think of any compliments.

'We've got loads of cash,' Toby replied. 'We've got the Viagra money.'

We'd heard about the Viagra scam from a couple on a jungle trip. Spenser and Aylan were 'Labradoodle' breeders from Leeds, with an impressive range of tattoos and a large number of beautiful new Indian gemstones decorating their many piercings. You can get Viagra at the drop of a hat in Goa, they told us. Tell a chemist in Calangute that you're having, ahem – marital problems – and he'll write you out a prescription quicker than you can say Hugh Hefner. After that, they're yours for about 30p a pop. Now I'm not advocating drug-dealing as a lifestyle, but with a street value of between five and fifteen pounds in London . . .

. . . we could pay for our entire holiday with a fifty quid outlay, and have enough left to take on the entire cast of Lady Love Vol. XXVII. It was a tempting prospect. Minimum effort, maximum profit. And with a colleague back in Toby's London office who was recently divorced and having prostate trouble, we were onto a surefire winner. Toby was happy to play Mr Floppy for a free holiday. After yesterday, though, the idea had lost its sparkle. Maybe there were better ways to spend the money we had saved . . .

We counted the cash for the umpteenth time. I knew Toby was on the brink. I'm not trying to paint myself as an angel here. I was just as surprised as Toby when the idea came over me. It was less of a leap for me, what with my personal connection to the cause. Toby fought it. I don't think he could quite believe what he was about to do with all that lovely lolly.

'Are we really going to do this?' he asked, with a sigh.

'Come on,' I said. 'Before we change our minds.'

At Sea View Cottages we found Father Mario bouncing his nephew's youngest little boy on his knee and singing softly.

'Father Mario,' Toby said, stepping forward to shake his hand.

'We wanted you to have this,' I said, pushing our Viagra fund across the table towards him. We watched him take the envelope. He didn't open it to look inside. We could have filled it with bits of newspaper.

'You're very kind,' said Father Mario, shifting the giggling child to his other knee. 'God bless you.'

'He'd better,' Toby whispered as we walked away. 'That's one hundred and seventy hard-ons he owes me.

UNDER THE BHODI TREE

'What you up to?'

Toby crept up on me at the iMac. I was peering intently at the screen from a distance that would have convinced any mother that blindness was inevitable.

'I'm surfing the interweb supermation highnet,' I said with a click of the mouse. 'I'm using technology to put me in touch with the spiritual. It's all very Robert M. Pirsig.'

'Pig sick who?'

'You know,' I said, turning to look at him, '*Zen and the Art of Motorcycle Maintenance*. The marriage of science and art.'

'Where's Sara?' Toby demanded, urgently. 'What have you done with my fiancée?'

I sighed and clasped my fingers across my chest, the better for thumb-twiddling. 'What did we take away from India, Tobe? Besides a fab tan and a generous dose of the squits.'

'Well,' he tried, 'Goa's a pretty good example of tolerance between faiths, isn't it?'

'That's what I thought, at first,' I said. 'But when you really think about it, what sort of state are they really in? Spiritually, I mean.'

He egged me on with a shake of his head.

'OK. The Portuguese turn up in at the crack of the sixteenth century and start converting the natives, i.e. smashing up temples and beheading anyone who fails to acknowledge Christ as their saviour.'

'Fairly typical sixteenth-century Christian behaviour.'

'Although not a good start to a peaceful coexistence. Of course, times change; eventually the colonial masters jump ship and Hinduism gradually reasserts itself.'

'But?'

'*But* it's rubbish. Hinduism *is* tolerant. It comes with its own range of collectable miniatures. But learning about someone else's beliefs and traditions only reminds you how arbitrary your own are, doesn't it?

'What about Father Mario?' Toby asked. 'I thought he'd put your mind at ease about the Catholic Church, at least. Or have you put that behind you completely?'

'Oh, I don't know,' I puffed, exasperated. 'Mario's a nice man. A good man. He can't undamn me though, can he? Especially after Rachol, it was nice to see a side of Catholicism I recognized – warm and welcoming – yet my personal problem with the Church hasn't gone away. And anyway, there are good people all over the place. Good Muslims, good Christians, good Jews. Their goodness doesn't put them closer to God than any of the rest of us. They still don't have any answers, other than their dogma.'

'So what's with the surfing?' He waved at the Mac, its fifty squillion colour screen brightly displaying a web page topped with a shiny gold 'Om'.

'I'm not quite ready to turn back from the East,' I said. 'There's a lot I like about their cyclical view of things. I'm increasingly convinced that the West is on a self-destructive course because its faiths are all so linear. World begins, courtesy of God, world just "is", then is destroyed in fiery torment. We're all so ready for the Apocalypse that it's becoming a self-fulfilling prophecy.'

'Woah!' Toby exclaimed. 'Should we stock up on canned goods and bottled water?'

'But it's got to be a healthier way of look at things, surely? A world without end, instead of a life spent waiting for the bombs to drop. I like the tolerance of other faiths, too. There's never been a Tibetan Inquisition.'

'And the webbage?'

'Well, we can't afford to go back to India, or jet off to China or Thailand,' I sighed wistfully. 'But if Mohammed can't afford a trip to the mountain, he can certainly catch a bus to the foothills.'

'You're losing me,' he admitted.

'I've found a really cool Buddhist nun in Haywards Heath,' I said. 'We're having coffee with her on Sunday morning.'

My previous encounter with Buddhism had been on a three-month trek though Thailand during one of the many 'gap' periods of my early twenties. I was enthralled by the ornate temples with the corners of their roofs hooked to catch Heaven onto earth and the fearsome statues of serpent *nagas* perched to guard against bad spirits. I was intrigued by the saffron-robed monks, padding barefoot through the towns with their brass begging bowls. At that age, I was more interested in soul music than soul-cleansing, and I left my Eastern inclinations at Bangkok airport.

In the ten years since I had tamed my traveller's urge and resettled in London, Buddhism seems to have enjoyed a boom. It certainly presents an appealing alternative to those raised on the carrot and stick incentives of Christianity, especially when it comes to checking out. For the grieving and dying, Buddhism's ideas of reincarnation and universal connection are profoundly soothing; they're certainly preferable to fretting about fiery damnation. In fact, if you're the sort who's squeamish about punishment and authority, Buddhism might be right up your street. There's no God, in the 'boss-man' sense at all – Buddha means Enlightened or Awakened One – so the authoritarian 'word of God' is a non-starter. Instead, Buddhism teaches that the human mind has limitless capacity to modify and grow. There's much to recommend in Buddhism for the here and now. After a decade of unfettered, guilt-free greed in the eighties, we've more or less come back round to the idea that for most people, life under free-market capitalism is a long, hard slog, with no million-pound pay-out on the horizon. With its casual rejection of all things shiny and expensive, Buddhism lets you leave the rat race without feeling like an underachiever.

Ani Chudrun is a Western convert to Tibetan Buddhism, back on British soil, but still stepping out in her saffron robes and cool skinhead. I was surprised to have found a bona fide Buddhist nun within easy driving distance. On the road there, I wondered what her home would be like, imagining a turreted temple at odds with the thatch and flint of the local Sussex architecture.

What we found, of course, was less exotic but nonetheless

rather wonderful: an elegant, white-washed Victorian house, extended in the 1970s to incorporate an airy garden room, with vast picture windows looking on to generous lawns. Some beautiful Buddhist images dangling on a washing-line at the bottom of the garden and a dozen fluttering, multi-coloured prayer flags wishing on to the wind, were the only concession to temple decor that I could see. We sat quizzing Chudrun about her unlikely lifestyle, and her definition of the divine.

'Our essence,' says Chudrun, 'is divine, a gift that shines through our base physicality like a crack of light in the clouds. Life is about managing the relationship between our physical self and our spiritual self. Sometimes it's easy, but sometimes you have to work on it to get the best out of both sides.'

She believed, she said, that we need to set challenges for ourselves, rather than picking an easy path, in order to achieve this balance. There are a multitude of ways to reach the ultimate melding of mind, body and spirit, but Chudrun advocates the teachings of Buddha as the fastest route to enlightenment. She has dedicated her life to this path because she believes total devotion to be the only way to achieve inner peace.

I wanted to know what Chudrun and her fellow followers felt about other faiths. Were they viewed as destructive? A harmless distraction? Or a valid alternative to the teachings of Buddha?

'As long as your motivation is pure,' Chudrun explained, 'the route you take towards enlightenment is less important than the journey.'

Nailing down her feelings about the opposition, though, proved tricky. While not openly dismissive, her final, cryptic response gave the impression that Chudrun herself, at least, considered the other great faiths to be little more than well-meaning distractions.

'If two philosophers meet and agree,' she announced, with a twinkle in her eye that said this was her final word on the matter, 'one of them isn't a philosopher. But if two holy men meet and disagree, one of them isn't a holy man.'

No prices for guessing who would earn the epithet in Chudrun's mind. Bald head, big on meditation; you know the feller.

The story of the original Buddha makes interesting reading. His original name is not precisely known for various records spell it differently, but one popular variation is Siddhartha Gautama. Born around 563BC in what is now Nepal, Siddhartha was the son of a rich man – some texts even suggest that his dad was King Sudhodana, the ruler of a modest kingdom in north-east India. At the moment of his birth, it is said, the blind were miraculously restored to sight to see the earth flooded by divine light. King Sudhodana asked fortune-tellers to prophesize his son's destiny and they all agreed that if Siddhartha stayed in the kingdom he would become a great emperor. However, they added, if he left his decadent life behind for a holy and frugal existence, he would grow to become the very saviour of the world. Tough choice for a young lad.

As Siddhartha grew older he became disenchanted with his luxurious existence and yearned for a sense of understanding and purpose. Disobeying his father's wishes, he went out into the world to see first-hand the pain and suffering of the masses outside the palace walls. Siddhartha began to wonder why such torment was heaped upon the people. He encountered an old person, a corpse, a sick person and a yellow-robed, shaven-headed ascetic – the four signs that prompted the search for the meaning of life – and he learned of holy men who spent their lives living purely in constant pursuit of the purpose of all existence. These encounters, apparently, were all the career guidance Siddhartha needed. He fled the palace, chopped off his royal locks and set off in search of the answers.

After six years on the road Siddhartha had increased in knowledge considerably, but true understanding eluded him still. In a move that displays both superhuman patience and a petulant sense of urgency, he settled down to meditate beneath the shade of a Bhodi tree. The Buddha-to-be decided that he would not move from that spot until enlightenment, or starvation, was achieved. After days of intense meditation Siddhartha achieved his goal, becoming the first human to whom all myriads of the secrets of creation were revealed. There are Buddhist followers who believe that although it seemed as if the enlightenment of Siddhartha happened relatively quickly, his spiritual struggle actually took many years over the course of countless previous lives. Despite the taunts and thunderbolts hurled down from Mara, the evil spirit determined to block his progress, Siddhartha is said to have stood firm, touching the ground beneath his tree and saying: 'The earth will bear me witness.' The story bears striking similarities to Jesus's forty days and forty nights spent in the wilderness, where it was the Devil that tempted and taunted him and tried to convince him to take the easy path.

As Siddhartha's teachings spread, the people renamed him Buddha. He spent the rest of his life inspiring people to follow the spiritual Buddhist path of the 'Middle Way', along with the four noble truths and the noble eightfold path, and helping those who came to him. He also founded the Sangha, the order of monks and nuns who devote their lives to the dissemination of his teachings. His dying words were: 'Hold fast to the truth as to a lamp. Strive to become fully awake.'

After the Buddha's departure from the physical realm, his followers fractured into different camps: the Theravada School, favoured in Thailand, Burma and Sri Lanka, and the Mahayana School, adopted by Tibet, Korea, China and Japan. Despite differences in their beliefs there is little of the mutual animosity so prevalent in denominations of other faiths. Instead, they respect each other's views, reasoning that what they have in common is far greater than what keeps them apart.

Meditation is a fundamental practice in Buddhism. It is the practice which, according to the Buddha's teachings, will quieten the mind for true self-discovery and prepare the soul for enlightenment. Indeed, it was meditation – along with exhaustion and hunger, no doubt – that prompted the very birth of the faith. I was curious to know what actually goes on in the brain during this 'transcendent' state.

Eugene D'Aquili, a veteran anthropologist of religion, and clinical therapist Andrew Newberg teamed up in the mid-nineties to carry out a set of experiments that they hoped would shed new light on this area. What they discovered was an incontrovertible and seemingly universal 'religious' experience. Whether their subjects were Franciscan nuns or Buddhist monks, D'Aquili and Newberg discovered the very act of deep prayer or meditation caused activity in the posterior superior parietal lobes of the brain to drop to extremely low levels. This area of the cerebellum is associated with the ability to navigate the world and recognize the boundaries of one's non-body. Tinker with it, and the line between 'you' and 'everything else' gets very fuzzy indeed. A lazy PSPL can lead to out-of-body experiences and an inability to distinguish fantasy from reality. This loss of self is central in all the world's faiths, which means that despite the difference in our religious traditions, we are all striving for the same thing. It is what the Buddha calls Nirvana, the sense of being close to God. In which case, might Siddhartha, sitting under his Bhodi tree, weak with hunger and fatigue, have conjured up his own 'truth' out of his misfiring synapses? Ask anyone with experience of LSD, and they'll tell you all about the – usually shortlived – spiritual revelations they've enjoyed on their acid trip. If this is the case Buddhism deserves credit for the appeal of its central delusion, and the Buddha himself for his powers of recruitment and persuasion. Then again, religion has a cast-iron get-out clause that D'Aquili and Newberg have been quick to employ, perhaps fearing a backlash against their work from the followers of all faiths. Their scans can tell us what happens to the brain under certain conditions, and what the likely symptoms of that brain activity – or inactivity – will be. Can they, though, state with any certainty whether any of the subjects' experience or memory of such an experience is valid? Can they prove that meditation does not literally tap into another level of reality? Of course not.

Chudrun told us she became a Buddhist because of a photograph. Travelling through Kathmandu in her early twenties, she had become transfixed by an image of a young Tibetan boy that was shown to her in a busy market crowd.

'He looked like a child,' said Chudrun as we sat in her sunny garden room sharing a pot of tea (English Breakfast, not Himalyan *chai*). 'But you could see more. It was as if he was older than his years.'

'Really?' I asked. 'You could tell that from a photo?'

She nodded.

'Hang on a minute. I'll get it.' She dashed out of the room.

A couple of minutes later she returned triumphantly, photograph in hand.

'I was working as a television journalist at the time,' she told us, handing over the precious snap-shot, 'and was instantly intrigued by it on a professional level. Look, it's an incredibly powerful image.'

Toby and I nodded in agreement. The boy looked ferocious yet naive, his proud, youthful face gazing straight into the camera lens.

'On the right side of his face he looks childish, unaware, but look at the difference on the other side,' she continued. 'He seems engaged in a wrathful, knowledgeable stare. It was this that touched me on a far deeper level.'

Chudrun learned that the boy lived in Tibet but the political situation there meant it would be incredibly difficult for her to travel there.

'But somehow I knew that the meeting would be incredibly important to me in some way and so I decided to wait,' she told us.

She returned to Sussex after her travels and a year passed. Chudrun couldn't get the boy out of her mind. She decided to go and listen to the Dalai Lama speak at Wembley and took the photograph she'd kept tucked away in her passport in the hope that someone there might be able to tell her if they knew of him.

'I casually asked a Tibetan security guard on the door – you've got to start somewhere, haven't you? Anyway, he looked at me as if I was stupid and foolish not to know.' She laughed.

'He told me that it was the seventeenth Karmapa. Honestly, I sat down on the steps at Wembley and wept. I was just so relieved to have a name, but of course still not really knowing exactly who he was.'

After hearing about the Samye Ling Tibetan Buddhist retreat on the Holy Island, near the Isle of Arran in the West of Scotland, Chudrun felt compelled to travel there to learn more. The Samye Ling Monastery houses a community of monks and nuns but also welcomes lay people with varying interest in Buddhism. It was here that Chudrun discovered the Karmapa Lama is the spiritual leader of one of the four major schools of Tibetan Buddhism, ranking only behind the Dalai Lama and Panchen Lama in the Tibetan spiritual hierachy. Bizarrely, the Samye Ling Monastery was affiliated with this line and the boy in her photo is the seventeenth reincarnation of the original Karmapa.

'When I went to see the abbot with the photo,' Chudrun recounted almost wistfully, 'and discovered that his brother was actually in Tibet with the Karmapa at that very time, I knew that I was home.'

After spending time at Samye Ling, Chudrun realized that she wasn't psychologically ready for her big meeting with the Karmapa. She had to prepare mentally rather than diving in for an autograph: 'I knew that I had to be ordained and go in robes.'

At the Samye Ling Monastery you can take ordination for a year rather than the traditional life commitment, but Chudrun ended up staying on for four years after that, following up her commitment by journeying to the Karme Ling Retreat Centre in New York, where she became ordained for life.

*

So who was the charming toddler that called Chudrun into service though a dog-eared snapshot? The present Karmapa – Ugyen Trinley Dorje – is the first high lama to have been officially recognized by the communist government of China. He belongs to the oldest line of Tibetan reincarnations, and according to the party line, his body houses a thirteenth-century soul.

Buddhists believe that the lineage of their teaching is paramount. Where other faiths rely on a written tradition through an unbroken chain of reincarnated teachers, the Karmapa has literally been telling the same stories and teaching the same lessons, albeit in various voices, for hundreds of years. He is the living record of his faith. The search for Ugyen began after death of number sixteen, in November 1981. But it wasn't until March 1992 that one of the four lamas sent out to find their next guru announced that he had discovered a prophetic letter from the previous Karmapa which had led to a boy from a nomadic family in eastern Tibet. There are all manner of strange tales about the time of the boy's birth – although all have appeared with the benefit of hindsight. Unknown blossoms bloomed, three suns were seen in the heavens, with a rainbow arching over the middle one, even the very music of heaven was heard.

Support of Ugyen's succession was already strong when, on 7 June 2002, the Dalai Lama announced his official backing. The Chinese government allowed a search team to travel to Tibet and he was formally identified as the seventeenth Karmapa. If all this priestly reincarnation sounds like a pretty smooth and friendly process for the lamas of Tibet, it's worth remembering that history – including religious history – is written by winners. At the time of Ugyen's rise to power an argument was raging between two of the lamas entrusted to track down the Karmapa's old soul in its new host body. While Situ Rinpoche, who had discovered the sixteenth Karmapa's revelatory letter, has always maintained its authenticity, his companion, Shamar Rinpoche, later withdrew his support after one of the monks charged with the Kamapa's safe delivery died in a car crash that some considered 'portentous'. Despite Ugyen's appointment to Tibetan Buddhism's third-from-top job – behind the Dalai and Panchen Lama – Shamar and Situ's dispute continues to this day. In 1994, two years after the search officially ended, Shamar produced his own candidate for Karmapa, Thaye Dorje. This second Karmapa has his own followers, of course. It's a situation that muddies Chudrun's version of the Buddhist reincarnation tradition considerably. At least one of the Karmapas, after all, is false. They may be harmless, they may even be helpful on some level, with their message of truth and brotherhood, but one or both of them are still wrong. The ability to embrace this kind of holy lineage relies upon the ability to ignore an obviously flawed and ultimately earthbound selection process. It must get in the way for many potential recruits, and a series of apocryphal supernatural details surrounding Ugyen/Karmapa are employed to help maintain a sense of heavenly mystery.

On the Holy Island with Chudrun was one of the lamas who made up the seventeenth Karmapa search party. He had known Ugyen's predecessor personally.

'I've never known a master die but I know that they often reveal themselves in some way to the people who knew them in their previous incarnation, ' Chudrun explained. 'Although before they die they do write a letter stating that they will be reborn, and state the names of the parents, town, date, house, etc.' She grinned. 'One of my teachers in Scotland was actually one of the group who went to find the new Karmapa and had known the sixteenth version before he died. Before his death my teacher had asked for one of his teeth. There's something powerful about relics from Buddha masters, particularly teeth that carry some sort of blessing. So the Karmapa had agreed that at the cremation when everything had got distributed my teacher would get one. Anyway, he never got it for one reason or another. So when he went to see the seventeenth Karmapa sitting on a bit of carpet in a tent, he told the boy that his predecessor was going to give him something but he never got it. Ugyen just pulled up the carpet he was sitting on to reveal one of his milk teeth ready for my teacher.'

When Chudrun finally got to meet the Karmapa their encounter wasn't quite what she'd hoped for.

'It was very difficult,' she explained. 'By that time there was way too much expectation. I even believed we shared a past life connection, but it was all ego.'

Chudrun had watched as other pilgrims had shuffled up to meet the boy lama, noting his different reactions as each person made their abeyances. Finally it was her turn.

'It was like when you see someone you think you know – in a crowd or across the street – and you go running over to them. Only when you get over there, you realize it isn't anyone you know at all.' She looked over at her framed picture of the Karmapa, shaking her head slowly.' He looked at me with real wisdom. Not arrogance. It was a look that said, "Do you really know me?" And of course I didn't. How could I have known him?'

Despite her self-confessed naive expectations, Chudrun's journey to the Karmapa became a starting point of her personal path to enlightenment, the goal of all Buddhists.

'Buddha taught us that the state of enlightenment exists right now in everyone's minds. But we have to work to recognize it.' She curled her feet up underneath her and paused. 'The easiest analogy is like the sun shining. The sun shines all the time. It's as bright as ever. But it doesn't look like that because we're seeing it from a distant and obscured perspective. Things like anger, pride, jealousy and aversion obscure our lucidity; they block out the sun. Meditation is the process that blows away the clouds to reveal the sun in all its glory.'

Besides meditation, there are various other things expected of the faithful Buddhist, if they're serious about seeing the light this side of the grave.

'Don't harm any living things.' That's the cuddly heart of Buddhism that attracts politically minded middle-class converts, as well as providing a core customer base for Britain's burgeoning veggie food industry.

Then there's 'no stealing'. Which is a lot easier if you're surrounded by other Buddhists, who tend to shun the materialistic life of iPods and easy-to-shift car stereos.

'Don't say unkind things.' That sounds like a freebie at first, a commandment you can stick to even when the others get tricky. But try it for a day. It's a tough assignment. When I gave it a go, I got as far as the ticket barriers at Embankment Station in rush hour. It was 9.07 a.m.

Drink and drugs are out as they cloud the mind and obscure the truth.

My personal favourite, though, is the requirement that, as a good Buddhist, you will not live 'in an over-excited way'. Now that's a fantastic cover for all manner of earthly failings, from greed to gluttony, but it's also the most straightforward, common sense advice offered by any of the world's premier league prophets, step one on the road to happiness: chill out.

Of course, if you're still really serious about joining the lama army, ordination as a monk or nun requires one more act of devotion to test commitment and shed distraction, a vow of celibacy.

'It's about focus,' Chudrun explained. 'The act of union is an incredibly powerful thing to put the body through. Not for everyone of course and not every time. But for me, like lots of people, a sexual relationship means discipline goes out the window. Having kids is tricky because of the attachment you feel, especially when it comes to illness and death. You just can't be clinging to the life you're in if you're devoted to the path of enlightenment.'

Despite her personal devotion, Chudrun naturally recognizes that ordination is a path few will choose in this life. For the general population, whose relationships are with each other, not God, she does feel that marriage is vital.

'It's the power of the vow,' she explained. 'And it's relevant right now for our society. It's more important than ever because these days marriage is more a matter of personal expression than social expectation. The decision to make a promise to someone out of loving motives, and to keep that promise no matter what, is a beautiful expression of human nobility and the power of love. It's good for the world.'

There's no formalized marriage ritual in the Buddhist faith, as the Buddha did not consider the union of earthly bodies to be a sacred ceremony. Buddhist weddings are simply an affirmation of the couple's commitment to live according to precepts of their shared faith. That said, in keeping with their relaxed 'the truth will out' attitude, Buddhists are free to marry the followers of any religion. If they turn away from the path as a result of their choice, well, that's their loss.

'The main thing is the determination of the couple and the clarity of purpose going into it. That's where I'd be wary. Mind you, pure love – absolutely honest and true – is the same as spiritual clarity,' Chudrun asserted. 'I just think loving God, or whatever you believe, is a more straightforward prospect. As long as you hold up your end of the bargain it's a relationship with a guaranteed happy ending.'

For the majority of us who chose corporeal coupledom over majestic celibacy, the Buddha did have plenty of sound advice on the subject of wedded bliss. He regarded the union as essential to the happiness and stability of society, but cautioned against a hasty or ill-considered union. To the Buddha, marriage had to be based on mutual respect; an alliance between equals. It was progressive for the fifth century BC. Buddhism developed in a society where women were subservient to men. So secondary was the wife to her spouse that *sati* – a widow's act of hurling herself on to her husband's funeral pyre – was still commonplace and considered the greatest form of honourable devotion to one's late husband. The custom was banned under British rules in 1829 but 'widow-burning' is still deeply respected in some rural villages. As recently as 2002, a 65-year-old woman, Kuttu Bai, threw herself into the flames at her husband's funeral in Madhya Pradesh. Local journalists revealed that her two adult sons did nothing to stop her.

The inequality of women in the society that gave birth to Buddhism ran far deeper than household hierarchies. Under traditional Hindu beliefs, no woman could hope to be freed from *samsara* – the endless cycle of reincarnation – before she had first managed to come back as a man.

The teachings of the Buddha meant a giant leap forward for spiritual and sexual equality. Ironically though, it is the history of female acceptance to the burgeoning Buddhist faith that, when it came to the crunch, turned this would-be seeker of the truth away from the road East, possibly once and for all.

Tell me if I'm getting the wrong end of the stick, but is the whole base of Buddhism the understanding that young Siddhartha, sitting under his Bohdi tree, was receiving the direct, absolute, no-room-for-discussion word of God – and by this I mean the illusive, transcendental force behind everything? And didn't this make it quite clear that all living things, let alone Joe Public and Her indoors, were equal and sacred in the great scheme of creation? Explain to me, then, why the omniscient mouthpiece of the divine initially ruled out female admission to the monastic *sangha* on the grounds that little lady brains would have trouble getting to grips with his big, new ideas.

Giving credit where credit is due to a man of remarkable reason and foresight, the Buddha did actually live to see the ordination of the first Buddhist nun, his aunt Prajapati – although not without great persistence from her, in the force of equal resistance from the Enlightened One. It is actually Siddhartha's cousin, Ananda, who is credited with persuading the Buddha of the error of his thinking. All things change, Siddhartha was reminded, and women too might change, if given the opportunity. But why did he need persuading? Perhaps he was a man of his times, fighting to shake off the shackles of his own cultural prejudices, following his life-changing revelation. But I don't buy it. Either you're a spokesperson for the divine, or you're not.

*

So much for Buddhism, then. My big hope from the mystical East. There was always Islam, of course; one of the great faiths we had so far shied away from. Although if I ultimately objected to cuddly old Buddhism on the grounds of sexism, I doubted I'd be overly eager to embrace the biljab and a life of wifely obedience. For that matter, I had realized that none of the really popular religions had a particularly impressive record on gender relations. My own lot had given women a pretty stark choice; virgin or whore. Not much in the way of career options.

Chudrun had also left Toby with mixed feelings about the path of enlightenment. He pointed out to me that there were hints at darker days in her past; drug use and depression. Chudrun encountered Buddhism at a vulnerable time and her faith helped to steer her off a self-destructive course. In that sense her personal path can be seen as a positive thing. Nevertheless, when Toby hears tales of righteous salvation from the path of doom he can never quite stifle his groans. And I do understand where he's coming from. They say there's never a copper about when you need one, but holy men can often smell a crisis of the soul from forty miles downwind. Certain cults and congregations specialize in the recruitment of the down and desperate runts of society. Like hungry hyenas, they home in on the limping calf, pouncing with promises of a new life and purpose. Chudrun did not fall prey to cynical evangelists; she found Buddhism as much as Buddhism found her. But was her religious conversion – her salvation from self-destruction – really so different from the born-again residents of maximum security prisons?

The difference between Toby and me is that I'm not so sure it matters. And the kick in the arse for cynics like Toby is that even the charlatans often get real results. They *do* turn people's lives around for the better. Clapping Christians might be annoying, but they're surely preferable to heroin addicts. No born-again Christian, to the best of my knowledge, ever mugged an old lady to pay off tambourine dealers or fund his cardigan habit. So why did it rile Toby so when the junkies and joyriders turn their backs on the criminal life in favour of prayer and penitence?

His explanation, from an irreligious standpoint, is that to embrace a new set of arbitrary beliefs is an odd way to deal with one's personal problems. And I too suspect that many converts are simply overwhelmed by the concern shown by their newfound friends in church, temple or meeting room. The offer of a fresh start and a loving community is hard to refuse when you're at rock-bottom. All that is required to maintain this new life and enjoy a happy ending is the suspension of disbelief.

All well and good, but is it enough in the long term, merely to paper over the cracks of past trauma with prayer? The 'clean slate' introductory offer of religious conversion is an enormously seductive concept, whether you're a serial child-killer or a recent divorcee with a guilty conscience. However, it effectively puts pay to any notion of psychological exploration and the pursuit of greater self-awareness. Without the closure of honest self-discovery, destructive character traits – like shortness of temper or addictive tendencies – will find subtler, but no less nasty, ways to manifest themselves.

Aside from his belief in the redemptive power of psycho-therapy over blind faith, I suspected that some of Toby's dismissive attitude towards vulnerable converts was simple sour grapes. No sceptic has ever scoffed at the compliance of the faithful, or dismissed their cosy, off-the-shelf philosophies, without acquiring at least a tinge of green to their cynical skin. How easy it would be to surrender and turn sheep, to exchange the burden of lifelong uncertainty for featherbrained acceptance. For all that, neither of us concluded that Chudrun's chosen faith has encouraged her to bury her past. It's obvious, rather, that she has come to terms with the path that led her to her personal saviour. Indeed, the Chudrun of today is a genuinely calm and calming presence in a room. Neither extraordinarily beautiful nor urgently charismatic, she nonetheless radiates a sort of cool, peaceful energy, like mental air conditioning. An hour in her company is enough to sell anyone the benefits of tantric meditation. 'I'll have what she's having,' you say, while your logic picks holes in her matter-of-fact statements about reincarnated priests and multi-dimensional reality.

I was slower to scoff at Buddhism's whackier points of doctrine. I saw in Chudrun a role model, I think; someone who had reached the point I was striving for. For all sorts of reasons – some profound, some undeniably frivolous – Buddhism appealed to me as a replacement faith more than any other obvious option. It was, a huge disappointment to find out that, however inspiring and friendly its practitioners, I could not simply flick a switch, turn on the faith and get happy. By the time we left our Sussex lama waving on the doorstep of her whitewashed cottage, we had made a friend, but my last hope of a quick spiritual fix was dashed. Barring the alien cults and sun worshippers, what on earth was left?

THE BRIGHTON BAHA'IS

The answer came in a radio news bulletin following the death of government weapons expert David Kelly. Toby and I were packed like pilchards into our tiny kitchen, washing the dishes from a Sunday lunch of Saturday's leftovers. Toby's ancient, leather-clad Roberts radio was blaring out jazz standards on a station he has trouble admitting he enjoys.

'The lovely Diana Krall singing there . . .' In Parky's mellow, gentlemanly tones, the line sounded like a chance encounter at Kensington garden party. I was daydreaming about canapés and scintillating conversation when the radio news drifted into my conciousness.

'. . . attended the funeral of Dr Kelly, a follower of the Baha'i faith, in . . .'

'What's Baha'i'?' I asked, jolting Toby from his reverie with a flick of dishwater from my pink Marigolds.

'Hm? Oh.' Toby furrowed his brow and tried to find a frame of reference. 'It's Middle Eastern, isn't it? Bit of Buddhism, Judaism, Christianity, Islam, all sorts.'

'I don't understand,' I replied. 'Do they believe in all those gods, or none of them?'

'I dunno,' he protested. 'I think they're one of those trendy Hollywood faiths, like Scientology and Kabbalah. Flavour of the month, then it's out with the icons and in with this season's new minimalist look.'

'Oooh,' I cried, bouncing on my toes, 'have we got enough money in the kitty for a field trip to LA?'

'You're 'avin' a larf, intcher?' he answered. 'If you want to get familiar with the followers of yet another holy book, you're going to have to find a local chapter.'

'Found one,' I called from the study, five minutes later. 'Brighton,' I added, appearing at his side with a computer printed address. 'They're in till six. Get your skates on.'

'But it's Sunday afternoon,' he protested weakly as he dried his hands on a tea towel. 'It's the Sabbath. We're not allowed to do anything except eat and watch telly. So sayeth the Lord.'

'Whose Lord's that, then?' I answered, unimpressed. 'Come on. No peace for the wicked.'

A Sunday drive along the leafy highways of Sussex is not an unpleasant experience. On any given Sunday, Toby and I are more than likely to jump in our Skoda and worm our way through the South Downs to the sea. On this particular Sunday, however, it was clear that Toby was in no particular hurry to arrive at our destination. Jerked out of his lazy mood, he was now heading for a impromptu rendezvous with Ron and Michael, two of Brighton's Baha'i brethren. They were the welcoming type – that much was obvious, considering the spontaneity of our visit – but beyond that, neither of us had any idea what to expect. A chance reference to a civil servant on the one o'clock news, and half an hour later we were on the road to an anonymous, suburban address where, for all we knew, a team of skilled brainwashers were waiting to indoctrinate us in their shady Middle Eastern cult.

Ron and Michael, it transpired, were far from the steely-gazed mesmerists we had conjured in our minds. They opened the painted glass door of the Brighton and Hove Baha'i Centre to us as one, grinning as they ushered us into the white-walled hallway of a large Victorian family villa. Handshakes and greetings were exchanged, and Toby and I were seated at a long table in the high-ceilinged front rooms.

'I'll pop the kettle on,' said Ron.

'I'll help,' said Michael, and the pair disappeared into the back of the house.

'They seem nice,' I said in relief.

'They don't seem dangerous,' Toby agreed. 'They look more like Rotary Club members than cult followers.'

'Baha'i is not a cult,' I said, frowning. 'It's a religion. For Heaven's sake, don't go calling it a cult around those two.' I waved at the open door.

'Well, I don't know,' he mumbled, slightly aggrieved. 'I mean, this is all rather sudden, isn't it? We might be walking into a Moony mind trap, for all we know.'

'Well that's obviously not the case, so relax, will you?' I said. 'Read some of the literature.'

I gestured at the fan of colourful brochures, laid out on the table. Baha'i publishers apparently favour the same gaudy style employed in those multilingual, photographic souvenir books that clog newsstands in tourist cities and the dustbins elsewhere. Toby grabbed the topmost tome, decorated with an

Israeli sunset and bearing a title which, while somewhat inelegant, was certainly direct: *The Baha'is . . . Who They Are, What They Believe & What They Do*.

The Baha'i faith, which preaches the international brotherhood of humanity and the essential unity of all religions and gods, was founded in the mid-nineteenth century at a time of unrest and insurgency in the Middle East. From his home in Shiraz, southern Iran, a young man known as the Bab, or 'the Gate', had caused great upheaval and gathered a considerable following, with the revelation that a new era of human history had begun. The Bab's message of peace and brotherhood was combined with the promise that the time of prophecy was at hand, and that a great teacher would rise to unite the world.

The Babis suffered widespread oppression and cruelty, arousing the interest of the European press, and the Bab himself spent more than half a decade under lock and key, bouncing from prison to prison in an effort to limit his charismatic sway over fellow inmates and gaolers alike.

Like another Middle Eastern prophet with a penchant for peace and love, the Bab was permanently silenced by the authorities in front of a sell-out crowd. His death by firing squad in Tabriz, near the border with modern-day Turkey, was followed by a time of dreadful persecution for the leaderless Babis. Twenty thousand people died, with the most prominent followers the first to follow their prophet into the next world.

Only now do we meet the true hero of our tale, Bahá'u'lláh, a young Babi nobleman on a self-appointed mission to rally the dejected survivors of his spiritual community. In the absence of any higher authority, Bahá'u'lláh proved adept at leadership and worked tirelessly to restore the good name of the Babi faith. Imagine the entire British royal family going over Beachy Head in a runaway carriage. Everyone else is toast, but Zara Philips's scrunchy gets caught in a twig on the way down and hey presto – Queen Zara I. Now, I'm not saying Zara would relish the prospect of her family's annihilation, but as for the unexpected promotion, well, I'm sure she'd warm to the role. And so did Bahá'u'lláh. In a few short years, the modest, intelligent and dignified young man, who bore the scars of his imprisonment during the persecution, had usurped the very prophet he championed. The Babis, satisfied that they had found the Bab's 'great teacher' became the Baha'i's.

Gaoled, discredited and exiled, Bahá'u'lláh nevertheless managed to augment his reputation worldwide with his expanded message of kindred mankind. In his lifetime, he wrote more than a hundred volumes on dozens of spiritual themes, which his followers believe to be the recorded word of God.

On top of this publishing output that would make Barbara Cartland turn greenish-pink with envy, Bahá'u'lláh was also a keen correspondent who kept a constant stream of letters flowing from his home to every corner of the world. Nearly 30,000 of his ecclesiastic epistles have survived, many of which have been published in anthologies of Bahá'u'lláh's writings.

At the beginning of the twenty-first century, the Baha'i faith has some six million followers and is the second most geographically widespread faith on the planet after the Christians, who have a much bigger marketing budget and a 2,000 year head-start. There is no clergy and no sermonizing, although discussion groups are popular where numbers allow. The principle devotional practices are: prayer, once a day;

fasting, once a year; and meditation, whenever they've got a quiet moment. They are also encouraged to reflect upon a passage from Baha'i scripture once a day. The Baha'is are not given to public preaching and, although they have an obligation to share the message of their faith, they are not aggressive in their efforts to convert newcomers. Instead, Baha'is prefer to lead by example. 'Let deeds, not words, be your adorning', said Bahá'u'lláh. His followers are optimistic that their congregation will swell as the unquestionable truth of his teachings seeps into the global consciousness and, slowly but surely, the numbers are growing.

In keeping with their softly softly tradition, Ron and Michael left us alone with the literature for a good old time – long enough for us to learn that the Baha'i International Community busies itself with a range of activities, from peace-building and human rights to global education and sustainable development – before reappearing with a china teapot in a knitted cosy and all the necessary trimmings for what was, as it turned out, a cracking cup of tea.

Softly spoken and so smiley that I began to wonder whether there might be a drop of laudanum in with the tea, Ron and Michael skipped through their life stories, before introducing the hypnotic wisdom of Bahá'u'lláh's sacred writings.

Ron was a typical – i.e. non-practising – C of E Christian who had been on the verge of a Catholic marriage to his first wife, some forty years ago, when a familiar dilemma presented itself to the highly principled young groom. 'I had to promise that my children would be brought up Catholic and I couldn't do that,' he explained. 'It wasn't my responsibility to impose my beliefs on children. I hadn't really thought about spirituality at all as an adult, but after that it was on my mind all the time.'

Admiring the Salvation Army's dedication to charitable work, Ron briefly flirted with the idea of joining them, but his disapproval of their 'only we shall be saved' attitude kept him from a life of brass bands and carol singing. After that, Ron branched out, attending meetings on every conceivable spiritual subject, from Krishna to colour therapy.

'Then one night I saw an ad for Baha'i on a bus,' said Ron, offering slices of marble cake around the table.

'The number thirty-six for Damascus, was it?' Toby quipped, accepting a slice of cake.

'Not exactly,' laughed Ron, putting us even further at ease. 'I went to a meeting, yeah, but I wasn't an overnight convert. I'm a socialist at heart and back then I was starting to get really disillusioned with politics. I was looking for new answers, but I went along expecting to find some weird little old lady, like the colour therapy woman. Only it was interesting. There were some good speakers at that time. Mind you, I went to two years of interesting meetings before I decided I was ready to commit myself.'

Michael's path to the Baha'i faith was similarly circuitous, and inspired by the same drive to find meaning.

'I was working in a newspaper office in Brighton,' he explained. 'Not exactly a hotbed of theological thinking, you might think, but I was exposed to a lot of people's ideas. Me and my brothers got into the stories about Lobsang Rampa, this Tibetan monk, into reincarnation, transmogrification, all that. Very well written.' He paused, shrugging. 'We all fell for it.'

Dr Tuesday Lobsang Rampa was a Tibetan holy man who,

in 1956, took the UK by storm with his bestselling book, *The Third Eye*. The autobiographical study of Rampa's mastery of Tibetan Buddhism included vivid and fantastical descriptions of his childhood in Tibet, and the psychic powers bestowed upon him by the surgical opening of his 'third eye'. It created a huge upsurge of popular interest in Eastern mysticism, but among the faithful, alarm bells were ringing. A group of Tibetan scholars hired private detective Clifford Burgess to check the validity of Rama's claims. His investigation led to one Cyril Hoskins, the son of a plumber, with a vivid imagination and a lifelong interest in Eastern and occult studies.

Cyril and Lobsang were, of course, one and the same. The discovery sent shock waves through the reading public. The author of *The Third Eye* was quick to reply. He had indeed been born Cyril Henry Hoskins, in Plympton, Devon. However, on 13 June 1949, while 'photographing an owl in a tree', the branch beneath him had snapped, plunging him headfirst into the ground below. Suddenly, Cyril found himself floating over his unconscious body, connected by a silver cord. And floating towards his sleeping self came the astral form of a man of oriental appearance. The oriental man snipped Cyril's shimmering umbilical chord, leaving him to float off into the astral planes. He then took residence in the fallen body, and awoke as Dr Tuesday Lobsang Rama, Tibetan Master and bestseller to be. So you see, it was all still definitely true.

Remarkably, the good doctor's incredible body-snatching tale was enough to keep his core fans happy. He went on to publish a further twelve books of homespun Buddhism, though none achieved the success of *The Third Eye*. Most devotees – Michael and his brothers included – dismissed their erstwhile guru as a charlatan. That Lobsang's fantastic explanation was apparently told from Cyril's perspective gives a clue as to the gullibility of the local boy lama's surviving fans.

The exposure of Lobsang Rama derailed Michael's quest for the truth, but it did little to quash his interest in Eastern philosophy. Although he lacked Ron's fondness for public meetings, he read voraciously across a broad range of theological topics before happening upon a leaflet advertising a local Baha'i group. It took some time before he plucked up the courage to attend.

'I spoke to a little old Persian gentleman,' said Michael, offering us a second slice of marble cake, politely declined. 'I asked a lot of big questions and he told me some home truths. I'd always had evasive answers from people in the past, but this guy was straight, so that was it for me. We talked for four hours and I asked him what was involved in becoming a Baha'i, right off the bat.'

There's no trial by paddling pool or penile surgery involved in conversion to the Baha'i faith. It is enough to alert the democratically elected National Assembly of one's sincere acceptance of the message of God.

'You have to accept the Baha'i message of this age,' explained Michael, 'and that Bahá'u'lláh is the messenger. There's no hurry. People come along for years and never sign up. Fear of commitment, maybe. Baha'i morality takes some adjustment. You have to change your life. No drink, no drugs. That can be tough for some people, but it's the law.'

'I used to think up all manner of excuses to keep drinking,' said Ron, chuckling. 'But there was this lovely young girl of fourteen or so coming here, and she said why would God make some laws absolute and others sort of bendable. Well, she got me, didn't she? If you accept the laws of God, you just do and that's that. It's not like you need alcohol to live. Occasionally you might misbehave, but that's between you and God.'

Ron and Michael are, I suspect, typical Baha'i' converts in some respects. Both have a long-standing interest in spirituality and religion. Both have dabbled in other Eastern faiths. Both have been unwilling to compromise their own highly tuned personal morality when faced with the failings of their former faiths. For these intelligent, left-leaning, deep-thinking, soul-searching individuals, the Baha'i-faith offers a tailor-made solution. Why reject individual faiths for their inadequacies and errors when you can embrace them all as part of a greater scheme, evolving, all-encompassing and inevitable.

For each age of man, said Bahá'u'lláh, there has been a lesson. God's message has been revealed episodically, by a series of true prophets, of whom he was declared the latest. The lesson for this age is one of unity across the boundaries of faith and nationhood, of a spiritual solution to the economic and political problems of the modern world. What better end, for Ron and Michael, to a search that might otherwise have dragged out to their dying days?

With the last slice of marble cake still unmolested, and the last of the stewed tea cooled to room temperature, we left the china on the table and moved across the hall into a larger room, walled with books. Ron knelt on the floor, fiddling with a VHS recorder while Michael offered us the comfy chairs. We watched a video of a huge international Baha'i conference in New York city. Tens of thousands of attendants cheered and clapped as an endless line of delegates in their national costumes filed across the stage.

'Baha'i is truly global,' said Ron, sitting cross-legged on the floor. 'God made man in His image, the Bible tells us that.'

It was odd to hear the Old Testament God of wrath and revenge popping up in Ron's gentle, progressive faith, but I suppose that's the point with Baha'i; just as the message and humanity change, so God changes also, manifesting in a form that is appropriate to time and place. God's chilled out a lot since the fiery OT days, but a lot of what he said back then still stands, OK?

'And if He made man in His image,' Ron continued, 'well, that's all of us, isn't it?'

'You've got to think a bit broader than physical likeness,' added Michael. 'Colour's an accident. It's the spirit and intelligence of man that's essential. That's the God in us. Man is born noble. If you maintain your purity of heart, you maintain your closeness to God.'

'I mean, look at that feller,' said Ron, pointing to a man on the TV, with a wide, white bone through his broad, black nose. 'Brilliant.'

We had met a fair few holy men on our travels, but Ron and Michael, the Brighton Baha'is, were our first holy 'blokes'. If it weren't for their spiritual aversion to real ale, they would have looked perfectly at home on the dominos team of the local boozer. They hadn't tried to hypnotize or abduct us; there hadn't been anything in the tea except tea. The hour or two Toby and I spent in their company had been a cheerful introduction to a growing faith with a strong, liberal morality. And yet, despite all this, the ride home from the Baha'i centre felt like sobering up after a lunchtime session.

Egalitarianism is the cornerstone of the Baha'i faith and its organizational structure is, on the surface, refreshingly democratic and transparent. Nevertheless, behind the Local and National Assemblies, the Auxiliary Board, the Continental Board of Counsellors and the Universal House of Justice lies a tradition of benign dictatorship that began with the Bab and Bahá'u'lláh, passing to his son and heir, Abdu'l-Baha and on to Shogi Effendi, the first guardian of the Baha'i faith, and the supreme authority on the writings of Bahá'u'lláh.

Toby, who is automatically suspicious of any individual who claims to know the mind of God, or his long-departed prophets, raised the issue on the drive home.

'I knew that would bother you,' I sighed at the inevitability of his cynicism. 'You just hate the idea that someone might know better than you.'

'That's not it at all,' he protested. 'When you introduce human hierarchy to a divine organization, you're damaging your credibility and belittling the value of personal discovery.'

'Struth,' I said. 'Don't get so hung up on the pay scale, look at the staff benefits. I happen to think Baha'i is a step in the right direction. I like the idea of uniting the world's faiths. A big part of my problem with religion is the conflict it causes. One faith, no enemies, right?'

'Wrong. One faith versus the non-believers. The ultimate holy war.'

'We're looking rather far ahead, don't you think?' I asked. 'And besides, I'm not sure the Baha'is would be the type to go in for jihad, if they ever had the numbers for global revolution. In the meantime, surely the message that all faiths are one and we should live in loving unity is worth thinking about.'

The Baha'i vision of global, cross-cultural brotherhood is, of course, to be applauded, but isn't as all-encompassing as it first appears. Despite its inclusive mission and broad, empathetic morality, the Baha'i faith is not an institution where anything goes; it is a proscribed religion, with very definite ideas about history, legitimacy and truth. Central to Bahá'u'lláh's teachings, as I have said, was the belief that the creator has revealed himself to man through a series of divine messengers. And it's a select list: Abraham, Krishna, Moses, Zoroaster, Buddha, Jesus, Muhammad, the Bab and His Nibs. It caters for a good deal of the world's god-fearing population, but it also reveals a decidedly Eastern bias, ignoring other early religious traditions altogether.

'If all faiths are one, revealing, piecemeal, the greater truth, then what of the druids, eh?' Toby pointed out. 'Were they just sitting up a myrtle tree, pissing into the wind? Now I'm sure pre-Roman paganism wasn't far up your average nineteenth-century Iranian scholar's list of pet subjects, but Bahá'u'lláh was supposed to be relaying an international message in the very words of God. Surely the Big Man would cover all the bases?'

'What it comes down to is this,' I replied, as his latest rant tapered off. 'You're never going to get your head around organized religion. You're too fearful of authority.'

'Too mindful of corruption, you mean.'

'You say potato. Anyway, it's pointless trying to find a faith that fits. There isn't one. You're highly moral, which is just as well, but any presence God has in your life is always going to be one on one. And only an occasional visitor, I dare say. Your God is the kind that pops in when your brakes fail and shoots off again as soon as you're safely on the hard shoulder. I'm used to more than that. As odd as it may seem to you, I like the organization. I like the support. And I like a lot of what Baha'i stands for. It might have seriously attracted me once.'

'But?'

'But, as much as I hate to admit it, you make a good point about the missing links in Baha'i's global view. Druids, Aztecs, Aboriginal Australians, Native Americans – all cultures with equally valid belief systems that aren't even on the Baha'i radar. I know it sounds frivolous, but it reminds me that their faith, at the end of the day, is just one man's version of the truth. That's what it always comes down to, isn't it? Bahá'u'lláh. I can admire his message and yet I don't think I'm capable of accepting anyone's word as gospel any more. I'm glad the Baha'is exist – they could teach a lot of self-righteous separatists a thing or two – but who am I kidding? Maybe it's time for me to let go of organized faith altogether or I'll spend my life picking them all to bits. It's time to work things out for myself.'

As tempting as it had been to jump ship and join a faith that reflected my thinking in so many ways, I realized on that journey home that Baha'i, despite its wonderful message, was just another prophet's say-so finally and that I could honestly no longer see the point of replacing my lost religion with another batch of arbitrary dogma.

Ghandi, who knew a thing or two about uniting divided peoples, once said that he believed 'in the fundamental truth of all great religions of the world. I believe that they are all God-given. I came to the conclusion long ago ... that all religions were true, and also that all had some error in them.'

He may have had something. In most belief systems, there are basic teachings that transcend their historical and cultural origins, over and above the standard rules about murder, robbery and inbreeding. When you strip the great faiths down to their bare bones, there are similarities that are undeniable.

Let's start with the omniscient creator: Yahweh, God, Allah. The overriding point of view across every religious group is that there is only one God. The next most popular view in each group is that it's theirs. Even the many Hindu deities are aspects of the greater God, Shiva. It's possible that one lot is right, but are their claims any more valid than those of the teenage film fan asserting that his fantasy-trilogy of choice is the best movie-going experience ever? History tells us that there'll always be another blockbuster – one with a bigger budget and better effects – to capture the imagination of the next generation. And faith evolves, too. I mean, how many followers of Mithras have you met lately? I'm guessing none, but there was a time when only Christ had a bigger European fan club. How soon we forget. Two thousand years and you're yesterday's God.

The great faiths also promote the idea that earthly life is full of suffering, and that paradise awaits us if we toe the line. Naughtiness of all kinds – jealousy, greed, pride and the actions they prompt – increase our suffering. Love, respect and honesty will take the heat off. At the heart of humans' suffering, whether the idea is related as a 'fall' legend, or remains abstract, is man's spiritual separation from his creator. The major faiths all offer their own special devotional diet; a sure-fire ticket to salvation, enlightenment or heavenly reward. But the more I have listened to the truly faithful over the years, declaring their unswerving beliefs in opposing versions of 'the truth', the more I have come to doubt that any of the robe and ritual brigade can reasonably assert that, whatever the other maps say, they know a shortcut to the supernatural.

The British Humanist Association website states that as the

very idea of God is implausible, there's no point in wasting your time trying to pick and choose from the various gods or deities available. Humanism strips away religious dogma altogether, promoting the idea that universal human morality can be achieved without the threats and superstitions of religion. Humanists live good lives, based on reason and empathy, not because of instruction from outdated so-called 'sacred' texts. But I find there's something peculiarly arrogant about Humanism's defiant atheism, however laudable their ethical code. Isn't absolute atheism a kind of faith, after all? A pompous certainty that one's own theory is incontrovertibly accurate. Dare you to prove otherwise. I've always been the sort to revel in the coincidences and mysteries of life. I like to think I'm a rational person but there's room for a little magic in the world, if you ask me. The Humanists would rationalize away every profound or unexplainable movement of my life. When I thought hard about the possibility of joining their ranks, I not only rejected their ideas, I actively pitied them.

I was beginning to realize that when I reached my journey's end, a truly satisfying conclusion would be too much to hope for. In fact, I was starting to feel as though I was chasing my tail.

GO YOUR OWN WAY

Despite a succession of weekends ferrying me to and from the unlikely haunts of south-east England's more exotic religious communities, it was completely obvious Toby was delighted to have a spell at home, a precious concept in our year of perpetual motion. We both cleared a couple of weekend freelance jobs that would help with the mounting credit card bills from our junior jet-set lifestyle; we even went to Ikea and put some curtains up. I admit, it was nice to be still for a while.

But I discovered quickly that it was only while we were somehow moving forwards, towards any sort of explanation for my seemingly endless magic porridge pot of questions, that I was happy. The search for spirituality seemed an end in itself. Perhaps it was because it eased the guilt of apostasy by proving the depth and sincerity of my decision to depart from my Catholic roots. Perhaps I was at the mercy of activity in my temporal lobes? Maybe my eagerness to keep looking – despite the increasingly obvious fact that satisfactory answers would have to come from within – was a result of some lingering tribal predisposition to be recognized as part of a congregation. And if so, would I really need the blessing of brahmin or bishop before I was ready to stop running and face life?

Our charming but conclusive encounters with the Buddhists and Baha'is of the South Downs had left me despondent. Weeks after we had turned our backs on the golden beaches of Goa, we found ourselves in the sun again, albeit a pathetic one, leafing through the Sunday supps in the back garden. I had been staring at the same page of recycled paparazzi shots of celebrities 'coming a cropper' for more than five minutes. Of course, the sight of Naomi Campbell falling on her spoilt arse in a pair of Slade-high platforms never gets boring, but Toby noticed the telling slouch in my shoulders and knew that my mind was elsewhere. He touched my knee under the table.

'What's up?'

I snapped to attention. 'Hmm? Oh. It's Goa.'

'Missing the beach?' he asked, innocently.

I puffed air through my nose and rolled my eyes. 'I wish. No. And it's not really Goa, specifically. That's just where I go to in my head when I start thinking about all those Eastern religions. I'm in a funk, to be frank.'

'So the great faiths didn't come up trumps,' he consoled me, rather feebly. 'Did you really think they would?'

'Oh, I don't know,' I snapped. 'All that Mystical East jazz. It's a total cliché, isn't it? But I couldn't help wondering whether it all might fall into place for me in India. All that yoga and veggie food. It's just so me. That's why I chased down Chudrun when we got home. I'd make a great Buddhist, Tobe. I've got all the right clothes.'

'Only weak-minded trust fundees find themselves in India, and I've got a feeling that has as much to do with the opening of their lungs to the local weed as it does with the opening of their third eye to the Enlightened One. So you've got the clothes, you just lack the conviction.'

'Exactly. I understand now that organized religions are all much of a muchness. The rules differ here and there, and it's each to his own at storytime, but they're all essentially man-made, aren't they? Dig away for long enough and you dent your shovel on some stony little issue that just rubs those earthly origins in your face. The chauvanism in Buddhism. Baha'i's pick 'n' mix prophecy. If I carried on sifting through the faiths I think I'm at the point where I'll just find the problems with each one of them. But at the end of the day, the most pertinent point about Eastern faith is that God's not overly hung up on whether you participate or not. That takes the pressure off believing anything else they say altogether. It's a completely liberating idea and, if nothing else, I think it's helping my apostatic guilt.'

'It probably helps the Hooray Henna-rys when they ditch their robes to take up their desks in the City twelve months down the line.'

'You're really quite bitter, aren't you, Tobe? Why is that?'

'A combination of middle-class guilt, financial envy and the scars of a childhood in Thatcher's Britain spent north of Watford.'

'Sounds like you've got a handle on your anger, anyway,' I said, half-jokingly.

'Self-awareness is my saving grace. And is apostatic a word?' he asked.

'It is now,' I said. 'I needed it. The point is – before you went all *Socialist Worker* – I find it easier to entertain the idea of reaching my own conclusions, faith-wise, if I can think of God as a little less judgemental, a little more creative and nurturing, Eastern style. And I might even be coming round to the prospect of not having to commit myself one way or another. Because surely it makes sense that a being as powerful and insightful as God isn't going to get His knickers in a twist over one empty seat at the Sunday service, right?'

'The *Bhagavad Gita*,' Toby chimed in. '"I am neither hateful nor partial to anyone."'

'Well, there you are, then. If that's the case, why bother worshipping at all?'

'"But if someone serves me in love, I am a friend to them, and them to me,"' he completed the quotation.

'Argh!' I squealed. 'Round and round in bloody circles.'

'I don't think it's something to sweat about,' he countered, evidently surprised to find himself arguing on the side of religion for a moment. 'I think it means God's there for you, whether you acknowledge it or not, but that it might be worthwhile getting to know him because, well, because he's a cool person to have at parties.'

I spread my fingers on the tabletop, leaning in purposefully. 'Doctrinal faith? Bibles and legends? Saints and prophets and rules and rewards? Forget 'em. The moment mankind gets involved, you're moving further away.'

'You sound like me,' he said, amazed.

'Well, maybe I do,' I said. 'Don't be smug.'

'Groupthink', a term coined by a psychologist called Irvin Janis in 1972 (although George Orwell got their first with the phrase 'doublethink' in *1984*) is the word used by psychologists to describe the mental state of that great mass of people who just can't seem to make up their own minds. These are the people who opt into the popular point of view because conformity and social acceptance ultimately means more to them than their own self-determined opinions and tastes. A united vision and a close community may make for a hassle-free life, but research into group dynamics and organized behaviour has shown that even different opinions in a community lead to better decision-making and social progress. Organized cohesiveness, meanwhile, often leads to stagnation, complacency and isolation from the wider world. The better an idea is established among the majority of any group, the more likely any remaining 'free-thinkers' will be to submit to the groupthink urge, surrendering their own instinctive inquisitiveness for an easy life. Wherever church numbers drop, the advantage of groupthink is lost. Without the power of peer pressure, whether subconsciously hurled like stones at a heretic, dominant faiths have to rely on the same powers of persuasion as smaller groups. And what they're finding these days is that, left to browse without interruption by aggressive sales staff, your average spiritual shopper doesn't give a monkeys what everyone else is wearing. If the hat fits, they'll wear it.

For these people labels no longer matter. They don't feel the need to compartmentalize everything into neat little doctrinal bundles. They come to their own conclusions, building a personal morality around their innate sense of right and wrong. Of course, I'm talking about people who a) have made the decision to at least think about morality and the human spirit, and b) have the benefit of having grown up in a world with its own overarching moral and religious systems. Bespoke faith is an increasingly attractive option as the authority of traditional oligarchies diminishes, and the parish church is redeveloped into starter homes.

Tristan Morell, a Brighton astrologer, tarot reader and clairvoyant, has come to terms with his own idiosyncratic belief system, regardless of the raised eyebrows from cynics he has no doubt had to weather. Tristan's personal faith neatly disposes of many of the problems that arise from adherence to formal religions. He doesn't have to worry about rigid or oppressive rules and has the advantage of being able to be vague with a clear conscience on any point of theology that he simply hasn't got around to pondering yet. At other times, when an idea or theory makes sense to him, his convictions are absolute. At the heart of Tristan's world view is a sincere belief in his own 'supernatural' powers: clairvoyancy and the ability to communicate with the dead. It's an eccentric starting point, although it would be impossible for cynics to disprove Tristan's claims conclusively. None the less, his easygoing, non-judgemental vision was immediately more appealing to me than the better known, but often equally potty, explanations of existence offered by religion's major players.

As Toby, Tristan and I chatted in his seaside flat on a sunny, Sunday afternoon, I had to remind myself more than once that, as I could no longer necessarily believe a billion Christians, there was no sense in siding with one Tristan. Then again, faith and – in particular – the afterlife are so much more immediate and tangible in Tristan's world.

As we settled in Tristan's kitchen with a bottle of wine, it seemed we already had company from the next world.

'Oh,' he shivered, looking at the goosebumps that had erupted along his forearm, 'my skin's prickling. Spirit's with me.'

I grinned to myself as I shivered along with him. I'd been drowning in cynicism for months and it felt familiar to get swept up in something unexplainable. I wasn't the same gullible girl any more; that person had disappeared in the wake of my first epileptic seizure. But nor was I quick to condemn. I felt as though I'd reached the top of a hill and had begun rolling down the other side. I was recognizing some of the things I'd seen on the way up, but they were whizzing past at speed as I hurtled towards my ultimate destination. The weird thing was that I felt the presence of 'Spirit', too, even before Tristan told us it was there. I know some people – including Toby, no doubt – will think I'm a loon. Maybe it was an electro-magnetic fluctuation, or just a hidden draft, but there's no denying I felt it.

Tristan didn't make a great deal out of his apparent gifts. He didn't flap like a charlatan about supernatural forces and destiny. He just shrugged as he said, 'This is how I see it', relating, without trying to explain, the conviction that his extrasensory experiences are externally inspired and authentically insightful. He has plenty of regular clients who'd be quick to agree. He believes in an agency, which he calls 'Spirit'. It is the force behind his work – like the wind to a mill – but it is also a sort of companion or guide, constant and benign.

'Each of us,' he asserts, 'houses a spark of energy that's part of something bigger. Something universal. Whatever you want to call it – God, Allah, energy, Spirit – it's a life force running through all there is. And the whole point of it is love.'

I nodded and shuffled forward on the window ledge I'd perched on.

'So do you believe in the continuity of individuals beyond death?' I asked, feeling like a sceptical intruder with my dry words.

'And if so,' added Toby, 'do you think we hang on to ourselves and join the soup, or remain distinct?'

Tristan thought for a moment, still subconsciously running his hand along the bumpy skin of his forearm. 'Oh, yes,' he answered eventually. 'I believe we carry on. We're energy, not this stuff.' He gestured at our bodies and his. 'I don't think you have to join the soup to become part of some larger consciousness. You have to let go of earthly ideas of self.' He grinned over at me as I sat rubbing the bloated belly of a bronze Buddha statue. 'It's good luck to do that, you know.'

I rubbed a little harder.

When I was a kid I had death all worked out. In my mind, a plank was lowered from trampoline-like clouds by a long and quite sturdy piece of rope, the body was placed on the plank and burly angels hauled it back to Heaven. I didn't know what happened up there, but I assumed it was good and probably involved party food. Of course, I soon found out that death wasn't so simple. Instead, it became a designated meeting place where I would see my loved ones again. The pain from loss almost eclipses the joy of love, but not quite, and so we love anyway knowing that one day we must all lose the people we care about. Having faith helps to offset that pain. But now I wasn't so sure about the existence of Heaven; I desperately wanted alternatives. I was hoping that Tristan, a man with the ability to peep behind the veil, might be able to shed some light on where love goes when we die.

For many, death doesn't signal the end for loving relationships. After all, people don't ever really leave us, we just get used to not seeing them. Some cultures take this quite literally. In

China, for example, ancestor worship is the native religion. Death and mourning for the Chinese deceased form part of their most revered ceremonies; on 5 April the Ching Ming Festival is held. The Japanese share a similar observance on the same day, but is it referred to as *Hansik*.

Ching, in Chinese, means pure or clean, and Ming means brightness. This holiday is also sometimes referred to as grave-sweeping day because it's when families descend on the cemeteries to remember their ancestors and clean up their graves. Fire-crackers are lit to frighten evil spirits away and to alert the deceased relatives that they are there to pay their respects. Before settling down to a graveside feast, offerings of flowers, food and drink are laid out on the gravestones and paper effigies of money and any other materialistic possessions such as cars, clothes or jewellery are burned for the deceased's use in the afterlife. Terry Wong, a Chinese/Irish friend of mine, told me that real possessions are also often put in the coffin alongside the deceased. When his grandfather died they had buried him along with his driver's licence, glasses, a pot of tiger balm, his best shoes, the suit he bought for his daughter's wedding, his passport, his washbag and a scan of the grandchild he didn't live to see. The precious family black jade, however, stayed this side of the veil.

The ancient Egyptians regarded death as nothing but a temporary interruption, a pit stop on the path of the everlasting soul. To guarantee this continuity they paid homage to their gods during and after their lives on earth. When someone snuffed it they were mummified to enable the soul's eventual return to the body. Furniture from the deceased's home, along with food and drink, were left on offering tables outside the burial chamber, presumably so that the recently dead could have a snack in the afterworld. Funerary texts such as spells or prayers were written on the inner walls of the burial chambers to help the dead on their dangerous journey past knife-wielding serpents, fire-spitting dragons and ravenous, five-headed reptiles to the next life. When they got finally got there, no doubt knackered, they had to confess to a total of forty-two gods, and convincingly proclaim their innocence of crimes against Heaven and earth. They then had to have their heart weighed for judgement – like members of a gruesome Weight Watchers splinter group. If their hearts weighed equal to a feather, representing Maat the goddess of truth and justice, the person achieved immortality. If not, they were barred entrance and their hearts were gobbled up by the croco-lion hybrid goddess Amemet.

The Greeks had plenty to say on all manner of subjects and are notable for having had the good sense to write them down. The philosopher Epicurus (341BC to 270BC) once scribbled: 'Death does not concern us because as long as we exist death is not here, and when it does come, we no longer exist.' He has a point. And yet the question of whether life continues after we slip our mortal coil has always agitated the minds of the religious, spiritual and scientific. We all have our theories on what happens when we die – whether it's fluffy white clouds and a free harp, reincarnation or simply oblivion – and which vision you favour is probably all down to whether you think you've got an immortal soul. Is the soul the aspect of humanity that recognizes God? Is it, as Buddha says, an aspect of universal truth – of God Himself? Or is our belief in the soul nothing but wishful thinking, a trick of the mind to keep our thoughts from morbid obsession?

Alejandro González Inárritu's film *21 Grams* proposed the

idea that at the moment of death every human being loses exactly 21 grams in weight. Could this last-minute weight loss mark the departure of our invisible, eternal soul, the same 'energy' that Tristan believes in, finally departing our cumbersome bodies to become part of a larger consciousness? Unfortunately, in this case, it doesn't look likely. The 21 gram soul theory originated from a Massachusetts doctor, Duncan MacDougall, in the early 1900s. Dr MacDougall felt sure that if we did indeed possess a soul it would have to exist in material form and should therefore be measurable. In 1907 he set out to test his theory. He converted a hospital bed into a rudimentary but sensitive set of scales that could weigh folks as soon as they breathed their last. Six terminally ill patients were recruited for his inaugural spiritual weigh-in. As well as the moribund humans, he repeated the weighing experiment on fifteen dogs, which, in accordance with his belief, should lack souls. MacDougall neatly concluded that humans lost around three-quarters of an ounce at the moment of death, while dogs lost nothing. As soon his findings were published in *American Medicine*, the critics pounced. He was repeatedly asked why the weight change took longer in some people than others and challenged about the efficiency of his scales and the variability in his data. Despite all protestations, MacDougall was never taken seriously. All corpses lose weight over time. Minute intercellular structures called lysosomes release enzymes that break the body down into gases and liquids. Changes in weight are inevitable. MacDougall's consistent reading may look like the self-prophesized results of a believer with a point to prove. But just because the soul can't be weighed and labelled doesn't mean it's not there.

Near-death experiences (NDEs), have been experienced by

people in every culture around the world and further investigation in this field may hold some answers as to where we, or our souls, go at death. The fact that survivors share a strikingly similar experience despite widely divergent cultural backgrounds suggests more than imagination at work. But are NDEs really a window on the waiting room for the next life? Modern research, both medical and mystical, may yet make progress towards an answer. Psychologists now discuss enlightenment and healing transformation. Biologists examining the brain near death, note the release of huge amounts of endorphins. The side effects of such a dose? Long dark tunnels, bright lights ... sound familiar?

Perhaps NDEs are just another physical process after all. Before you bin your Gideans though, consider the extraordinary anecdotal evidence of respected Seattle paediatrician Dr Melvin Morse, which gives me hope.

Having narrowly avoided death by drowning, a seven-year-old girl started drawing pictures. Her blow-by-blow description of the emergency room struggle to save her life – complete with her illustrations from a bird's eye point of view – took Doctor Morse by surprise. The little girl had been pronounced clinically dead after nineteen minutes under the water. But while hope faded in the emergency room, the unconscious – no, *dead* – seven-year-old was apparently struggling back to her body from somewhere near the ceiling, driven, she later said, by a desire to return to her mother and unborn brother. She drew the expected baby in one of her illustrations, taking care to fill his chest with a bright red, outsized heart. When the boy arrived, months later, heart disease was diagnosed.

Coupled with his patient's uncanny recollection of events which she cannot have witnessed, this apparent act of childhood clairvoyance persuaded Dr Morse to examine the idea of perception without consciousness. He has recorded dozens of interviews with children who have had near-death experiences, as he believes their experiences to be less culturally influenced than in adult cases. Dr Morse encourages his patients to interact with the benign presence that is a common feature of NDEs, believing that only by challenging the experience can we figure out whether near-death visions are internally or externally produced. His findings have been published in medical journals and he's working to detect physical changes in the right temporal lobe of the brain as a result of post-death experience. He believes that by studying the neuroscience of an NDE, we are learning more about an area of our brains that we barely use, which is responsible for paranormal abilities and the power to heal ourselves, both spiritually and physically. Morse believes that anyone can unlock that part of the brain through prayer, meditation, perhaps even through any mundane, repetitive action. In his mind, if we can unlock the secrets of the right temporal lobe, we're possibly stepping into another realm.

Of course, none of this goes any further to settle the question of life after death. Even near-death, after all, is just that. What we can say categorically is that nobody has ever been able to prove that there isn't an afterlife. But what do we have to look forward to if God isn't the final destination? What happens to love itself, to the intensity of relationships and the bond of the supposed soulmate? How can it be that we find our perfect someone only to lose them all over again?

Atlanta psychiatrist and marriage expert Frank Pittman once said, in the March 2004 issue of *Psychology Today*: 'Nothing has produced more unhappiness than the concept of a soulmate.' And he's right. A huge percentage of romantics are in danger of aiming too high and taking the risk of missing out on perfectly solid opportunities along the way in the pursuit of an illusion. After all, if we spend our lives looking for that perfect someone to 'complete' us, the chances are we'll never feel complete. And if a soulmate really is the one and only true eternal partner given to us by God, a divine marriage already exists and perhaps we should be promising more than 'until death do us part'. I read an article once about a Hindu gentleman in India who was caught on a stepladder attempting sex with a female elephant. When asked what he was trying to achieve, he announced that he believed that Nellie was a reincarnation of his deceased wife. When pressed on exactly how he knew, he explained that he had recognized the twinkle in the elephant's eye.

Love is a potent, sometimes all-consuming force – and as Tristan believes, the point to it all. Its sudden absence can be unsettling physically as well as emotionally. My grandad pined away to nothing in not much more than a year after his beloved wife's death. In his final months he surrounded himself with the souvenirs of their shared memories, boxing up the rest of his possessions in preparation for their anticipated disposal or distribution. Without Violet, Alec saw no point to living. He was a lifelong romantic who was never without his well-thumbed pocket-sized volume of their favourite love poetry. On one of our last meetings he passed the little book on to me. The gold-embossed corners had rubbed white and the margins of almost every page were crammed with Grandad's scribbled notes. It was one of the best gifts I have ever been given, because it was given with such love, though at the same time, it was heartbreaking. As he surrendered his beloved verse to me, I knew that my wonderful grandfather was going for sure. Although we all adored him, a greater love was calling – but then Violet had always been a bit bossy.

I'm sure most of us don't want to believe that death is truly the end, and a great many people seek out the Tristans of the world, hoping to prove our pet theories of life beyond the grave. Science is blind to the beyond, but can the metaphysicists of the modern world – the astrologists, psychics and mediums – do any better? And yet, while scientists' predictions fail and hypotheses mutate, it seems the spiritual community has just as valid an insight into the workings of the universe.

For Tristan, the continuation of the spirit beyond death is not a matter of question. That we survive beyond our corporeal demise is the basis of his personal belief system. He explained that once you embrace the idea that we are all sparks of energy – housed in a temporary flesh-box – death shouldn't be a problem. Like the ancient Egyptians, he argues, we should see death as a mere skin-shedding exercise. In his mind, reincarnation is the next logical step – and the next, and the next, until we reach our most perfect state. Through past life regression, he believes himself to have been reincarnated a number of times.

'I didn't actually think it would work,' he told us, while topping up our glasses and hunting in the fridge for another bottle, 'but I was actually amazed at the results. I thought I'd probably have been some female scrubber in Tudor times because Elizabeth I is one of my heroes. But amongst other past lives it transpired I was a male architect in the horribly repressed Victorian era, of all things.' He wrinkled up his nose with distaste. 'I'd been rich but miserable, because I was gay and unhappily married to a woman. But in this life I came out as soon as possible, at sixteen in fact, yet have always had money problems. Life is about finding a balance.'

There's more than a smattering of Buddhism and Hinduism in Tristan's tailor-made philosophy, minus self-denial – although after a somewhat wild youth, he acknowledges the importance of moderation – and the endless written texts.

'But I do believe that something is judging us somewhere,' he mused, 'and what you give out you get back so don't create problems for yourself on a karmic level.' He jiggled his eyebrows and looked thoroughly naughty for a moment. 'But we all know when we're being bad really, don't we?'

At a Hindu funeral the priest recites the fifteenth chapter of the *Bhagavad Gita*, a profound, soul-stirring dialogue on the battlefield between Lord Krishna and Prince Arjuna, comprised of eighteen chapters with a total of 701 Sanskrit verses. This chapter is about the conditioned life struggle of *jivatma*, or the 'living soul', in the material world, compared to the spiritual realm where every soul is infallible. It is an incredibly hopeful and inspirational passage:

The soul is never born nor dies; nor does it become only after being born. For it is unborn, eternal, everlasting and ancient, even though the body is slain, the soul is not. As a man shedding worn-out garments, takes other new ones, likewise the embodied soul, casting off worn-out bodies, enters into others which are new. Weapons cannot cut it nor fire burn it; water cannot wet it nor can wind dry it. The soul is unmanifest; it is unthinkable, and it is spoken of as immutable. Therefore, knowing this as such, you should not grieve over the inevitable.

Reincarnation is a core belief for many in the East, but many cultures across the world have toyed with the idea at some point or another. These days it's a powerful alternative to the predominant Western idea of Heaven and Hell. In fact, a great many of the Church's early pillars wrote and taught about reincarnation and the pre-existence of souls. In the Old Testament souls gathered in Sheol, the grave or a place of shadows, a meeting place for souls. In the New Testament there are a few passages describing how souls await to be resurrected when Jesus returns. But Christian past-life advocates, such as the Plato-loving Gnostics, were persecuted out of existence after the Fifth Ecumenical Church Council of 553, as they were viewed as dangerous heretics. The Literalists – the school of Christianity adopted by the Roman empire in the fourth century, later becoming Roman Catholicism – took control, although this was more to do with clashes of power rather than spiritual enlightenment. Any contrasting ideas at this time were politically dangerous because they opposed Emperor Constantine's vision of Christianity.

Islam, however, teaches the continuous progress of the soul. It believes that God has given us both body and spirit and the spirit is the nucleus from which a higher form of life grows within us. During our lives our actions shape our spirit and when we die the spirit remains, formed from our deeds – whether good or bad – and does not return to this world after the death of the body but moves on. There is comfort to be found here, because if we are to embrace the theory of reincarnation we must also accept that if we are born, perhaps poor or handicapped, that these are punishments for transgressions in a previous life. And if this is the case should we feel guilty for our pain or have no sympathy for those that suffer? Or even applaud the rich and fortunate for a presumed previous life of altruism? These attitudes are not acceptable in Islamic teachings. Instead, their belief is that we are all born with a pure soul and it's up to every individual to shape it into something beautiful.

Tristan shyly told us that he believes he knew his partner, Barry, in a previous life and experienced a soul connection when they met this time around. And many of us experience that feeling of familiarity with a stranger, that inexplicable bond. Call me soppy, but a great part of me desperately wants to embrace the idea of reincarnation wholeheartedly, although I hate to think that any horrors in this life are pay-back for evil deeds from the last, because if we do meet up again and again . . . and again, love truly never dies.

Although there is much anecdotal evidence of eternal life and liberation through rebirth, there is, to date, no conclusive scientific evidence in its support. But despite the fact that Tristan's beliefs may seem left-field to some, it's not as unlikely as it might sound, and there are people from the scientific community who are actively trying to advance the study of past lives. The leading figure in this field has been Dr Ian Stevenson, the former head of the Department of Psychiatry at the University of Virginia, and now Director of the Division of Personality Studies at the University of Virginia, who has offered convincing scientific evidence for reincarnation. He collected and documented thousands of cases from children from over the world who claimed to have memories of a previous life. Dr Stevenson researched the dead individuals each child remembered being, and confirmed facts from the deceaseds' lives that matched the child's memory. In his book, *Reincarnation and Biology: A Contribution to the Etiology of*

Birthmarks and Birth Defects, there are even cases where claims of past life injuries correlate with birthmarks, injuries or birth defects. But Stevenson himself has stated that the evidence is only suggestive. He is as much admired as criticized for his work.

There are now many recordings of entranced people recounting the details from what appear to be past life experiences. There are even reports of foreign languages spoken by people who claim to have no conscious understanding of the tongue they use freely under hypnosis. Of course, there are cases where this can simply be explained away as surfacing memories that were hidden away and triggered under hypnosis. But not in every instance.

Tristan's work can be incredibly beneficial and helpful to many, especially with those who struggle to come to terms with someone's death; after all, we all want to know that our loved ones are all right. He told us about an Irish lady who came to see him in a terrible state. He explained that 'Spirit' had told him it was OK for him to tell us about her. Tristan is incredibly protective and private about his clients.

'When I do readings normally, I'll sit in front of the client and tell them what I see from the Tarot. But on this occasion it was very different,' he explained quietly. A girl had appeared standing beside him, playing with her beautiful long red hair. She told him that her name was Sarah.

'I asked the woman if she knew someone called Sarah,' Tristan continued, 'and also whether there was something about Sarah's hair falling out when she was alive.' The woman had burst into uncontrollable tears and, when she had calmed down, explained that Sarah had been her daughter who had died of leukemia. Before the illness had taken over and the cruel side-effects of the drugs kicked in, Sarah had loved her beautiful mane of hair and had been horrified when it had started to fall out in clumps. But when she appeared beside Tristan she was happy in spirit, and was thrilled to have her hair again. The experience helped the woman come to terms with her daughter's death. Before visiting Tristan the woman had lost her faith as an Irish Catholic. Sarah's death had kick-started the same process that I was experiencing. Her visit to Tristan, whose work and beliefs clash with her Catholic conditioning, had managed to resuscitate her faith where the priests had failed.

'So she's got her faith back and immediately has to start worrying again about colluding with the Devil?' Toby teased.

'Yes, I know.' Tristan laughed. 'Irony upon irony. But I was just glad that she was happy.'

Among Tristan's regulars are a varied selection of faithful adherents to major religions, including a surprising number of Christians, Jews and Muslims.

'They're not supposed to, I don't think,' he said. 'But if you ask me, if whatever God they believe in is letting me do this – helping me to do this – how can it be a sin? I'm not forcing it to happen. It doesn't hurt anybody. I'm just happy that I can help to give people hope in some small way. It feels like I'm doing something worthwhile.' Then he added, 'Oh, that sounded naff!'

According to Tristan, religious devotion doesn't seem to be as relevant in the spiritual world as it is here on earth. He is in contact with spirits who have lived through various religious experiences at various times in history. One might assume that if a devout Christian, say, popped his clogs and found he could still communicate with the physical world, the first thing he'd communicate – as loudly as possible – would be: 'For God's sake, say your prayers because they're bang on the money.' This, though, is something that spirits never seem to bother with, 'even the ones who are warm and loving', says Tristan. Should we assume from this that while faith is personal, doctrinal religion is irrelevant?

'I think it's only irrelevant if it's irrelevant to you,' Tristan mused vaguely, when I put the question to him. 'What's in your heart is important. We shouldn't underestimate the power of creation. There is a force behind it all and a morality that's essential to that force. Yes, we all do wrong things, but if what's in your heart is genuine – the right intentions – then that really should be all that matters. If all the Christians are right then all the Jews are wrong, and on and on it goes. That's got to be rubbish, hasn't it? I once had an argument with a Jehovah's Witness on a live radio show. He said every reading I did was evil and something to do with God being angry with Saul for seeing things. So I asked him why God made Saul clairvoyant in the first place then? That stumped him'

'So what do you say to die-hard cynics?' I asked him in conclusion, reluctantly gathering my things to leave and giving Buddha's belly a final rub.

Tristan downed the dregs of his wine and shifted forward on his chair. 'There's a wonderful Chinese proverb,' he said, a smile playing across his fine-boned, handsome face. 'People who say that it can't be done shouldn't interfere with the ones who are doing it. I really believe that. I sit here, every single day, doing it. You know? It's a weird way to make a living – believe me, it's a weirder way to live – but it works.'

HEAVENLY HEALING

As Tristan helps people with his work, based around his personal beliefs and talent, there are also healers whose own beliefs are based around their ability to channel love from a higher universal force. It's this supposed force, or energy, that practitioners claim can permeate their patients' bodies. I was intrigued by it.

In my experience, which is undoubtedly linked to thirty years with our beloved but crumbling NHS, and one visit to an insurance firm's dodgy Harley Street quack, most doctors leave their personalities on a peg by the surgery door. The medical profession is often accused of lacking compassion, the very thing that religion and spirituality get Brownie points for. However, after years of suffering some consultants' God complexes, it seems that patients are ready for change. With alternative therapies given ever more credence by the medical establishment, are we ready to let spirituality back into the hospital ward?

Despite the relentless advance of medicinal science in the twentieth century, the failures of science to tackle big killers, particularly cancer, has left an open window for many new approaches to healing. All manner of theories, from colour therapy to the power of prayer, are scrutinized as possible partners to traditional medical care. So is a truce between medicine's cold science and spirituality's warm holistic approach on the cards? At the Community Centre for Enhanced Health Technologies (CCTAS) in Yeumbeul, Senegal, the region's traditional healers, who brew age-old remedies from indigenous plants, established a computer database in a bid to preserve their knowledge. If the herbalists and healers can embrace the technology of the establishment, perhaps the men in white coats will be encouraged to log on for a closer inspection at the softer side of patient care.

Of course, holistic healing is nothing new. Here's what Plato had to say on the subject: 'The cure of the part should not be attempted without treatment of the whole. No attempt should be made to cure the body without the soul. Let no one persuade you to cure the head until he has first given you his soul to be cured, for this is the great error of our day, that physicians first separate the soul from the body.'

From reiki to rolfing, all alternative therapies have one thing in common: they treat the patient as a whole rather than focusing on specific symptoms or body parts. That's not to say that your reiki master is going to say no to a cast on his broken arm, but when it comes to illness – as opposed to traumatic injury – healing is seen as a restoration of balance in mind, body and soul. These are the Three Musketeers of human happiness, and on holistic healing, it's all for one and one for all.

Not surprisingly, there are no official qualifications available in the art of healing with love. Nevertheless, there are a great many practitioners whose sincere faith in their own abilities sets them apart from the cynics and charlatans. The responsible spiritual healer will always agree that their work should be done alongside, not in the place of, conventional medicine, and that the doctor should remain in control of the patient's overall care. The National Federation of Spiritual Healers, founded in 1954, provides a code of conduct that forbids members from making diagnoses and countermanding any official medical advice. The federation's preferred dynamic is one of close liaison and mutual consultation between physician, healer and patient. Fusion, you'll have noted, is something of a theme in holistic medicine.

Spiritual healing has been practised since the beginning of recorded history in all dominant civilizations and cultures. Only when conventional medicine was developed were the more psychological aspects of healing gradually eroded. Traditional and spiritual healing has weathered centuries of ridicule and even persecution, but has survived, and today enjoys a new generation of faithful adherents. The Prince of Wales's Foundation for Integrated Health exists to positively promote complementary health practitioners in the UK, and NSFH figures show an estimated 20,000 spiritual healers are working in Britain.

Patients who lean on religious practice as an adjunct to medical care often report great benefits. Studies show that religious or spiritually minded patients are likely to enjoy a more positive attitude in general. Their self-esteem is often higher than the faithless and they seem better able to cope with even life-threatening crises. Faith really comes into its own when you're facing death. Maybe that's a big part of its purpose. But even for those who have replaced religion with a humanist idea of compassion and empathy, driven not necessarily by supernatural forces, but by a profound and freely chosen moral philosophy, the idea of love as an agent of healing, beyond the understanding of conventional science, can still be valid.

Juliusz Wodzianski is a spiritual healer who channels a force that he believes is 'pure love', abundant and tangible in the world around us. He makes no claims of divine insight, but believes in a benign, spiritual force that envelops and animates all life on earth. I was curious about his methods so on a free weekend Toby and I went to visit him in his north London home.

Juliusz works his healing by opening his heart to the invisible force of love and channelling it into his patients. As he explains: 'It is simply a matter of tapping into the universal love that is omnipresent and available to all of us. No tools are needed, there's no mystery or ritual and the process is completely safe.'

Of course, cynics might argue that that's because he's not actually doing anything at all, but Juliusz maintains that the energy he channels enters the mind, body and soul of his subject, travelling to the site of pain like magic Nurofen.

He argues that the human body has remarkable self-healing capacities but that it sometimes needs a push in the right direction, which healers can provide. He believes that other forms of energy channelling, such as crystal-healing or reflexology, can be just as successful as his own, and sees them as nothing but formalized versions of his own art. In his view, all forms of healing work with the power he calls love, but the method of access differs. 'People like to differentiate everything,' he asserts, 'make it complicated. But often it's just about seeking out a USP so the populace buys into it. It's all just about love. Simple as that.'

According to Juliusz, everyone has the power to heal. 'There are absolutely wonderful healers walking about the world who have never heard of the concept of healing,' he told me with a smile. 'Who wouldn't want to do it? And yet the way they conduct their life – the way they respond to other people and help them in distress – makes them the most wonderful natural-born healers.'

It's easy to see what he means. It's not hard for any of us to shoot someone a smile instead of a frown, drop a few pennies in a charity box, or chat to a pensioner in the post office queue. And there's no denying the emotional lift that the kind good deed provides, whether you're giving or receiving. If there's any truth in the notion that happy means healthy, the accumulative effect of these small acts of love could hold the secret of eternal youth for a society that's ready to kiss and make up. It would be nice to think we'll get there some day.

Patients who have undergone spiritual healing generally agree that it helps mitigate pain and is deeply relaxing, and even traditional naysayers acknowledge the benefits of effective stress relief in combating physical and psychological illness. Collected data appears to show that patients who have received spiritual care often recover more quickly, and relapse less often, than those who have not. It could all be in the mind, of course, a benefit of blind faith that boosts the immune system. But if it's working, who cares how?

Juliusz himself has witnessed remarkable results from his work. 'One of my clients had been given a few months to live,' he remembers. 'She came to me in a terrible state. She'd had a double mastectomy and was very conscious of it. But after a few weeks of treatment she started to feel better about her body. She even started swimming again. She asked to see her consultant as she was feeling so much better and had another scan. It was completely clear. Her consultant had explained that the body can go into remission, which of course it can and does, but the transformation in her health occurred when her attitude towards life changed. That's how I saw it, and that was her view, too.'

Juliusz doesn't lay claim to curing his patient. He doesn't even claim to fully understand the healing process. We all know that unfortunately this is often down to luck. He simply states in his calm, assuring way that he helped her find the space to explore her own emotions and feelings, and that through their sessions, she found she had a huge amount of residual anger from a previous relationship.

'Once she started externalizing it her whole being changed,' says Juliusz. 'To watch her unfold was amazing. Like watching a flower grow. Anger is one of the key things to look at. People bury their emotions, ignore their spirituality and block out love. That has a great effect on the body and the mind.'

For Juliusz, spiritual healing has nothing to do with religion. Love is channelled from the world, through the healer to the client, and works irrespective of either party's beliefs. Juliusz doesn't channel energy from his own body, a sensation he describes as 'debilitating', although some healers do claim to use their own 'energy'. A darker side of Juliusz's work was revealed when he explained that from time to time he has suffered extremely unpleasant and unsettling healing sessions. Occasionally, he claims, he sees a client who carries so much negativity or ill intention that they literally block his own body's reserves of 'love', leaving him weak and drained. But despite the occasional exorcist moment, Juliusz has no room in his personal philosophy for the age-old spiritual dichotomy of good versus evil, light versus dark, God versus the Devil. And he has personally managed to reduce religion to a single, uncomplicated four letter word. Do I have to spell it out for you?

There's no doubt about it, personal faith is a positive thing. It breeds happiness and contentment in those individuals brave enough to stand alone, regardless of what society may think. But I found that I couldn't even begin to think about creating my own belief system without first trying to find out exactly what love was without God. If it isn't something that is divinely inspired is it merely a biological response and if so, what's the point of getting married or even just committing ourselves to one person for the long haul? In short, if we took away the artifice of society, would love survive?

'There's a Buddhist proverb,' I told Toby as we shared washing-up duties one Saturday evening. 'You're not the only one who can quote things. "If you meet the Buddha on the road, kill him." It means when someone tells you they have all the answers, they can only be lying. I haven't decided whether there's a God or not. But I know now that any relationship we may have in the future will be strictly one-on-one. I really like this idea of personal faith.'

'And as for love?'

'Love is real. It's felt. And it's a wonderful feeling. If that's all it comes down to, ultimately, I think I can live with that. It does break my heart, though. We invest so much in love. We attribute it with such mystical power. It would be a shame to see it reduced to animal instinct. I'd hate to think that without the social and family structures promoted by religion, mankind would just be running around rutting like rabbits.'

'Just because love might be predominantly physical doesn't mean it can't be "special" without God. However we got here, the human experience is miraculous, and love is one of the defining aspects of our lives,' Toby said. 'It's at the heart of every truly worthwhile human endeavour. It drives us on and pushes us to extremes. It's our nature to love, and it always has been. What if I told you that human beings have been hooking up in loving couples since before the dawn of religion? What if I told you that love is older than God?'

'How old is that, then?' I asked, snorting.

'I dunno,' he answered. 'Three and a half million years?'

'Pretty old,' I said, 'but God's older than time.'

'It's older than religion, though.'

'I'll give you that,' I said. 'But prove it.'

'Fine,' Toby replied. 'The next trip on this little spiritual odyssey is mine. No nuns, no priests, no yoga and no icy baths. I'm going to prove to you that love was doing just fine long before the church stepped in and told everyone they could all carry on doing what they were doing, but they had to swap rings first.'

'Where are we going?' I asked, brightening at the thought of sunlit, tropical locations.

'To see a friend of mine who knows about these things.'

'Does he live in a beach hut? Or just off the beach? Or within driving distance of a beach? Somewhere warm?'

'Probably not warm, at this time of year,' he admitted. 'Coastal, yes. Tropical, no. No more questions, OK? It's a surprise. Besides, why are you so keen to fly again? Wasn't India and Lourdes enough for you?'

'A-ha! So we *would* have to fly.'

CAVEMAN LOVE

As soon as I crowbarred our destination out of Toby I started to grow as nervous as I was excited. We were going to New York.

Memories from my last attempt to storm America were still painfully fresh in my mind. Despite returning there a more sophisticated woman, even if I say so myself, dressed in sombre clothing and flat shoes, the moment we landed Stateside I transformed into a gibbering wreck.

'Stop looking so guilty,' Toby reprimanded as we approached Immigration at Philadelphia airport.

'I'm trying,' I hissed under my breath. 'I'm doing my yoga breathing.' I pecked him on the cheek. ' If they deport me or lock me up again remember I love you?'

I stepped towards the counter, my knees weak.

'What is the purpose of your trip ma'am?' the po-faced officer asked.

I flicked my eyes nervously towards Toby, who had strolled through and was waiting for me beyond the barriers.

'Um, pleasure,' I stuttered.

He met my gaze. 'Is that your travelling companion?' He tipped his head in Toby's direction.

'Yes,' I replied. 'He's my pleasure, um . . . fiancé.'

I smiled sweetly but the Immigration man was unimpressed.

'How long have you known him?' he snapped.

I wiped my sweaty palms on my trousers. Beads of perspiration clustered on my brow. 'A few years now. We met at a publishing house. Anyway, we . . .' I filled him in enthusiastically on the minutia of my daily existence.

'. . . and then I started work for—'

'Thank you, ma'am.'

My passport was stamped and I ran for freedom.

I sat guarding the bags while we waited for our connecting flight and Toby explored electronic what-nots in the shops. My heart was still pounding from passing through Immigration.

'You OK, love?' said a tall guy with salt and pepper hair.

'Oh yes, sorry, I always get caught up in the drama of flying.'

I stuck a thumb in the direction of the 'Shitty Shitty Bang Bang' connecting flight outside that was expected to flap us to New York. He sat opposite me, placing his laptop carefully beside him.

'Me, too. Actually this is the longest flight I've done so far. I bloody hate it. I'm Pete, by the way. From Staines.'

I smiled. 'I'm Sara.'

We shook hands over the pile of luggage between us.

'It's all worth it though when you get there, isn't it?' I added.

Pete's face broke into a wide smile. 'In my case, today, most definitely.' He sighed with a faraway look.

I shuffled forward eagerly. 'Sounds intriguing. Work, holiday or romance?'

'Romance,' Peter replied. 'At least, I hope so.'

I cast my trashy mag aside. 'That's even more intriguing.'

He chuckled. 'It might sound crazy or weird to you.'

'I love crazy and weird.'

'OK. I met a girl on the internet: Nora. We've been emailing each other for about a year and, well, I guess we fell in love.'

'That's so romantic,' I cooed.

'I know.' His smile faded. 'It would have been perfect, but I was already living with someone.'

'Oh, complicated.' I nodded.

Pete nodded, too. 'Tell me about it. We were drifting. No excuse really, but Nora and me, we just got on. We shared the same passions, tastes, you know? We've got similar backgrounds. We just click. And this will be the first time I actually meet her.'

'Wow!' I exclaimed, then paused. 'Hang on ... the first time?'

'Yes.' He laughed and nodded. 'This is where I might sound crazy,' he went on. 'I've left my girlfriend, my job, everything, to start a new life with a woman I've never met.'

I slumped back in my chair. Love *before* first sight? My toes were tingling. 'Wow, that's incredible. But, excuse me, what if you don't fancy each other?'

'We do.' He shrugged.

'Well, yeah, mentally, but, y'know ...' I trailed off.

He laughed. 'You mean, not fancy each other in the sack?'

I nodded, my face burning.

'The internet's not a text-messaging service, you know. We've seen each other in various, er, ways. We've filmed ourselves for each other and we've, um ...' He blushed a little.

'Right. Yes,' I replied quickly.

'And in a way,' he regained composure, 'I think it's a better way to meet someone. As a man I'm always fancying women physically first. I see a pair of tits and think *she's* got a nice personality. Then when all the hormones have calmed down, I work out whether I'm attracted on a mental level. Which I'm not most of the time, if I'm honest. So I suppose I'm trying it the other way around this time. Does that make sense?'

'It does actually, Pete.' I nodded. 'It's much more important being attracted on a cerebral level. Although we girls have known that for years. After all, the body goes all saggy but the brain doesn't.'

'Unless you count Alzheimer's,' he pointed out.

'Um, yes.'

Pete from Staines flipped his laptop open. 'Want to see some Jpegs of her?'

'What kind?' I asked, to be on the safe side.

'Nothing saucy, love,' he laughed. 'Just give me a mo. I'll shut down the private folders,' he jiggled his brows suggestively in my direction, 'if you know what I mean.'

As I watched Pete pick his way through a homemade scrapbook of Nora porn I realized that email and text-messaging had taken over from the love letter. Since Samuel Johnson stomped around in coffee shops, intellectuals have snivelled about the terminal decline of letter-writing. But ignoring the lack of stamps and envelopes, there are probably more written communications today than at any other time in history. Hi-tech love notes are darting through the ether like cupid's arrows sending us sweet nothings. That said, where's the heartfelt consideration in a stream of texted, vowel-light 'I lve u'? In short, without going back to basics and sharpening up our good old-fashioned pencils, are we missing the point?

Apparently people used to take their letter-writing very seriously. In 1730, Alexander Pope asked all of his correspondents to return the letters he had sent them. It then took him several years to rewrite and publish them. Mark Twain, Lewis Carroll, Jane Austen and Dylan Thomas refused to send out mail until they had tinkered with epistles to the point of perfection, just as they did with their professional work. The art of words is lost when firing out a quickie on your laptop or mobile. While electronic messaging is convenient it promotes shallow shorthand. Yes, a quick 'I lve u' can help a couple feel connected, but familiarity breeds contempt. Who hasn't felt a pang of irritation over a misfired, well-meant message from a loved one? Voicemail costs 10p a pop, you know.

Eighteenth-century letter-writers really went to town with their efforts too, although the materials they employed were markedly less cumbersome. Women would be treated to soppy quill-scratched sentiments about their fragile beauty and vulnerable charm on fine parchment paper. The envelope would be sealed with wax and gathered with masses of silk ribbon. Presentation was as important as the contents. If our love notes mirror the spiritual condition of the society we live in, then the most anyone can hope for is a string of cheap thrills and quickies before the email connection is dropped.

I asked historian Dr Rebecca Earle from the University of Warwick whether love letters reflected social niceties or whether they were a release. She explained that love letters, like all letters, emerge out of particular social contexts and in some way reflect these contexts, but this doesn't mean that the person writing them didn't regard them as a form of release. Indeed, by the mid-eighteenth century the middle classes and aristocratic society in England and France conciously became more emotional in general, people were encouraged to express their feelings much more, and this became a convention in its own right.

It seems the oldest known love letter was found in Iran and supposedly dates to about 4,000 years ago. A dewy-eyed fellow called Gimisa decided to drop a note to his girlfriend, Dasbuaj, arranging a date. It was written on a stone that weighed sixteen kilos. How's that for a love letter? It explains its survival anyway. Dasbuaj would have had a job tearing it up when Gimisa dumped her. But Gimisa started a trend that would keep Clinton Cards in pocket for life. Throughout history men seem to have played the main part in letter-writing. Dr Earle explained that the rates of female literacy varied from country to country over time so it's hard to generalize on the subject. But if the lady couldn't write for herself she could just hire herself a professional. There is also a school of thought that says that in England the rise of Protestantism in the seventeenth century encouraged people to devote time to examining their own consciences on a regular basis and that this led to a big increase in diary-keeping and letter-writing.

At the beginning of our relationship, Toby did things the old-fashioned way, complementing the steady flow of smutty emails with a series of hand-written, hand-delivered letters, his heart laid bare for all the world to see. And maybe, ultimately, that is the point of a real love letter. Dr Earle feels that it is a loss to historians that people don't write so many letters any more as they haven't yet figured out how to save electronic messages for posterity in the same way they have letters. Hopefully they'll figure out a way some day.

Emails can be deleted or denied. But, while lovers can generally presume safely that their letters are strictly FYEO, a written record of heartfelt sentiment can bite the arse of the wayward harder than a pitbull with tetanus. Signing your name to a pen and ink letter means commitment.

Our flight from Philadelphia to New York turned out to be the kind of budget airline that charges for blankets and counts the peanuts into your hand, one by one. In the City of Brotherly Love, they scanned our shoes for Semtex and our faces for signs of anti-American sympathies, then waved us through Immigration to pick up our connecting flight.

'That's not *really* our plane, is it?' I spluttered as Toby and I trundled along the travelator to Gate 7. 'It's . . . too small.' I stumbled as my feet hit the stationary floor at the end of the moving walkway. 'It's got a propeller!'

Toby grabbed my arm to steady me and followed my horrified stare into the windy, wet night beyond the glass walls of the concourse.

'Twin propellers,' he said. 'So if one of them—' He changed tack rapidly. 'Propeller-driven planes are just as safe as jets,' he tried, unconvincingly.

'I'm not getting in that antique,' I said, shakily. 'It's going to crash and we're going to die. It's always little propeller planes that crash.'

'Where do you get that from?' he asked. 'How many light aircraft crashes do you hear about on a weekly basis, exactly?'

'Ah, well,' I began, 'you don't hear about them, because only a few people die. Only twenty or thirty people at a time. Not newsworthy, on an international scale. But, believe me, they drop out of the sky like butterflies at a gasworks when the weather's bad.'

'If the weather was that bad, they wouldn't send us up in it,' he pointed out, pleadingly.

'Well then, what if a seagull flies into us? Hmm?' I crossed my arms and dropped one shoulder, pouting emphatically.

Toby sighed and pulled me down into a seat that faced the airport's grey internal walls. 'I sincerely doubt that seagulls are a major threat to modern commercial aircraft,' he began, earnestly, 'but, baby, if there's a seagull out there with your name on it . . .'

I slapped him on the thigh and let out a reluctant chuckle. 'We'll be OK?' I asked, nodding expectantly.

'Of course we will. It's only a half-hour flight. You can have a nap.'

'Are you awake?' Toby whispered. Our tiny plane had been buffeted by strong winds since we cleared the runway.

'I can't open my eyes,' I whispered back, through gritted teeth. 'I don't want to watch us die. Oh God, oh God! Oh God, I wish I believed in God.'

'That is the weirdest prayer I have ever heard,' Toby remarked, peeling my white-knuckled hand from the armrest between us. The seat-belt light pinged on above us. He stifled a cry of pain as my nails dug into his palm.

'Ladies and gentlemen, we'll be experiencing some turbulence presently,' came the chirpy announcement. 'Please return your trays and seatbacks to the upright position and remain in your seats with you seat-belts buckled while we ride it out.'

'Ride it out?' I asked. 'Why did I let you drag me on to this bloody barnstormer, Toby? We should've come by ship.'

'What? Drop a grand a piece and risk four days of your

Titanic fantasy? I think not. Don't panic, sweetie. Woah!' We dropped through the clouds. 'This is nothing. Jesus!'

'Back off,' I snapped. 'He's mine. At least until we touch down. Our Father, who art in Heaven ...'

After a kangeroo touchdown Toby and I decamped to our hotel room and flopped out on the bed.

'Well, I'm glad we survived,' I said. 'Horrible flight.'

'I could think of worse ways to go,' Toby replied.

I sat up. 'What? Worse than burning in agony in a ball of flames? I'd say that was quite a bad way to go.'

Toby shook his head. 'No, I mean dying together. You and me. It's romantic.'

'In a pointless kind of way maybe. I'd still save you though, if I could. Father Liam said putting the other person first is love.'

'Everybody knows that.'

'Hmm,' I rolled over to the bedside table to grab a handful of cheesy Cheetos, an addiction from my last trip rekindled.

'Of course, that's not always the way with real relationships. Remember Brian and Shelley?' said Toby.

'Nope.'

'Yes, you do,' said Toby. 'The couple who broke up on their honeymoon?'

'Um ...?'

'They were on a walking safari?' Toby continued, waiting for me to signal my recognition. 'The guide spotted a lion close by.'

'I don't know this story at all,' I said firmly.

'You do. You were in the pub when Alex told me.'

'Refresh my memory,' I sighed, humouring him.

He *hadn't* told me. I probably hadn't been there at all.

'OK,' Toby said, 'so the guide spots the lion but tells the group they won't be bothered because it looks like it's recently been fed. Only the lion has other ideas, and starts padding towards them. Everyone panics, and Brian and Shelley bolt for the nearest tree.'

'Go on.'

'So Brian's running, like buggery, with little thought of his new wife, but Shelley puts on a sudden burst of speed and overtakes him. Then – this is the clincher, right – Shelley reaches the trees first, Brian, hot on her heels, reaches up and yonks her out of his way. He practically climbed over her to save his own skin.'

'That's awful,' I exclaimed. ' I thought it was going to be a nice story.'

''Fraid not,' said Toby. 'The lion left without eating anybody, but by that point, Brian and Shelley had been forced to face some uncomfortable home truths. They flew straight home separately and had the marriage annulled. They didn't really love each other at all. Not when it came to the crunch.'

'But they must have been in love to begin with,' I argued. 'Why would they bother with all the hassle of a marriage if they weren't?'

'Maybe they liked wedding cake?' Toby suggested.

'So? Crash someone else's wedding. How can you think you're in love, get as far as tying the knot even and then find out it was all built on false assumptions – like the assumption that your bloody husband won't abandon you to hungry predators?'

Toby squeezed my hand. 'I'd save you from lions,' he said earnestly.

'You wouldn't have to,' I reminded him. 'I'm faster than you.'

'You reckon,' he chuckled. 'Nightmare situation. Who knows for sure what they'd do in a spot like that?'

'I do,' I protested. 'I wouldn't have time to think about the consequences. You can call it selfish if you want to be cynical, but I wouldn't want to live at the expense of seeing you eaten.' I shuddered. 'Mind you, that might change once we have nippers. I'm not jumping into a snake pit for you when there are kids to think about.'

'A-ha,' said Toby. 'And there you have it. Altruistic acts always have an ulterior motive when you get down to it.'

I flicked a precious Cheeto at him. 'I hate it when you go all Hawkins.'

'It's Dawkins,' corrected Toby, rolling his eyes.

'Whatever. So tell me, why do people risk their own lives to save strangers, eh? Why do they devote their precious time to alleviating random human suffering? Why bother even sticking a few pence in the charity box?' I demanded.

'Guilt,' Toby suggested. 'Empathy is a pain in the arse trait of human nature. We never do enough to help, although we fully understand the suffering of others. The occasional small act of kindness has a disproportionately big pay-off in terms of self-image. Charity eases the conscience. Kindness counters guilt.'

'I'm the Catholic, Tobe.'

'Guilt is universal,' Toby asserted. 'That's why the Pope picked up on it.'

Loathe as I was to give credit to my hard-nosed fiancé's thoughts about altruism – the most broadly applied, least obviously rewarding form of human love – there was some sense in his cynical assessment. For starters, altruistic cooperation is not limited to mankind. Vampire bats are known to regurgitate their own food for underfed companions, an act with no apparent benefit to themselves. Longer, closer observation reveals the advantage in such cooperation. During social grooming, the bats can easily judge a full tummy from an empty one. Those who share their food with the undernourished essentially earn a 'reputation' for kindness that pays off in reciprocal acts when they themselves are light on lunch. By contrast, bats who keep their bellies full, neighbours be damned, find themselves friendless and famished when their own feeding fails.

It has been suggested that this 'altruistic' behaviour might have evolved during the last Ice Age, as once common food became more scarce. By sharing food the vampire bat assured its species' survival. So perhaps the complicated motives that underly human generosity and sacrifice have similarly practical evolutionary roots.

Richard Dawkins, one of the big hitters of contemporary evolutionary theory, and an unshakeable atheist, maintains that even the most costly act of altruism, for example, sacrificing one's life to save a child, is motivated by our genes' drive to survive long-term even at the expense of their current host. But even if human sacrifice and kindness is an accident of evolution – if altruism is no more a product of love than greed is a product of focused hatred – it should not be belittled.

We are not automata. We are not simple creatures, who eat and sleep and shag and shit and nothing much more. In every aspect of our lives, we strive to overcome our animal nature. We are civilized, sophisticated, loving. We expect Brian to save Shelley, or at least not to hamper her own efforts to escape the lion, because for human beings, the emotional and social conventions of human society have become more important to us even than our own survival. And love itself sits at the very top of the pile of revered human traits. It transcends the prerogative to save our own skins. Ignore its power and, when the crisis has passed and the lion slunk away, people like Brian will find few sympathetic to his course of action, and even fewer who are ready to admit that they might do the same thing themselves.

Such is the power of love. Sometimes death is preferable to dishonour.

We sat in a diner near the East River, drinking weak filter coffee while the kitchen staff slaughtered the three pigs that would be required to provide our huge American breakfasts.

We were joined by Will Harcourt-Smith, older brother of Toby's best man-to-be, Alex, and his Manhattan-born girlfriend, Amira. Will is a paleo-anthropologist who left University College London for a research and teaching position at the American Museum of Natural History. In a city where people play to type, he revels in the licence that his English Gentleman persona grants him to exercise a mischievous and well-honed brand of pomposity. He was outlining his favoured methods of patronizing students when the food arrived. Bacon and eggs, pancakes, hash browns, sausages. Everyone eyed each other's orders hungrily as the waitress set them down.

'And the raisin oatmeal?' she asked, holding the last dish aloft.

I raised a reluctant hand. A bowl of uninviting slop, sprinkled with hard, black raisins, was deposited in front of me. My shoulders drooped and my bottom lip quivered.

'It's all watery and grey.'

'You ordered it,' Toby reminded me.

'Healthy option,' I said, pouting. 'What was I thinking?' I sipped at a spoonful of oatmeal, recoiling from the taste like a kitten with mustard.

'Send it back,' he teased. 'We'll find you some wheat grass later.'

'I can't send it back,' I hissed. 'That would be rude.'

'This is New York, for fuck's sake! Rude is what they do. Go on. Send it back. Get yourself some eggs. Mmm.' He stuffed a forkful of bacon and eggs into his mouth. I called the waitress over.

'Excuse me,' I began, meekly, 'I don't like American oatmeal.'

'And I don't like British rock music,' said the waitress, sighing heavily. 'I'll get you some eggs.'

I apologized profusely and repeatedly as the waitress carried my oatmeal back to the kitchen.

'It's really not a problem,' said Amira. 'So, you guys are getting the guided tour, huh?'

'Yes,' I said. 'I can't wait. I love going backstage.'

'It's a museum, not a theatre,' Toby pointed out.

'Yeah, but you know what I mean. The "no public access" bits. The back rooms and corridors.'

'There's a room entirely dedicated to spiders,' chimed Will.

'Dead or alive?' Toby asked, concerned. He's never been good with spiders. A chink in his manly armour.

'Both,' he grinned back. 'Show you, if you like?'

'No. Thanks,' I said, coming to the rescue. 'Tobe's a complete ponce when it comes to spiders. Aren't you, darling?'

'Thanks.' He stole a sip of my cold, unfinished coffee.

'What exactly are you interested in?' asked Amira.

'We're on a spiritual love quest,' I said. 'Toby's brought me here because he thinks Will can shed some light on love from a scientist's perspective.'

Amira chuckled and tapped Will's hand across the table. 'They came a long way,' she teased. 'You better come up with the goods, Doctor Love.'

'Sara's being a bit vague,' Toby said as Will coloured. 'We're really here to answer a few specific questions.'

'Which are?'

'Is love a cultural phenomenon, or a basic human condition? Are human beings naturally monogamous? And which came first: God, or man?'

'Nothing too ambitious, then,' said Amira.

The waitress returned with a plate of toasted muffins and griddled eggs. I apologized again, thanked her enthusiastically and grinned approvingly at my second breakfast.

'Here's another one for you,' I said, cutting into the perfectly cooked, golden-yolked eggs. 'Which came first ...'

We left Amira among the redbrick high-rises of Tudor City and jumped on the subway to the West Side of Central Park, and the predictable, neoclassical frontage of the AMNH.

Inside the museum is a treasure trove of spectacular fossils and awesome, state-of-the art exhibits, mixed with kitsch survivors from the sixties. We stood in front of an exhibit in the latter category: a panoramic scene of prehistoric Savanna, with a papier-mâché volcano puffing cotton clouds on the horizon and a pair of hirsute hominids – male and female – plodding across the ash-strewn landscape, hand in hairy hand.

'This exhibit is a reconstruction of the Laetoli Trackways,' said Will, his booming, authoritative tones immediately drawing a small crowd. 'A leftover from the days of wax and wonder, I'm afraid.'

'I like these old-fashioned models,' I said, having previously jumped a mile at the animatronic dinosaurs and surround-sound whale song as we wound our way through the museum. 'Art meets science.' I indicated the prehistoric African landscape, painstakingly painted on the exhibit's curved backdrop.

'Colin Farrell meets Gerard Depardieu,' said Will, tapping the glass in front of the muscle-bound male.

'Who's his lady friend?' I asked. 'And hasn't she heard of waxing?'

'Which brings us to the purpose of your visit,' said Will.

'You mean our research into prehistoric feminine depilatory practices?' I asked.

'That's not something Toby mentioned in his emails,' said Will. 'The subject, I thought, was love.'

'Oh yes,' I said, turning to Toby. 'You were going to prove to me that human beings had been falling in love since before the invention of marriage. Is this them, then? Fred and Wilma Flintstone? Because, I've got to tell you, this Madame Tussauds stuff doesn't cut the mustard.'

'They're not just pretty waxworks,' Toby protested.

'Pretty?' I said, scrunching my face at the furry couple. 'I worry what you see in me, Tobe. I really do.'

'Laetoli Trackways,' harrumphed Will.

'Tell her, Will,' Toby said.

'It's a diorama of a part of a set of footprints – the Laetoli Trackways – found in East Africa in 1976.'

'And?' I asked.

'And they tell us more than you might think. Most fossils are records of an animal, yes? But these footprints are effectively fossilized behaviour, a record of a shared moment in human evolution.'

'How so?'

'Well, for starters, they're 3.6 million years old. When they were found, they were the oldest evidence of bipedal hominids ever uncovered. And their very existence is a matter of pure chance, like much of archeology. They were formed thanks to a very specific combination of circumstances. The local volcano, Sadiman, errupts – there it is on the backdrop – and every living thing in the area quite naturally decides to start walking in the opposite direction to the big smoking hill of death. Then it rains, turning the plains into one huge muddy field. And finally, as our hominids trudge on, there's another volcanic ash fall, trapping the prints they leave behind them.'

'I still don't see what this has to do with love,' I said. 'Though it's all very interesting.'

'Look at the exhibit. There are two sets of prints, one smaller than the other. Probably a male and a female. Moreover, their paths are so close that they must have been walking arm in arm. What you're looking at here is a reconstructed snapshot of the first recorded human couple.'

'Hell of a date,' Toby chimed in. 'A picnic in the shadow of Mount Kerblooey.'

I furrowed my brow and tugged at my ear impatiently.

'They might have been more than girlfriend and boyfriend,' added Will. 'The smaller of the two sets of prints shows signs of a burden on one side. It's all speculation, so our exhibit doesn't allude to it, but there's a solid chance that our apeman's lady friend was carrying something on her hip.' Will mimed a hip hold. The effect, despite his muscular bulk, was rather camp.

'A baby,' I said, my eyes widening with surprise.

'Precisely,' said Will. 'Like I say, we can't know for sure. Might've had a limp or something. But it paints a pretty picture, doesn't it?'

'And when you say human . . .' I said.

'I mean early human,' said Will. '*Australopithecus afarensis*. Small, hairy, stupid. Human to a tee.'

'Isn't there a danger that we're romanticizing here?' I said, my new-found scepticism tempering my delight at the trackways' implications.

'Of course,' said Will. 'Because we're human, too. We romanticize everything.'

'I've often wondered if our attitudes and emotions are driven by evolutionary experience *and* higher thought,' Toby said.

'Eh?' I said.

'OK. Back when we were fresh from the trees, we were still prey to beasts like the sabre-tooth cats. So as time goes by, we invent the spear and the slingshot and the electric toaster, and Snaggletooth ends up as an animatronic in a travelling exhibition. But we retain our fear of fanged predators, and because we've developed language and culture and stuff, we tell stories about vampires and dragons and demons.'

'It's an interesting thought,' said Will. 'Come with me.'

He led us into the next hall to a row of recognizable primates. On a shelf lined with dark velvet rested a tiny skull, almost, but not quite, like that of a human child. Will pointed to the rear of the head. Two perfectly round puncture holes told of the owner's violent dispatch. I shivered.

'Perhaps love *is* just a collision of instinct and sentience,' said Will, steering us back on course. 'And all the ritual and romance that surrounds it is a human invention.'

'Exactly.' Toby agreed. 'We evolved to bond in at least superficially monogamous family units because it's the best strategy for successful child-rearing. The Laetoli Trackways appear to demonstrate that, although there's room for argument. If they do, that's evidence for monogamy, "love", if you like, that predates formal religion, by a few million years. Today, with a few thousand millenia of evolutionary and cultural progress under our belts, everything's warped from its original meaning; predators have become nursery rhyme monsters, lust has become love.'

'I see what you're saying,' I said,' but it's hardly a cheery message, is it? Love is ... what? An evolutionary response.'

'May I?' asked Will, ever the gentleman. Toby waved him on.

'If you ask me,' Will began, 'you're missing the point, which is that, however we got here, we are Homo sapiens. Thinking man. There's something special in our capacity to analyse the world around us, and ourselves. If we think we've stumbled upon another piece of the puzzle, whether it's a fossil or a Martian microbe, it shouldn't detract from the basic wonder of human experience. Because love, more than many of life's little surprises, is wonderful, after all.'

'You soppy old sod,' Toby said, punching Will playfully on his beefy shoulder, and immediately regretting it.

'But I've always thought of love as inherently spiritual,' I said. 'Soulmates and destiny and all that. Reducing it to the physical symptoms of a biological function is so depressing.'

'So don't,' said Will. 'Understanding how the machine works tells us nothing about who built it, or what the machine is for.'

'We're the machine,' Toby whispered to me.

'You're a twat-machine,' I whispered back.

'Science is concerned with the physical, not the metaphysical,' Will continued. 'Too many people see science and religion as diametrically opposed and mutually exclusive. I never quite understood why. There's always room to marvel at the unknown and some things, however much we struggle to understand them, are destined to stay that way.'

'Destined?' I asked. 'You haven't got a touch of religion yourself, have you, Will?'

Will shrugged. 'I consider myself a spiritual person. I call myself a Christian.'

I took in this unexpected information with lips pursed and head cocked.

'I'm not sure it matters what you call yourself, though,' continued Will. 'I just don't think it's healthy to deny the spiritual side of life completely. I think therefore I am, right? Well, I feel too, and a lot of the time I want to thank someone for that. Sometimes not.'

'I hear you,' I said, smirking. 'Thanks, Will. You've been rather helpful. Really helpful, actually.'

'Have I?' asked Will, looking baffled. 'Glad to be of service. Want to see the spider room?'

'No!' Toby said.

'Right,' said Will, message received. 'Lunch, then. I need to grab my coat from the office upstairs. We can take the lift they use to transport dinosaur skeletons.'

'Can we really?' I asked slightly worriedly. A lift didn't sound *that* exciting.

'It's more impressive than it sounds,' said Will.

*

'I can't believe I got a run-up in an elevator. It was massive!' I squeaked excitedly as we sucked beer from the bottle through quartered limes. We were lunching in a Cuban café on Amsterdam Avenue.

'I told you it was cool,' said Will, appeased after the museum elevator's initial failure to impress.

'Still,' Toby said, 'it's a long way to have come if the lift is going to be your favourite thing about the trip.'

'Oh, I liked other stuff,' I said. 'The hairy couple and the monkey head.' I shovelled a forkful of red beans and rice and grinned at the boys in turn.

'She's doing it deliberately,' Toby assured Will. 'We were listening.'

'Of course I was listening,' I said, swallowing. 'If you want to know, I've had another epiphany.'

'Have you got your Tegretol pills?'

'Shush. I'm serious. Will, let me ask you a question.'

'Shoot.'

'What's love? Give me the scientist's answer. The pond-scum to primate version.'

'Well, as we said in the museum, I suppose it's an emotion that's evolved to ensure that the long task of human child-rearing is successfully shared by monogamous parents.'

'You old romantic,' I said. 'Now ... What is love?'

'Erm,' said Will.

'Come on, Will, you big lug. You're *in* love, I've seen it. You know what love is, cast off your lab coat and let rip.'

Will coloured slightly and took a swig of his beer. 'Love's the be all and end all, isn't it?' He smiled. 'There's a magic to creation that will remain permanently beyond our comprehension. That's because we *are* creation – we're part of the software. We'll never be able to see the hardware, not from this side of the screen. If you acknowledge the awesome and the unknown, there's always room for faith. Faith in a God; faith in love. Faith in love is the easy part. Love is like time: it's an abstract idea that's tangibly real to every human being. Let's be honest, it's the *only* thing that makes any sense at all, half of the time. So what if it is just an accident of evolution?' He paused, poking the lime segment into his beer bottle and swigging back the foamy leftovers. 'Bloody happy accident.'

I grinned. 'Thank you, Will.'

'What for, precisely?' he asked.

'I've been listening to Toby telling me something along those lines for months. That faith and science aren't mutually exclusive, that there's room for God. Rome, at least, seems to automatically oppose scientific explanations for things. Why doesn't it see science as the study of God's methods, rather than an attempt to obliterate Him.'

'It smacks of a deep-rooted insecurity,' said Will. 'The more rigidly you stick to a religion's doctrine, the more your belief starts to sound like folly. I think we should be able to distinguish between the myths told to illuminate prehistory and the moral spirit of a modern faith.'

'It's refreshing to hear a balanced view,' I said.

'From someone with authority?' Toby asked, peeved. 'Why don't you take my word for these things? I read *New Scientist*.'

'From someone with *faith*,' I replied, picking rice off his shoulder. 'It's easy for you. You can soothe me with platitudes about losing the Church and keeping God. I know you're just humouring me. I know you mean well, but encouraging me to cling to some vague idea of spirituality is like giving a dummy to a starving baby. It's been good to listen to someone who has a handle on the science stuff and remains Christian.'

'I'm sorry,' said Will, 'but from where I'm sitting, you two are getting yourselves all worked up about nothing. Find a way to express your spirituality that is true to your moral heritage, but let go of the fear of punishment. Don't worry about getting it wrong. God has to care more about love than He does about ritualistic allegiance, right? Lead a good life and you're quids in. *Just stop worrying.*'

'Easy for you to say,' I said, smiling despite myself. 'You're quite cosy in your tweedy C of E faith. I think I need to meet someone who's been through what I have and come out whistling.'

'A born again Atheist, you mean,' said Will. 'How are your literary contacts, Sara? Could you track down a brilliant ex-archbishop with a penchant for stirring it up among his former employees? He's published all over the place.'

'If he's in print, I can find him easily,' I said, brightening and scribbled the name he gave me on a napkin.

'You're a mine of information, Will,' I said, as we settled the bill and climbed into our coats. 'If we manage to track him down, I'll send you a jar of Marmite, or a box of proper teabags or something. Where do you get this stuff?'

'World Service,' said Will. 'You can take the boy out of Bloomsbury . . .'

A DIAMOND ON THE DOWNS

I stared at my hand in disbelief. It seemed impossible, almost surreal. It wasn't there. I could barely breathe. I sat quietly for a moment on the suitcase we'd taken to New York that hadn't yet made it up to the loft. My eyelids were clamped together in attempt to shutter out the truth. I knew that the next time I opened my eyes and saw my ringless finger, it would all become real.

'Babe?' Blissfully ignorant of my loss, Toby stuck his head into our bedroom. 'Why are you throwing clothes around?'

A pair of navy boxers arced towards him, landing on his shoulder. He grinned at me and picked them off. I couldn't speak.

'Sara? Have you been crying?' He stepped into the room, his smile drooping at the corners.

I collapsed on to a pile of crinkled shirts and the tears came. Toby scooped me out of the dirties and sat me on to the bed.

'Come on, sweetheart,' he pulled a pair of tracksuit bottoms from my shaky hands, 'what's the matter?'

I stared into Toby's blue eyes and a fresh rush of misery surged through me. I couldn't tell him that I'd lost the most beautiful, important and expensive thing he had ever given me. The one thing . . . I tried to steady my staccato breath and fought for the words.

'I've . . . I've lost my ring,' I gasped. 'I can't find it anywhere.'

I watched Toby pale, his calm escaping like a puncture. He grabbed my left hand, searching for confirmation. He looked back at my face.

'Your engagement ring?'

I nodded silently.

'Are you sure?' he asked, panic rising in his tone. 'Have you checked—?'

'I've checked everywhere,' I snapped. 'I've been looking for it for hours. It's gone.' I sobbed again.

Toby thought for a moment. 'When did you last take it off? Could you have left it somewhere?'

I shrugged and shook my head. 'I don't know. I mean, I don't take it off, do I? I don't know when it went. It's just a part of me . . .' I trailed off, glancing at my hand. The base of my finger was dented slightly where the ring had been. 'It's like suddenly finding that one of my ears has gone. I kind of knew something was missing, I didn't feel complete somehow. And now I know . . .' I trailed off as fresh tears followed old track marks down my face.

'You must have taken it off, Sara,' said Toby, losing his cool and gradually turning redder. 'Rings don't just fall off fingers. I mean, it did fit. We had it fitted!'

'I lost a bit of weight but you couldn't get it past my knuckle without a squeeze.'

Toby picked up a sheepskin rug and shook it pointlessly. He

got dust and a safety pin. 'Rings don't just vanish. If you can't remember taking it off—'

'I didn't take it off.'

Toby rolled his eyes. 'OK, you say you didn't take it off. It must have slipped off somewhere in the cold.'

Then he clapped a hand to his forehead and looked panicked. 'Cissbury Ring,' he groaned. 'Tell me you've seen it since we got back.'

'I can't,' I admitted. 'We might as well give up now.'

Cissbury Ring – the appropriately named site of my catastrophic loss – is an Iron Age hillfort on the South Downs of West Sussex. It's wild, beautiful and bloody massive. If my ring was up there we'd seen the last of it, for good.

'It was really cold yesterday.' Toby prompted. 'Did you wear gloves?'

'Yes.' I sighed, biting nervously at my lip.

'Shit.'

We stared at one another across the room. Neither of us able to verbalize what we were both feeling.

'Do you think we should borrow my dad's metal detector and go back?' I asked hopefully.

'Don't be mental,' Toby tutted. 'The place is huge and we covered every corner!'

'Sorry.' I shook my head. 'I'm just desperate.'

'I'll call the police,' Toby replied sensibly. 'There's no way it'll've been handed in, though.'

He sighed, involuntarily scanning the floor of the room for a platinum glint. It wasn't just me that was hurting. The skin around Toby's eyes looked bruised and patchy, as it always does when he's tired or worried.

'I'm so sorry this has happened—' I began.

'It's just one of those things,' he replied quietly.

It wasn't. Saying 'it's just one of those things' is just one of those things people do when 'one of those things' has properly screwed up their day. I knelt down and started pulling dust-covered objects out from underneath our bed.

'I know. It's just an object. No one got hurt or maimed. But it still really hurts, doesn't it?'

'Yeah.' Toby nodded sadly. 'And it was beautiful.'

I spied something sparkling halfway under the bed.

'Hang on . . .' I wriggled underneath, stretching out for the magpie treasure. 'What's this?' He sprang to my side, his eyes wide with anticipation.

I wriggled out again, clutching a tiny ball of tinfoil.

'Bollocks,' said Toby.

'I can't bloody believe it. I can't bloody believe that my beautiful ring has gone. My parents were bloody right,' I croaked. 'I don't deserve nice things.'

Toby laughed, despite himself.

'Your parents told you that when you ripped your clothes so that you could fasten them together with safety pins. You were fifteen, things have changed. Probably.'

I rested my forehead in my hands. 'I can't bear the thought that someone is going to stumble across my ring and trundle home with the best find ever. They won't know how much it meant to *us*.' I stood up and brushed myself down. 'I knew there was something funny about Cissbury Ring. Mound of crap!' I mumbled bitterly. 'I bet it was the bloody highway man.'

The area around Cissbury Ring is rife with legends. On Midsummer's Eve they say that fairies dance there. And they're in good company: serpents, tunnel-dwellers and smugglers' treasure are all said to lurk below the hill. UFOs have been sighted above it. The Devil himself even built the place, they'll tell you. My favourite story, though, is the tale of a local highwayman, a malevolent fraudster, who left a trail of devastation in his wake. He was eventually captured, but before being executed for his heinous crimes he swore that he would never rest. A little while after they had buried him, his corpse was found above ground. Legend states that it took several attempts to bury him before he stayed where he was supposed to, but still he refused to rest. His ghostly form has been seen riding a horse near the road where he was buried. And he's still helping himself to visitors' valuables. Including, it would seem, my ring.

Toby and I sat for a while in silence as the enormity of our loss soaked into us like summer rain. Toby's mum, Penny, had given him the money for my ring the summer before she died. I had been welcomed into the Starbuck clan with open arms and Penny in particular was thrilled by the prospect of a wedding. The money had been her blessing and it gave me a connection with her that would last far longer than the brief period of our friendship. The ring was only an object, it's true, albeit an expensive one, but it was irreplaceable on an emotional level. Loaded with memories, it was a constant and comforting reminder of the love in my life.

Toby and I hunted the house for five and a half hours that day, unearthing things we hadn't known were lost in the first place. But no ring.

Someone told me once that when prehistoric man wanted a mate he just tied a woman's arms and legs together to stop her escaping. I'm still not sure whether they were kidding. He'd woo her hog-tied for a while, then eventually her legs would be released, and if she didn't make a bolt for it, well, job done. I, for one, am glad to be living in the era where engagement means getting jewellery, not rope burns.

When Toby asked me to marry him he opted for a fairly conventional route. It's tried and tested, after all. I mean, some go for an exotic locale, but who wants to be stuck in an air balloon at the crack of dawn when she turns you down? Not worth the risk.

The ring-giving itself is hugely significant and the history of this practice is complex and fascinating throughout different times and cultures. It's been suggested that the oldest record of nuptial ring-giving comes from ancient Egypt. They believed that the circle was an emblem of eternity and the ring a powerful, never-ending symbol linked to eternal love, a love without beginning or end. It was these great minds which chose the fourth finger of the left hand for the ring as this was where a special vein called the *Vena Amortis*, or Vein of Love, was supposedly thought to run from, straight to the heart.

The Romans first introduced the betrothal ring as an iron hoop, the *Anulus Pronubus*, later made out of gold for the gentry. They were a soppy bunch and as early as the fourth century AD cringeworthy inscriptions embellished the inside of their bands as they often do today. I'm putting my phone number on the next one. Just in case.

My ex-engagement ring was platinum (I swear to God my heart just skipped a beat at the mention of it). Jangling yellow gold evokes too many Essex-bound teen memories and I've heard, probably from the jewellers hoping for a platinum sale, that white gold yellows over time. Traditionally, though, engagement rings had to be yellow gold. As far back as 860AD,

Pope Nicholas I decreed that a gold ring was necessary to signify an engagement. The Blessing of the Rings signified the wholeness in the state of marriage, in which nothing is missing and everything is possible. The precious metal proves the groom's financial sacrifice for his lady's hand in marriage. And the traditional diamond, it was believed, was a magical object, created in the flames of love. It's still customary to blow a fortune, only now the marketeers have managed to push their product up to two months' salary instead of the traditional one.

The wedding band is perhaps even more significant than the engagement ring. Many couples refuse ever to take them off, a demonstration of their faithfulness to each other. The cynically minded might argue that a wedding band is a patriarchal invention designed to tag the taken. Maybe they're missing the point, which is that the meaning of a ring – engagement or wedding – is felt first and foremost by the wearer. I hadn't realized what mine meant to me until I was sifting through sacks of decaying rubbish in my back garden on the night after I lost it.

UNWEAVING THE RAINBOW

'Dee and Lee?' Toby grinned, handing me my drink. 'Well, you've got to hand it to them for seeing it through. I've known people who called off entire relationships because their names were too close.'

'Like who?' I asked, scanning the room for my friends' arrival.

'Paul and Paula,' said Toby. 'Which was a shame, 'cause they were perfect for each other.'

'Well, technically Dee's a Deborah.' I shrugged. 'Lee calls her Deborah. Dee's her college name.'

'Easier to slur after six pints of snakebite,' said Toby. 'That explains the lasting union, anyway.'

He looked over my shoulder and squinted into the distance. 'I think they're here. Is that Dee? Or just a mental woman?'

I turned to see my beaming friend racing towards me, her arms outstretched and her hip-long tresses swinging wildly behind her.

'Both,' I replied, preparing to charge.

I hadn't seen Dee for ages. Money, kids and the M1

had conspired to keep us apart. As always, though, when true friends reunite, it was as if we'd seen each other only yesterday.

'I can't believe you lost your beautiful engagement ring.' Dee sighed over her second G&T, stroking my finger where the band had been. 'It's heartbreaking.'

Toby and Lee sat in the corner talking mortgages while Dee and I huddled together whispering conspiratorially, one witch short of the full set.

'I know,' I moaned. 'It's crazy, but I still find myself looking for it everywhere we go.'

Toby butted in as he gathered up the empties for another trip to the bar. 'Me too,' he said. 'I caught sight of something shiny in a drain today and had to stop myself kneeling down for a better look.'

'It might turn up yet,' said Dee optimistically. 'I heard a story the other day about a woman whose ring turned up in a wood pigeon's stomach a year after she lost it.'

'Really?'

She paused and tucked a long strand of hair behind her ear. 'Might have been a cuckoo.'

Then I spotted a band of gold glinting on Dee's left hand.

'What's this?' I asked, waggling her wrist. 'All this talk of *my* ring. Have you gone and got married behind my back?'

Dee shook her head firmly and chuckled to herself. 'As if. Course not. Lee wears one too, mind.'

I turned to inspect his chunkier version of the same gold ring. 'Why?' I asked. 'If you're not interested in getting married?'

'Because other people are,' said Dee, sighing.

I raised my eyebrows in query.

'It's just easier,' she explained, staring thoughtfully at the ring and spinning it with her thumb. 'We've got two kids and unmarried parents aren't universally popular, you know. It's not a problem, it's just easier to let people make cosy assumptions. What they don't know hurts no one.'

I laughed and helped myself to a handful of salt and vinegar crisps. 'Where are you living then? Victorian-ville?'

She rolled her eyes. 'No, love, just Leeds.'

I sat up in my chair. 'Are you serious? Do you really wear your rings for the busybodies' benefit?'

Dee nodded. 'Oh yeah. Course, they all know damn well that we aren't actually married, but as long as everyone is happy to pretend, we don't run into problems. We don't give a shit what they think about us, but we don't want Rosie or Noah to suffer from any stigma. After all, we love the little bastards.'

Dee laughed long and hard and I flopped back on the faded velour bench; a cloud of dust puffed out and dispersed like a shy genie.

'But don't you think it's all just too stupid for words, this ring business?' I said. 'Surely it should be enough that you're committed, happy, supportive parents? God. Do I sound naive?'

'Not at all,' Dee replied consolingly. 'And as to your question, you'd think so, wouldn't you?' But, believe me, society's not quite there yet, twenty-first century or otherwise.'

I reached for my wine, dipping my elbow in a sticky puddle on the table. 'What about it, though?' I asked. 'Will you ever get properly married, do you think?'

'Oh yeah, I'm sure we will at some point,' said Dee. 'But we haven't really got the cash and it's not exactly top of the list with two children to clothe, feed and *edumercate*. To be honest, it's a pain in the arse.'

'Not the cherry on the cake?'

'Nor the hundreds and thousands on the trifle,' she grinned.

'But what about your rights?' I asked. 'And stuff?'

Dee looked confused. 'Rights to what? Party?'

I laughed. 'With the kids. I mean, if one of you dies or something, what happens to the children?'

'That's a cheery thought.'

I clapped a hand to my mouth apologetically.

'Sorry. It's still all a bit hypothetical to me. It must be very different when you've got kids.'

'I did get a little twinge,' she admitted. 'It depends. If both parents are on the birth certificate and are match-fit to carry on looking after their kids, the children would automatically go to the surviving parent. The decision can be made in a will, or court order, but it can all still get nasty, of course. If nothing gets sorted before one of the parents snuffs it, the whole thing can become a bit of a free for all. A guy I know, Sam, had a girlfriend who died in an accident. They hadn't thought about the future of their kid, Jake. They were too young to worry about all of that. Sam wasn't on the birth certificate as they weren't together at the time and his girlfriend hadn't written a will. She was in her twenties, for Christ's sake. Why would she have a will? Anyway, now her grandparents are applying for Jake, and it's getting downright dirty. Sam's been taking anti-depressants. He's lost his job and now they're using that against him.'

'Does Sam want Jake then?' I asked.

'Yeah! He loves the little sod more than anything.'

I sat back in my seat and sighed. 'That's awful. It doesn't

seem right for a willing father to be kept out of the picture by force.'

'Tell me about it,' Dee replied. 'If you've got kids, you've got to worry about all sorts of rubbish.'

'It just seems ridiculous that for parents, whether they like it or not, it's still easier to be married. That is, if you don't fancy fighting through the courts if anything goes wrong, or being the local social pariah. Not very romantic, is it? Married because you have to rather than because you want to. It's archaic.'

'Yep.' Dee nodded seriously. 'We are stuck in Victorian-ville in some ways.' She looked over at Lee, who caught her eye and winked. Dee smiled and looked back at me. 'But it helps to be stuck there with someone you love.'

That night I lay awake, listening to Toby's snuffly breathing and working myself into a panic. I couldn't stop thinking about my friend's angle on marriage. I'd been so utterly consumed with trying to work out the right marriage, the right God, that I seemed to have lost the point of everything altogether. Dee and Lee aren't philosophically opposed to matrimony, but any thoughts of a wedding had to be shelved, at least temporarily, as they struggle to bring up two children on less than a stockbroker's salary. The rings they wear are a token of their love for each other. Sincerely given, they are also a disguise, designed to keep a judgemental society at bay. It's a shame, for one of a romantic disposition, but until the day when a wedding becomes a real romantic possibility, financially speaking, the very mention of marriage sends Dee's stress levels soaring.

Her situation is a common one these days, with rocketing divorce rates, the nuclear family breaking down faster than unstable plutonium, and the usual religious and financial complications of marriage all ganging up to strip the joy from your happy day. A walk down the aisle isn't always a stroll in the park. All too many couples encounter wedding horrors, from meddling mother-in-laws to violent faith-related family feuds. I know of someone, from a traditional Pakistani family, who chose to drive her car over a Sussex cliff when her parents proposed an arranged marriage in favour of her long-term Hindu boyfriend. It wasn't God that made her do it. It was the pressure of family expectation. And families never expect more than when there's a wedding in the works.

There's something about the ideal of that lifelong bond between husband and wife that still grips us, long after the days when marriage was a tidy means of patriarchal property distribution. Perhaps this is because marriage is an expression, at least in theory, of love. Everyone can sympathize with the pain of a broken heart, so it's all to easy to understand the profundity of a broken marriage. Now love is a matter of faith; admit that your love affair may not be for ever and it's halfway over already. So perhaps the marriage enjoys its enduring popularity for the same reason. It is an extension of the promise, however rash, that lovers make to stay together for ever. In an age when the chance of making it 'until death do us part' is approaching 50/50, we have learned, for the sake of romance, love and hope, to suspend our disbelief in the institution of marriage.

There are some people who seem to prefer weddings to marriages, though, and live their lives accordingly. Udaynath Dakshiniray, from Orali in East India, is a liver-spotted father of twenty-nine kids, famed for having married some ninety times. He has, by his own admission, every intention of finding ten more lucky ladies to complete his century. And with proposals from Europe and America flooding in, thanks to the unstoppable march of the worldwide web, Udaynath is sure to make his target. Unmarrieds, he says, are looked down upon and unfairly treated. Marriage is a mission. It is his duty to marry these poor unfortunates, thereby overcoming the social stigma they face.

As a righteous polygamist Udaynath is in good company. Krishna, one of the most revered and widely-worshipped deities in the Hindu pantheon, was quite the playboy during his earthly lifetime. The blue dude had over 16,000 wives. (God help him if they were all in monthly sync.) According to legend, a demon called Narakasura who reigned in terror over the land of Pragjyotishapura, abducted 16,000 daughters of the gods. The gods, who were understandably miffed, asked Krishna if he could help them retrieve their missing progeny. After a huge battle, during which Krishna slayed the demon king, he successfully freed the ambrosia-reared cuties. However, as the women had been held in bondage, their chastity was soon brought into question. Despite the girls' protests, their families rejected them as they were no longer pure. Lord Krishna, however, decided to give them the benefit of the doubt and promptly married the lot of them. A whopping good deed, no doubt, but I'm sure it had its perks for him.

For thousands of years, polygamy was common across the world. Early societies rarely restricted the number of wives a man could have, although polyandry usually elicited more of a head-choppy-offy response. Even as recently as the seventeenth century, polygamy was practised and accepted among relatively mainstream Christians. Whittling down your wives to one at least puts the focus of marriage back on love and that special bond. But with the bond so easily broken today, the question I want answering is: why does anyone bother?

Despite recent parliamentary bills which give unmarried cohabiting couples more legal rights, there are still innumerable disadvantages to remaining single when it comes to inheritance tax, rights over children, pensions and property. Common law marriages – the presumption of commitment in long-term, unmarried couples – have not been legally recognized since 1753. So it's fair to say that society, legally as well as morally, conspires to maintain marriage's stronghold on male/female relationships.

For millions, of course, there is also the religious imperative, undertaken at a holy venue. In Britain, however, religious duty is slipping down the list of reasons to get married. Since civil wedding ceremonies were first permitted in England and Wales under the 1836 Marriage Act, there has been a conspicuous shift away from religious to civil ceremonies.

For my part, marriage had always been about a sacred promise, sealing the certainty that your chosen someone would never let you down. Once I had snagged the man who shared my sentiments, we'd get down to having children, bringing beautiful, well-behaved mini-us's into an unshakeably safe, carefully sculpted family environment. As an adopted child, that security, and the uncomplicated bond of blood, has always been something I've craved. Take it from someone who carries the baggage, no matter how loving and secure your family, for an adopted child fear that the family's status quo could alter is always present. All it takes is the interruption of those lurking genetic relatives, or the unexpected birth of bona fide brother or sister, and the doors to the family fortress are flung wide open.

If there was a time when adopting a child was tantamount to an admission of failure in one's marital bed, then that stigma gradually abated in recent years. In fact, adoption seems almost trendy these days with poster-mum advocates like Angelina Jolie and Rosie O'Donnell shopping for orphans and keeping their figures in the bargain. And maybe avoidance of stretch-marks isn't the best reason to go the ready-made baby route, but who's really complaining? Not the orphans. Parenting is surely one of the most rewarding, terrifying, altruistic and challenging things that we ever hope to undertake. We all know there'll be tears, tantrums and several years of teenage torture along the way, but the joy, optimism and pride is supposed to counterbalance that stuff. When you adopt, though, you've also got to deal with the ticking time-bomb of an identity crises waiting to explode. For Mum and Dad, that probably means reliving their own tale of infertility, miscarriages, failed IVF treatment, whatever, while sharing the burden of guilt over junior's burgeoning philosophical angst. It's a lot to handle and I take my hat off to my own folks.

Of course, it's completely natural for an adopted child to be curious about their genetic roots, just as I'm sure any parent who puts a child up for adoption will doubtlessly speculate about how their genes are doing out there in the world. Even if there is honesty from the outset between an adopted child and their new parents, there will always be a space for the missing history of the child's conception and birth, and a sense of loss, or lacking, that never quite goes away. It's difficult for any parent to have to watch their child suffer physically or emotionally, but there is no way to protect them from the baggage of adoption. I can understand why so many children used to grow up in blissful ignorance of their origins. Tell the truth and at every stage of an adopted child's development there will be questions that the parent might not be able to answer. Who do I look like? Who do I take after? Why was I given away? What's wrong with me? Rejection by one's own parents – even for the most altruistic intention – is, if you'll excuse the phrase, the mother of all rejection complexes. And no amount of love can ever quite erase the knowledge of that first, devastating kick in the head.

The last couple of decades of pre- and peri-natal research have brought a clearer understanding of what a foetus actually experiences in the womb. Among recent theories is the assertion that a strong spiritual or emotional connection exists between the mother and her unborn child, even before the birth. In *The Primal Wound: Understanding the Adopted Child*, Nancy Verrier argues that parent/child bonding is a continuous string of psychological, physiological and even spiritual events that start in the utero and continue through the post-natal stage. She believes that when a child is separated from its mother at birth the interruption in the long bonding process causes deep-rooted problems: 'the resultant experience of abandonment and loss is indelibly imprinted upon the unconscious minds of these children,' she claims. Whether or not you buy into her theory, the phrase she applies to the trauma of adoptive separation, 'the primal wound', certainly rings true to my ears.

It's easy to assume that an on-tap supply of love from doting adoptive parents would be enough to make everything OK. But if, as psychologists tell us, we start learning to trust right at the outset of our development, and that the shape of this learning determines our ability to form relationships in later life, then surely the separation of a newborn from the one human being with whom it has shared any kind of relationship will have a damaging impact. I know, on a level, that the issue has shaped me. Despite a family life that has been rock solid, I struggled for a long time with romantic love. At the back of my mind I was always worried I would be abandoned again, and I found it hard to believe partners when they tried to reassure me that I was loved. To protect myself from rejection I would pre-empt my boyfriends with a first strike dump, or deliberately stir things up so that they'd hopelessly fulfil my prophecy of abandonment. And each time they left, the hurt and anger dug themselves in just a little bit deeper.

I count myself as one of the lucky ones though, my 'primal wound' having left only a faint scar. My parents are loving, inspirational and so very kind. They tell me that I was chosen because of my smile. Apparently I grinned at them like I was theirs already. It was the same with my brother, Kismet. It doesn't really matter how we get here, just as long as we do.

However happy the outcome, though, and however loving one's family, if we're honest, adoption will probably always feel like a second choice. I'll admit when I was younger I never dreamed of getting married and 'adopting'. I stuffed cushions under my velour tracksuit like all the other little girls. Natural childbirth is the obvious route, no point denying it, and deep down we're all curious to see how our genes would fare in the next incarnation. But what I appreciate as an adult is that adoption does nothing to lessen the essential joys and trials of parenthood. However they arrive, the presence of children in one's life is an all-encompassing responsibility. Once the commitment to raise a child has been made, then that child deserves to take first place in the hearts of its parents. Where there is purity of intention, and a surplus of love, a child and its family will always thrive.

However and whenever I have any future children, the one thing I have always remained very sure about is that I want to give them as much stability and commitment as possible although problems and trauma in life are unavoidable. And as old-fashioned as this might sound nowadays, this means I want to be married first. The problem here is that I was beginning to question and doubt the concept of marriage altogether. All my wedding fantasies were weighed down with a new-found cynicism and confusion. My family tugged one way, concerned that my marriage wasn't going to be blessed in the way they knew and understood. Toby pulled in the other direction, urging me to follow my own – i.e. his path. I felt as though I was stuck in the way of a gathering storm, more confused and vulnerable than ever before. I knew that I had muddied my opinion of marriage by dwelling on aspects that were never central to my belief in the institution; at the time exploration had felt like the responsible course of action. But now I found myself changing and I didn't like it. Once a hopeless romantic, an open-minded believer; now a godless cynic and a relationship pragmatist. I had peered up to the heavens and found them empty. Now it was clear that my spiritual malaise had contaminated my other great faith – love.

Many people marry for all the wrong reasons. In the UK, four out of ten marriages end in divorce. That was one statistic I was desperate not to become part of and, as I lay awake, next to my sleeping fiancé, I started to wonder whether losing my engagement ring had been an omen.

We'd been squabbling over silly things for months, but recently the arguments had escalated, becoming more angry and accusatory. The differences in our personalities had begun floating to the surface. Because *I* was changing, *we* were changing, our comfy dynamic shifting like a bucket of eels. Toby, I observed, seemed ever more angry at the world, while I sunk into spiritual despair. I remembered my ridiculous 'to do' list. A year to find God and get hitched. What on earth had I been thinking? After so many months of fruitless searching, the darkness of the bedroom hid the concern on my face. I had possibly lost my belief in God altogether. Now I needed to know whether I still believed in love enough to keep the promise I'd made to Toby. If this was really who I had become, would love still be enough to see us through?

There was a time when love enjoyed the same no-questions-asked devotion from me as God. As my faith faltered, though, all kinds of questions were inevitably thrown up. If the whole of human existence could be attributed to a series of blind, biological accidents, then could love too be quickly reduced to a handy evolutionary strategy, a trick of the mind to promote baby-making? Exactly the problem Will had raised on our New York visit.

When I contacted him by email, Dr Mark Lythgoe – an endocrinologist Ph.D. at the Institute of Child Health, University College London – was keen to drop the poetic metaphors of 'heart' and 'soul' when talking about love. 'He broke my heart,' we say as Prince Charming disappears over the horizon with a new damsel on the back of his horse. But, according to Dr Lythgoe, human love affairs – from the first frisson of attraction, to the declaration of undying devotion – are shaped by 'sexual brain chemistry'. This, then, is the path of true love.

Step one is all about lust. When we're out of the prowl for prospective partners, our sex hormones – testosterone and oestrogen – reign supreme. In men, for example, as well as providing that inexhaustible sex drive, high levels of testosterone provoke the development of certain 'masculine' facial features – strong jaws and cheekbones – that are more attractive to the opposite sex. Genetic indicators like facial features are linked to the more 'attractive' a prospective partner, the better their underlying immunity genes. Of course, attraction is never straightforward. There is evidence that women respond more to that classically 'masculine' face, for example, at times when they are most likely to become pregnant. At other times, more feminine-faced men – the comforters, the stability providers – win out. It's been suggested that as many as one in ten of us are ignorant of our true parentage, with our own genes conspiring to cuckold husbands and bamboozle fathers.

After lust, comes phase two: attraction. This is the part we mean when we talk about 'falling in love' – the sleeplessness, the shakes, the sudden susceptibility to second-rate, soft-rock ballads. And amazingly we can see phase two in action by looking directly into the brain. When you're 'in love', certain areas of the brain light up like a Christmas tree. These areas of activity are quite specific to love. They are different to the areas stimulated by the use of euphoria-inducing drugs like cocaine and ecstasy. They're so specific, in fact, says Dr Lythgoe, that there might one day come a time when a brain scan, not a band of gold, will be considered the ultimate token. The localized 'high' associated falling in love might also go some way to explaining the compulsive, sometimes socially self-destructive, philandering of some wayward partners: love junkies.

Those of us who overcome the addictive pitfalls of attraction can finally look forward to settling down. Phase three in the sexual brain chemistry of love is 'attachment'. This is the glue that keeps couples and families together, and leads to a deeper long-term bond than the heady nookie-neurotransmitters of previous stages. It's also the bit that many people find tricky, a head-on collision with their evolutionary roots and animal instinct. As attraction gives way to attachment, the body chemistry of both partners changes significantly. Testosterone and oestrogen give way to oxytocin, a subtler substance that promotes lasting emotional connections.

Oxytocin, 'the cuddling chemical', is released by both men and women during orgasm. It floods the senses and increases the bond between lovers. Of course, this means that in order to get your fair share of cuddles, you've got to be having regular good sex.

Things would be easier, concludes Dr Lythgoe, if, like the prairie vole, we found ourselves flooded with vasopressin – the monogomy chemical – at the end of a one-night stand, and thereafter were fiercely and permanently loyal to that one sexual partner. Instead, we rely on a combination of low-strength chemical cocktails – hormones and pheromones – and ongoing courtship ritual.

So there it is, the infinite majesty of romantic love, reduced to a set of psychosomatic symptoms and chemical instructions. When I first read Dr Lythgoe's take on love it knocked me for six, but the more I consider it, the more I see gaps in the medical explanation for man's most mysterious emotion. And from pole to pole, the fact is that, for much of the world, monogamy is held up as the ultimate model of human love. And, despite adoring the prairie vole's easy ability to 'love the one you're with', despite countless millennia when shag-and-scarper proved a wonderful evolutionary strategy (at least for the males of our species), we do manage to stay together. The lucky ones among us will even assert, as they pick out trinkets for their diamond wedding anniversary, that they 'stay in love'.

The sexual brain chemistry that undeniably sparks and shapes our love affairs does not tell the whole story. In a very real sense, it seems to me, human love is genuinely transcendent. It relies upon your communication and mutual experience. On compatibility of character, and of dreams and emotions that have nothing to do with making babies.

However we got here, whether moulded from clay by God, or sprung by chance from the primordial soup, human beings are more than the sum of our parts. We recognize this in ourselves – when we're not too busy eating, shagging and fighting – and praise the 'higher' aspects of humanity. Having read the label on the love bottle, and noted all the active ingredients, I am left with the conviction that there's still some spark of magic that cannot be reduced to a chemical symbol. Of course, I reasoned to myself, as I picked at Lythgoe's notes, that might just be my own brain chemistry talking, but what the hell? By accident or design, we're the higher life on this planet, and love lifts us higher still. Wherever God had gone, I decided, I really didn't want to lose his greatest gift.

YOU ARE CORDIALLY INVITED

Weddings are like health scares. For the first thirty years they're something that happens to other people. Then, all of a sudden, they're everywhere .

Before I turned thirty, I had been to a few family weddings. This particular year, Toby and I had already attended two and had been invited to a further three – with the possibility of even more on the cards. And thanks to the British summer's annoyingly narrow window of opportunity, and most couples' desire to tie the knot on a sunny day, all three were squeezed into a series of weekends on the dry side of the Wimbledon finals.

These days, I like to keep my weekends free for woodland walks and aimless pottering, so at first, the prospect of more than a month of back-to-back weddings was a bit daunting, along with the fact I had a severe case of wedding fatigue. Three things won me round. First, I reasoned, the happy couples were all friends. And like a mardy child on the edge of curiosity, I knew damn well I'd enjoy myself once I was there. Secondly, it would give me an opportunity to remember what the fuss was all about and hopefully see why people bother making a vow to stay together at all. And thirdly, I was supposed to be planning a wedding of my own. And, if I played my cards right – and if Toby and I got back on a romantic track and stopped bickering – I could crib all the best bits from every wedding and trump the lot of them!

The Wedding of Vandana and Gavin
Vesey Suite, Sutton Coalfields Town Hall

A Hindu marriage is a sacred occasion for more than just bride and groom. Traditionally the ceremony is seen as uniting two souls and entire families. For that reason, the guest list at a Hindu wedding can quickly get out of hand. Vandana, though, had been strict with her family (not wanting Gavin's far smaller family to feel too outnumbered on the day) and had managed to keep numbers down to 400. For a Hindu wedding this is considered quite cosy.

Sutton Coalfields Town Hall was heaving when we arrived. A kaleidoscopic sea of exquisitely embroidered saris lit up the rooms more than any flowers. It was mayhem, with hundreds of people milling about, a constant hum of chatter filling every corner of the building, best men standing on chairs banging gongs into the joyous hullabaloo. Can I just reiterate here … 400 guests! Much later I asked Van how she went about throwing such a huge party and she explained that the whole process had been about compromise. It had been vital to her, as well as to her parents, that their families had an equal voice in the arrangements. In Indian culture, the extended family – aunts and uncles – all play an important role in wedding organization. So with each step Van and her parents took, her large, close family also had to be consulted. Then there was Gav – who might have been happy to call it a day after the registry office – to think about. After all, as Van pointed out with a grin, it was his day too. Considering all the potential pitfalls, though, Gav and Van's multicultural marriage was a triumph.

Visually it was amazing, with various symbols of successful life together displayed or sprinkled on a ceremonial fire, as bride and groom sat under the traditional tent, the *mandap*. Flowers signified beauty, coconuts fertility, rice and jaggery sustenance. Ghee fuelled the sacred fire and kumkum, a fire-red powder, was used to mark Van's and Gav's foreheads as their union was solemnized.

As I learned in Goa, a traditional Indian wedding can last for four days, but most of the time, even in India, people tend to opt for the cut-down version, which comes in at just under three hours. Of course, even this would seem a marathon for your average non-Hindu British wedding guest. But before you drop off in sympathy, this is where the real genius of the Hindu ceremony comes in. Because, from the moment the groom appears, holding a coconut decorated with the Sanskrit swastika – a Hindu good luck symbol that nevertheless raised a few eyebrows among the senior members of Gav's family – until the happy couple are drummed out of their *mandap* to start their life together, there's no obligation to sit quietly and watch the whole thing at all. The result is hours of organized, joyful chaos, with guests milling and moving about, nipping in to check on the bride and groom's progress, then nipping out again to keep the party going.

Van's brother, on camcorder duties, maintained a running commentary on the ceremony for the ignorant among us, while cheeky uncles swapped cigars and betel nut powder outside, and happy kids thundered from room to room in their Diwali best. Factor in the most delicious vegetarian buffet I have ever enjoyed and a raucous Bangrah disco that got everyone from seven to seventy on the dance floor ... Van and Gav's wedding went straight to the top of my ratings, for fun factor alone.

But what many people didn't know on the day was that a month or so before the wedding Van had been diagnosed with breast cancer. Against all odds on two counts – age and race – the diagnosis was to change their vision of newly-wed life beyond recognition, and rock two families to their foundations.

Van's first chemotherapy session was booked in advance for the week of her return from honeymoon. That my good friends knew this, faced the fear, and were still ready to make their profound, public commitment to each other fills me with pride and love. Marriage means knowing that someone will never let you down. It's rare to get the chance to put that to the test before the deed is done. Gav and Van went into their wedding with their eyes open and their hearts full.

As Van said: 'For me it's about love. When I see my husband, my soul partner, I can feel myself light up and smile. When I'm feeling down I only want him with me. When I lie in bed and he's asleep, I watch him and think how lucky I am to to have found him; how gorgeous he is. When we argue, I can still see he loves me. And whatever life has thrown our way, he is still beside me, taking each step forward with me. I know he will never let me down.'

*

Mr and Mrs Frank J. May request the honour of your presemce at the marriage of their daughter Siobhán Marie to Thomas Glenn McMurray at Our Lady and St Etheldreda's Church, Newmarket

An interesting one, this. Two Irish families; Siobhán a Catholic and Glenn a Protestant.

'Should I take my knuckle-dusters?' asked Toby, as we polished our shoes before setting off. I didn't know what to tell him. In the event, of course, everyone was deliciously happy and very well behaved. A picture of Irish solidarity in the home town of English horse-racing.

The service, conducted in tandem by Father Paul Hypher and the Reverend Kevin Burdett, a Baptist minister, came pretty close to the model I had imagined for myself. Siobhán was a vision in a corseted white dress, with a beautiful posy of blue hydrangeas and bridesmaids wearing matching blue. We sang hymns, the kind everyone knows, like 'Lord of the Dance'. There was even a doddery old organist who had trouble on the fast bits of the 'Wedding March', and was really woefully inadequate when he left the keyboard to serenade the newly-weds with an acapella version of 'Ave Maria'. I bloody loved it. My folks would have entirely approved, too. (Although I could see Toby fidgeting throughout the readings and that 'peace-be-with-you' handshake confuses him every time.) It had all the authority and ritual I expected in a wedding. I hadn't been to church for ages – not a Catholic one – and it felt like home. I sat back on the hard wooden pew watching dust motes whirl in the coloured light that shone from the stained-glass windows and listened to the preachers as they tied up proceedings at the altar.

'... may the Lord in His goodness strengthen your consent

and fill you both with His blessings. What God has joined together . . .'

I shifted on the bench as the familiar prickle of discomfort washed over me. The ceremony was familiar, yes. Moving, and beautiful, too. And yet at that moment, I knew that I would probably never be able to have a Catholic wedding and feel that it was 'right'. Everyone likes a bit of nostalgia. However, as I soaked up the cuddly cosiness of Siobhán and Thomas's old-fashioned church wedding, I realized that I couldn't base my own wedding around nostalgia that my groom wouldn't share. When it came to the deeper meaning of a church wedding, I had to acknowledge the very mention of God gave me a sinking feeling. Was that how I wanted to feel on my wedding day?

'It was more than just a day,' Siobhán raved afterwards. 'It meant a lot that people had come from so far away to be there. It was the first time my Irish and American family were in all one place together, which made it so very special.'

Both Siobhán and Glenn see marriage as a vital institution. And for them it was clear that the marriage was a solemn occasion with a party atmosphere and a chance for everyone they loved and cared about to witness and celebrate their happiness.

*

Lovely friends
Please come and help us celebrate our wedding at
The Rivoli Ballroom, Brockley
Cabaret, Cava, Tapas and Tango all night long
Dress up up up
Will and Sophie

One more wedding. I pulled the overworn outfit out of the wardrobe for the last time that year and dollied myself up for an after-wedding party with a difference. My boss at the time, Sophie, was marrying Will, a man with as much joy for life as herself. A small civil service in Greenwich was followed by a wedding breakfast for twenty-five friends and family at a local restaurant. The pudding was a single, enormous Jaffa cake, Will's favourite. Later in the day, and this is where we came in, they opened the doors of the Rivoli Ballroom for another 250 riotous revellers. The ballroom, in Brockley, south-east London, has somehow avoided renovation long enough to have become a spectacular living museum. A genuine, honest-to-goodness, original ballroom. The kind where the Kray Brothers might have entertained Barbara Windsor and her bosomy buddies while Bob Monkhouse honed his compere act on-stage. Red velvet walls, walnut-panelled bars, mirror balls, large red lamps dangle from the curved ceiling, their light bouncing off a gold-strip cabaret curtain. Even the cloakroom is memorable, a vision in green and gold flake wallpaper.

The bride, to suit her surroundings, had slipped out of her 1970s trouser suit daywear into an incredibly sexy, silver bias-cut sequinned Jenny Packmam number. Will wore a hot red disco suit. Between the pair of them, they managed to upstage the venue.

Will and Sophie chose their unconventional two-tier wedding because they wanted everyone they loved to come and party with them, but felt that the exchange of vows should be more intimate. Sophie is an ex C of E devotee and now happily godless, so a marriage in church would have felt hypocritical. The Greenwich Registry route followed by a party was a novel way to enjoy both an intimate 'just the two of us' wedding and the biggest, flashiest, fastest party in Brockley's history, all in one day. And with their *pièce de resistance* – cabaret from Dusty Limits and his camp troop – to keep the crowds cheering, they honestly managed the best of both worlds. There was even a second – I'm guessing ruder – wedding ceremony for evening guests performed by Rev. Dusty, and topped off with an impromptu choir of 200 singing 'Going to the Chapel'.

'It couldn't have been more fun,' said Sophie afterwards. 'Or more spiritually satisfying to be able to celebrate with all of our dearest friends in the best way we know how. I don't believe in the happiest day of your life crap. Too much pressure. But you've got to admit,' she paused to let a huge grin spread across her face, 'it was certainly memorable.'

And it was. There was no denying it. Sophie and Will's wedding had inspired me to want something different myself. By freeing themselves from tradition, they had been able to tailor the day to express their personalities and their love beautifully.

Earlier in the year Toby and I had attended my first civil service wedding – a beautiful ceremony held at the Waldorf. I admit I rather missed the pomp and circumstance of the traditional church do: the disharmonious hymn singing, the well-worn readings, the silent, nodding authority of the man upstairs metaphysically rubber-stamping the day's events. But the ceremony lost none of its emotional impact. The intention had been sweet, heartfelt and sincere. Instead of making their promises to Heaven, Paul and Jackie made them to each other, which was rather lovely. More honest, at least, for a couple of non-believers. It was clear that Sophie and Will felt the same. For the first time I think I really considered the civil ceremony route. I'd talked about it before, of course, but not with any real conviction. I think I'd secretly assumed that my family faith would win out eventually. But the more I thought about this way, the more I liked it. It felt more human, more real to be taking on the responsibility of a long-term relationship and promising to make it work, as opposed to simply making the leap and expecting God to catch you.

But then there was always the worry of my family's expectations. Sophie confided that this issue had caused them some stressful moments too. Apparently there were times when the families had felt bamboozled by the whole thing. They simply couldn't understand the couple's vision of what constituted the ideal wedding.

'But that's families, isn't it?' said Sophie with a shrug. 'In the end, when everything came together, they could finally see what we'd been going on about. Either they're all disturbingly good liars or they enjoyed every damned minute of it.'

I admit it, friends or no friends, and for all the free food and party favours I was likely to receive, the prospect of attending all those weddings had been far from appealing. For starters there had been the worry that crossover guests would cotton on to the fact that I only own one decent dress. Then there were the gifts, a small price to pay when you consider the expense of wining and dining a roomful of guests, but 'nearly an armful' if you happen to have spent the last year prancing around the planet in search of spiritual equilibrium, when you should've stayed at home to earn some money.

If you'd paid a penny for my thoughts at the beginning of my month of matrimony, you would probably have walked off with your ears ringing, wishing you hadn't spent your money. By the time the curtain came down on the cabaret at the Rivoli Ballroom, though, marriage and me were back on good terms again. This is what I learned:

> That marriage is like diving. There are many ways to do it, but they all end up with the same result: take the plunge and you'll hit the water.

> That family counts, but couples count more. If your folks are trying to steer you away from your dream wedding for selfish reasons, they've forgotten whose day it is. Remind them, tactfully, or surrender to the meringue dress.

> That if you let yourself get bogged down in the details, the meaning of your marriage will only be obscured. Relax.

> I want a giant jaffa wedding cake, too.

ON THE ROCKS

It was during one of our 'cosy' Saturday mornings, set aside for soppy couply bonding and breakfast in bed, that Toby and I finally cracked. It was inevitable, I suppose, after months of tension, money troubles and low-key bickering as we wallowed in the mire of introspection and worried over the very foundations of love. In the end it was an innocent phone call from my mum that cut short our lie-in and kick-started the biggest row in our relationship. She only called to let me know that she'd bumped into an old school pal of mine, who'd been proudly juggling a couple of rosy-cheeked nippers. The grannie instinct had clearly kicked in.

'And of course they've both been christened,' Mum had announced cheerily. 'You'll be doing the same one day with yours when they arrive, won't you?'

And there it was; the spectre of my Catholic past. I hadn't even considered the aftermath – the fall-out – of my personal pilgrimage. My parents had tried to understand the reasons behind my retreat from the Church, an institution they still believed in wholeheartedly. But with faith colouring their own views, they could never fully empathize. I knew it must be painful for them to see me turn my back on our shared beliefs. It must be tough for any parent to watch their children reject what they have taught them, and the threat of eternal damnation for their only daughter could only sharpen such pain. If I could have eaten a magic sweet and believed again I would have. I honestly would. Of course, life's never that simple.

The conversation with my mum about christenings left my mind reeling. The daydream of a young family, and recollections of happy family christenings, stirred the memory of my faith. But that's all they were; memories of what my religion had once meant to me. Once again, like the first time at the Natural History Museum, I felt the loss both physically and emotionally. With my mum's chirping assumptions down the line, I felt as though I was back at square one, missing the God I might not ever rediscover. My parents seemed to have come to terms with the possibility that I might not have a church wedding. (There were, I later learned, a few worried phone calls to Father Dorricott and a lot of bedtime prayers on my behalf, but eventually they did seem to accept it might never happen.) But with kids, even hypothetical ones, entering the picture, the issue of faith suddenly seemed more urgent again to my God-fearing mother. It's understandable. The continuation of faith is as important to a true believer as the perpetuation of his or her genetic code. So in a faithful family, raising a godless child is like breeding a mule.

Realizing this, and wanting to avoid endless, painful conversations about salvation, I figured that surrendering to the idea of a christening, at least, would keep my folks off my back. And anyway, where was the harm? It would be as harmless as saluting a magpie, or picking up a penny for luck. It would also be the ritualistic get-together that would appease my entire family, pay lip-service to my own lingering Catholic ties and, moreover, be a great excuse for a party ... with presents. Unfortunately, Toby saw things differently. I should have seen it coming.

'Why?' he barked aggressively, when I casually suggested that we might dip the heads of our hypothetical babies. 'And after the christening?' he continued, rolling his eyes. 'What then? A Catholic school?'

'No, of course not,' I snapped back defensively, then added 'Maybe. I don't know. It depends what's best in the area we're living in.'

Toby's brow furrowed. His cheeks coloured. I deeply regretted crossing a bridge that might have least have waited until after the wedding. Although perhaps it was good that we had addressed it before it was too late.

'I want our kids to make their own minds up, when it comes to the big issues,' he insisted.

'So do I,' I protested, sensing that my push for common ground would fall on deaf ears.

'But that means enabling them to do so,' said Toby. 'Not brainwashing them from birth into a particular mindset.'

'You're not interested in anyone making up their own mind,' I said, tiring of Toby's aggressive stance. 'You just want everyone to agree with you. Which you know our kids would if we brought them up with this detached, outsider's view of religion that you're so bloody proud of.'

'And that's a good thing, right?' said Toby, his voice rising in pitch and volume.

I fought a wave of panic and rubbed at my aching forehead.

This bickering was getting us nowhere. I was getting nowhere. For a year I'd been running away from my roots, looking for a replacement for my lost faith, jogging around on an endless, circular track.

'It seems to me,' I began, breathing deeply in an effort to remain calm, 'that "we" are all about "you". Why can't you let me just do this? Why do I have to fight with you every step of the way? We're not having a Catholic wedding. Fine. But I'm fed up of compromising.' I was shouting now. 'I'm just fed up! You've made me feel as if it's an intellectual failure to believe in God. And what does it matter to you, Tobe? You think it's all bollocks? Fine. Let me have my bollocksy ceremony with my bollocksy imaginary babies. OK?'

Even as I screamed my indignation, I found myself annoyed with my own argument. I was sick of defending beliefs that I hadn't properly formalized for myself yet. And I'd had enough of compromising my own position in an effort to keep everyone else happy. The pressure from my family to come back into the fold would always be there, and I was beginning to wonder whether Toby would always be too wrapped up in his own principles ever to be more than glibly dismissive of their faith. It was a huge source of potential conflict, with me stuck in the middle. In truth, I wanted to run away from the lot of them.

The rest of the day was divided between long periods of silence and short bursts of shouting, as Toby and I descended from passionate debate to bullish declaration and finally down to the level of raw, painful insult. I berated Toby for his cynical, jaded approach to life, his unbearable insistence on playing devil's advocate every time I found something that interested me. He, in return, laughed at my gullibility and pooh-poohed the sense of wonder I found with the world.

By tea-time, there was nowhere left to go. We were way beyond the point where a hug and a smile might have diffused the situation. Every word exchanged was cross. We had never gone to bed on a row. Now we would be sleeping apart, by choice, for the first time in years. I couldn't see a positive outcome. I decided to go home and called my parents to let them know of my imminent arrival, stalling them on my precise reasons for my impromptu visit.

Toby drove me, in tearful silence, to the train station. I climbed out of the car without a word, slammed the door behind me and strode into the ticket hall, without looking back.

A NAME ON A BENCH

I stared morosely out of the train's greasy window on the journey down to Southend-on-Sea, allowing the rhythm of the tracks lull me like a rocking chair. A conversation Toby and I had shared months ago rattled around my mind. We'd been driving past the Angel of the North on the way back home from his aunt and uncle's Cumbrian farmhouse, and we had been so certain back then that all the soul-searching in the future couldn't and wouldn't come between us. How wrong we'd been. Soggy mole hills of used Andrex, both 'soft and strong', just as the pack had promised, surrounded me. I honestly couldn't believe that it had got to this point. When Toby and I ever reach the peak of a serious row, it's not unusual for one of us to threaten desertion. Neither of us ever actually walked out, though. I've gone as far as to snatch up the nearest bag, regardless of its contents, and flounce out of the flat, slamming doors until the red mist clears. But we're always friends again before bedtime. It's all part of a well-oiled routine designed to vent our frustrations in a way that caters for our sense of drama and passion. This time was different. I'd left the flat. I'd left town. I'd left Toby. And, I told myself, I wasn't coming back.

I ducked the hugs, and all of the clumsy, well meant offers of comfort from my parents, preferring the solitude of my childhood bedroom. I couldn't have articulated what had happened anyway. None of it made sense to me. Toby and I had been rock-solid before all this faith well-gazing began. We'd spent Sundays tangling our toes in bed, arguing about the artistic merits of *Hollyoaks*, not haring about the planet on some fruitless crusade. It all was my fault, of course. Maybe if I hadn't been such a slave to my all-consuming desire for answers, I would have noticed the cracks appearing in my relationship sooner. I'd put my true love last, ignoring his beliefs, when he should have been at the heart of my journey. The truth was our bickering had been growing worse for months. We were tired, confused and skint, and Toby's heartfelt proposal of marriage seemed a very long time ago. Endlessly raking over issues that most people save for drunken dinner parties and late-night phone-ins had exposed a hidden gulf between us. We might have fed off the differences in our world views, played to our strengths, and become more than the sum of our parts. Instead we had argued ourselves into increasingly distant corners. In the red corner, the cynical, loveless Papist, faithless but stubbornly loyal. In the blue corner, the free-wheeling iconoclast with a big mouth and one permanently raised eyebrow, playing advocate to a devil he doesn't even believe in.

Initially, I'd thought that I wanted Toby and I to change together, to settle on a positive spiritual outlook for the rest of our lives. But in truth I just wanted my faith – my old faith – back again because with faith life made sense. If Toby had experienced some sort of spiritual epiphany and started bowing down to the baby Jesus, well, I'm sure the moral support would have been nice. There's safety in numbers where faith's concerned; I've learned that along the way. The more people agree with you, the less you think about what you're saying. However, with hindsight, the very notion to harbour even a very small desire for a happy Catholic ending to our story was ridiculous. I had been foolish and naive. People spend their entire lives coming to their own conclusions through introspection and reflection, not because some jaded Catholic on the brink of marriage invites them to join their Sunday club so they can tidy up things for the God-fearing family.

I love that Toby digs for knowledge like a pig digs for truffles. The conviction in his considered opinions, once he's reached them – and even when they're unpopular – is something I admire about him greatly. And yet these very qualities are what drove me to question, and ultimately abandon, everything I had ever known, leaving nothing in its place. I resented that, and in the end, gnawing resentment had pushed me away from him. I couldn't help blaming him, still, for the ferocity of his attack and his knack for an argument. A frustrated announcement that he was 'past caring' and 'would marry me however and wherever' had come too late. Maybe if we'd bitten the bullet and shuffled down the aisle into the welcoming arms of Father Dorricott all those months back we wouldn't have got into this mess. We could have done what every other bloody couple does. We could have casually lied to my wonderful old parish priest for the required six months and left the Church in a cloud of dust as soon as the ink had dried on our wedding certificate, never to return again. But no, we took the moral high road and found ourselves up a ruddy great hill when the fog set in.

I sat huddled against the lukewarm radiator in my narrow old bedroom. Nothing much had changed since I had spent my allotted miserable teens in much the same position. Same carpet, threadbare where I'd danced out the theme tunes to my adolescence, the cupboard full of Babyliss crimpers, failed first novels, embarrassingly frank diaries and battered GCSE textbooks in covered wallpaper off-cuts. And the same single bed I'd always slept in. In a double bed, I might have piled my pillows into a roughly Toby-shaped heap and conned myself into believing everything was all right, so that I could get a few hours of much-needed sleep. In my cell-block single, I had nothing for company but my dark thoughts. It was going to be a long night.

At 9.00 p.m. my mother could bear it no longer. Her Irish instinct to deal with all trauma by preparing vast amounts of food had been successfully repressed since my afternoon arrival. But now, with two official meal times already missed, she had finally made up her mind to force-feed me.

'Do you want a cup of tea and a cheese toastie?' she asked, poking her head around my bedroom door.

'No, thanks,' I replied.

'A slice of my nice fruit cake? It's still warm . . . and a cup of tea.'

I shook my head. Even her fruit cake wasn't going to do it, nice or not.

'OK.' Mum pulled back a little dejectedly, as mums do when they can't help. 'Why don't you get some fresh air, then?

Take a quick walk to the river, maybe. You look grey. Are you eating lots of green veg?'

I nodded. 'I am. And I will, actually. Take a walk, that is. It might help clear my head. Thanks, Mum.'

She brightened immediately. 'Good idea, then you can come back and we'll have a late supper. What do you say to fish and chips? And I've got a treacle pudding and custard for afters.' She smacked her lips and turned, still chatting merrily. 'Something really, really stodgy. That'll sort you out.'

I'll admit, it was nice to get out. I tramped down to the river at the bottom of Ferry Road. An ancient crossing-point over the Crouch for pilgrims on their way to Canterbury. The ferry was still there halfway though the last century, taking school children and villagers to and fro. The last of the ferrymen, Jock, was a Popeye-armed stand-in for Johnny Weissmuller, the first of the movie Tarzans. By Hullbridge standards, that's quite a claim to fame. It was the river I came to as a starry-eyed schoolgirl to plan my own rise to movie or rock star fame, or to mourn the passing of another puppy love.

I must have sat there thinking for ages as the sun dipped over the estuary flatlands and the sound of bells from moored boats grew louder in the gathering wind. A small pack of skinny tracksuited youths rounded the corner and stood puffing at a badly rolled joint in the shadows. A cacophony of ringtones broke the silence and my train of thought. I decided it was time to go.

The scent of cardamom and coriander drifted over from the local tandoori. Another hour and the pub crowd would be sniffing their way over like Pavlov's pissheads. I zipped up my jacket, remembering a night like this from long ago. It was just before I'd left for Atlanta with the band. I'd sat on the riverside bench with Keith and Anthony, toasting our ambitions with a shared can of Stella. We carved our names on to the bench in an uncharacteristic act of romantic vandalism. To our young eyes, as we admired our handiwork, it was as good as having our names in lights. We were immortalized. We vowed to return, our impossible dreams accomplished, to toast our success, preferably with something colder. So much had happened since then and the reunion had been written off in another life. I knelt on the damp ground and squinted for a sign of our carvings. It was too dark to tell if our work had stood the test of time.

'Lost some'ink?' A broad Essex accent pierced the evening air.

I stood up, startled, to face a couple of pale teenage girls. Both had their hair scraped back far too tightly; the Peckham facelift. Rows of gypsy hoop earrings dangled like curtain hooks from their sagging spaniel ears.

'Um,' I replied, nervously, wondering whether they were carrying knives.

One of them thrust her cigarette lighter aloft like the Olympic torch. 'Will this 'elp?'

As a tiny blue jet flared into life, the lighter played a tinny, unauthorized version of Britney's 'Hit me Baby One More Time', which was cut short as the lighter snapped shut.

I cleared my throat, wondering if it was responsible, from a mature, adult point of view, to share my youthful act of vandalism with potentially impressionable, not to mention potentially violent, youths.

The other girl stepped forward. 'Only we've got our boyfriends coming, innit.'

I looked at them inquiringly.

'We need the bench,' said girl two, with a sniff.

'Oh, I see,' I replied. 'It's nothing, I've not lost anything, I mean. Thanks, though.'

'Whatever.'

I stood in the darkness opposite the girls, in their tic-tac tracksuits. Suddenly I really wanted to see my name etched on to that wretched bench more than anything.

'Actually, can I borrow your lighter a sec?'

The girl sighed and passed it to me. I scanned the bench with the light from its pathetic flame. The girls stood back giggling.

'What you looking for?' one of them asked.

'A name,' I told them. 'Mine. I know it sounds silly but I wrote it years ago and want to see if it's still there.'

'Nah, mate, know what you mean,' came the approving reply.

'Tagged my name on a bus in felt tip and it lasted six months before they scrubbed it. Fuckin' chops.'

I straightened up.

'Chops?' I asked.

'Y'know, chops. Porn. Phat.'

Oh God; I had no idea what she was talking about. Was I really too old to understand teenagers already? I'd be telling them off next.

'Well, it's probably best not to get into a habit of writing our names on things,' I mumbled. See? It had started already!

'Suppose so,' said the girls, eyeing me with new suspicion. 'You gonna be long, by the way? Baz and Tyron'll be 'ere soon.'

I turned back to my search. And there it was, the cluster of names that I'd been looking for. Smoothed and almost illegible, like a scar.

''Ave you found it?'

I nodded and both girls leaned in.

'Sara, Anthony and Beef,' one of them read out loud.

'That was Keith, actually.'

'Oh.'

The three of us bent over the bench together, staring down at the fading legend. It was a private moment, and it felt odd to be sharing it with two thirteen-year-olds from the Hullbridge ghetto. But there we were; two generations, at a pinch, brought together by vandalism.

'Oi, you ready?'

Baz and Tyrone had arrived, I surmised, assessing the pale, peach-fuzzed studs who had appeared from nowhere besides the bench. My cue to leave.

'I better be off, then. Thanks, girls.' I smiled.

'S'all right, man, innit.' They broke into a clumsy impression of Jamaican patois, presumably in an effort to impress the boys whose dope-leafed satin caps and baggy tracksuits pointed to a shared love of dancehall fashion.

I left them sucking their teeth and squeezing each others' arses, and turned for home.

It had been odd seeing those names on the bench. I'd been young, free and somewhat wild back then, and had thrown myself wholeheartedly into every relationship that had come my way. But love, real love, had been years away. I knew that now. Plato, whose deliciously slim volumes made excellent teenage posing tools, said that man and woman were sliced in two, like a flatfish, before birth, and were designed to seek out the perfect fit, the other half. The relationships I'd had had never quite made me whole though. There was always something missing, such as fidelity, sobriety or employability.

It had taken me years to figure out what I was looking for.

Years more to actually find it. And now, when my love and I should have been flapping around on the ocean bed, as one happy, whole flatfish, I found myself alone again. It was funny, when I lost my faith I was less than whole. My spiritual crisis left me missing a presence I had taken for granted. But I got by. There were tears, as well as anger, even desperation at times, but I never missed God that much, not when it came to the crunch. Now, twenty-four hours after I'd left Toby, I missed Him so much I thought my chest might burst. Outside my parents' house I sat on a low wall and watched for shooting stars. An idea was forming. It was my fault that Toby and I had got to this point, for more reasons than I've yet confessed to. It was up to me to sort things out.

It's confession time. Just after Toby and I set out on my quest to find answers, I hit a series of personal problems. It wasn't long since I'd had the first, scary grand mal seizure and I was finding it hard to adjust to the medication. I was putting on weight and, rather more frighteningly, I was experiencing serious trouble with my memory. Most of it was to settle down, although I am far more prone to malapropisms than I ever used to be and there are memories that I've given up trying to remember, but for a while my confidence was shot. I was nervous being out in public on my own just in case I had another fit, headaches confused me and I became introverted and shy. At the same time a friendship I had forged with my birth mother broke down with apparently mutual animosity. Rejection issues and other related demons that had never been far from the surface reared up and hit me all over again, as they did her, and sadly we blamed each other. Then, when an unsympathetic boss sacked me, I found an even lower level to hit. It was just one of those black periods that we all have to deal with every now and again, but at the time it was all too much. With my faith in tatters I turned to ... um ... magic.

Now, this might sound a bit wacky, but it's not really. Magic is a religion itself to many, although I wasn't consciously looking for it to be a replacement. Much doctrine has an element of magic to it – evoking supernatural entities and asking for things through prayer is a very effective form of witchcraft. Spells are often repeated mantra, just like whipping off a quick round of the rosary. Some forms of religion even have specific schools of magic – Judaism has the Kabbalah, Islam has Sufism, for example. Christianity itself has some incredibly developed rituals with its super-holy relics, faith-healing and exorcisms. So you see, if you embrace the possibility of religion, why stop there?

If you can open your mind to the possibility of magic, just for a moment, we're all subconsciously using its basic principles all the time, in sending pacts and wishes into the ether or acting on superstition. And although science mostly dictates that pandering to superstition and the supernatural is foolish, many of us still busy ourselves with specific rituals in the hope that fate won't catch us out. We just don't give it a name.

Magic, in its simplest meaning, is the manipulation of nature to get what you want. There are a variety of different techniques – from traditional Wiccan witchcraft to Chaos Magic, a much frowned-upon practice in which the magician pinches whatever they think will work from all the other methods on offer; a mix-and-match system similar to those who form personal faith systems. I'm sure many scientists would find the suggestion of a connection between magic and quantum physics ridiculous, but there are links that can't be ignored.

We are all made up from sub-atomic particles, one big lump of energy. Through the limited spectrum of our senses we all interpret the world differently. We are born alone, we die alone and nobody will ever share our experience of life. Quantum physics suggests that information and even matter and energy can travel backwards through time under certain circumstances. It has also found that observing something can inherently change whatever is being observed – matter obeying mind. This means that reality isn't necessarily fixed and each of us might have the power to change it. If we can believe that our thoughts have the power literally to change the universe, we can become or have whatever we wish. It sounds crazy, I know, but it's true to say that positive people often seem to attract positivity, and a run of bad luck often lasts when you feel negative about life. But generally people don't tend to believe that problems, or dilemmas, can be modified by intention alone. It's all too simple.

I did it the old-fashioned way – your classic Buffy-style witchcraft – evoking the entire cosmos with chants and candles. I was tapping into things I should never have meddled with, driven by a sense of urgency that had spun out of control. I didn't really know what I was doing, nor did I completely believe in the power of my rituals. Nevertheless, I became obsessed. I had by then abandoned the idea of God, so I had no one to pray to. But after a lifetime of asking Him to sort things out, I still wanted something greater than me to arrange things on my behalf. So I passed the buck from God to the universe and, when I might have been learning to stand on my own two feet, started casting spells instead. Night after night, I sat in front of a candle, desperately hoping that someone, or something, was listening. I wanted to find peace, have my questions answered and my love sworn true for ever. Messing with this might have stirred up all sorts of stuff – partly psychological, perhaps even externally – but you can't really know. But inexplicable, strange things began to happen around me, and everything seemed to be going wrong. I'd convinced myself now that I'd cursed us somehow, that some kind of parasitic spirit was stalking us. And despite my newborn cynicism, I had to try something radical, something familiar.

My parents were delighted when I returned home from my walk with a waggle in my tail. Enough stodgy food was eaten to sink a ship and I nipped upstairs to make a discreet phone call to a friend. She knew who to put me in touch with. That night I tossed and turned on my knackered childhood mattress, listening to the cacophony of my dad's snoring coupled with the ethereal scream of mating foxes. I missed Toby and my feet were cold without him. I picked up my mobile a couple of times and hovered over 'home' but stopped myself. We needed the time apart, although I did wonder what he was doing all alone.

The next morning I woke early to set off back to London. Mum was already at the oven, hovering an egg over the frying pan, but I managed to fight off all attempts of a fry-up. In truth I was nervous, because at 10.00 a.m. that day I was booked in for an exorcism.

I have to admit I was terrified. In my mind exorcisms constituted floating beds, Linda Blair's 360-degree spinning head and *Tubular Bells* – although I think this vision might have something to do with William Friedkin. Your 'trad' exorcism is thought to be a religious rite for driving evil from the possessed. The Catholic Church still believes in diabolic possession, and robed-up brethren still practise a lengthy ritual. The Archbishop of Calcutta, Henry Sebastian D'Souza, actually ordered a priest to carry out an exorcism on Mother Teresa just before she died in 1997 because he thought she was under attack from the Devil.

These days the spiritual community has a more gentle approach to demonic possession. As bin-men have become Refuse Collection Engineers, so exorcists are now known to their troubled clients as Spirit Releasement Therapists. Spirit Release, for all its ghouls and ghosties, is treated as therapy more than a religious ritual and has nothing to do with the Church. Spirit Release Therapists state that their aim is to free both the client and the attached spirit so both can continue merrily on their separate journeys, whereas old-fashioned exorcism was about confrontation and wrenching the spiritual squatter away. While the medical world remains inevitably sceptical on the matter, there are some who do embrace it. Dr Alan Lindsay Sanderson, for example, first came across the concept of spirit attachment and spirit release in the early nineties, while working as a consultant psychiatrist in the NHS. Through his work he began to believe that the spiritual dimension could influence human behaviour and that spiritual attachments could be caused by emotional disturbance. These days, Dr Sanderson has left the NHS and is the founder of the Spirit Release Foundation, only stepping down as chairman in 2004. He uses spirit release therapy with many patients, apparently finding it to be highly effective when used to treat conditions such as addiction, depression, relationship problems, anxiety, sexual problems and multiple personalities.

I was very much hoping that it would work for me. I hadn't heard from Toby.

THE EXORCISM

Note to cynics: DO NOT READ.
You won't believe it, anyway.

I left early for the journey to north London's Caledonian Road
and arrived on the grubby strip with time to spare. I stood by a
bus stop, squinting at a bag-battered printout of the relevant
A–Z page. A shaft of pale sunlight filtered through the unbroken sheet of cloud just long enough to dazzle me.

I'd been told not to drink any coffee before my exorcism, as
caffeine can hamper the hypnotic process, and without my
morning jolt, sleep still hung over me like fog. One thing,
though, was crystal clear: twelve hours and one good kip after
I'd hatched this latest soul-cleansing scheme, the whole thing
felt faintly ridiculous. I mean, an exorcist? Why couldn't I just
drag Toby to Relate, like a normal couple?

I rubbed my eyes and decided to walk up the Caledonian
Road. When I found the address I needed I stood at the door
for a while, dithering. A milk float pootled by, its empties
jangling with every bump. The driver, a milk-white man-
mountain with a riot of ginger curls, waved at me and poked
his head out of the open side, grinning.

'You lost, love?'

I smiled back unenthusiastically and shook my head. Although in a way he was right. I'd been lost for ages, staring at the corner of a much larger map, with no idea what lay beyond.

He left with another cheery wave and buzz of electricity, closely pursued by a bow-legged pensioner waving a 'no milk today' note in one hand and a pint of silver top in the other.

I turned to the house and took a deep breath. I was going in.

I don't know what kind of pointy-chinned mystic I was expecting to answer the door. An ominous turban-wearing guru, perhaps, with crystals dangling from every *chakra*, or a mousy academic type with just a hint of 'seen too much' in his eyes. In the end, my exorcist, Zoë, turned out to be a pleasantly attractive thirty-something whose only badge of spiritual abnormality was a marked sense of peace and quiet, unusual in a city-dwelling chick of her age. We chatted for a while about the reasons for my visit and she did her best to reassure me that I wasn't crazy. She'd heard much worse. Which was some comfort, even if what it really meant was that there were people out there possibly harbouring even wackier fantasies than my own and had so far escaped confinement in a psychiatric secure ward. I nestled in Zoë's squishy leather sofa and let her tell me what *she* thought was going on.

Spirit release therapists believe that at the point of death a spirit usually journeys towards 'the light', but doesn't always get there. Sometimes confusion steers a soul off-course. It might remain a ghost in a familiar place, or attach itself to a living person. Sometimes spirits stick around to help out needy friends or relations, or to exact revenge for some harm suffered in life. Sometimes they stick to you whether you want them to or not. All sorts of things can cause spiritual attachment, such as sudden death, the bond of love – or meddling with magic.

According to Zoë, it's quite common for conscious disembodied spirits to intrude upon an individual's psychic space and attach themselves to it merging with his or her unconscious mind and sometimes asserting their will over that of the living host. This process of spirit attachment can, she asserts, have horrible effects, causing a steady decline in one's mental and physical health as foreign spirits takes control.

According to this way of thinking, many things we tend to put down to stress, such as memory problems, succumbing to addiction, unexplained fatigue and depression, even symptoms of schizophrenia, are actually symptomatic of possession. Some psychologists would probably want to keep an eye on Zoë, just for voicing such ideas. I prefer to keep an open mind.

I told Zoë about all my amateurish magical dabbling, as well as my mounting spiritual malaise. I felt faintly silly to be talking so earnestly about hexes and charms in the cold light of day, and I told my story more than reluctantly at first. But Zoë took me seriously, scribbling copious notes, asking questions, listening without comment. Soon I was completely relaxed. Whatever I'd let myself in for, I felt confident I was in good hands.

'People are often subject to psychic attack,' said Zoë eventually. 'Sometimes from spells or curses that other people generate, but also often because of *pacts*.'

I raised an enquiring eyebrow.

'They may have been made in this life, or in a previous one,' she said. 'Or, you might unwittingly form a pact when performing magic. A pact is an agreement – a link – between two souls. It can be positive or negative.'

According to Zoë, while I was locked away in my bedroom, burning candles and broadcasting my wish list to anyone or anything who might be listening, I'd neglected to protect myself from disembodied spirits who coveted my physical form and wouldn't think about hopping on board. The books that I'd read had said nothing about safe hex. There was no mention of the spiritual STIs and the dangers of other-worldy-one-night-stands. I'd just said the magic words, waved my arms about a bit and thrown open the door to a room with hidden nasties. In all honesty, I'd hadn't taken it that seriously. I'd been hoping for results, certainly, but hardly expecting them. And who wears wellies when they're not expecting rain? Zoë believes that a person can sometimes take on the attitudes, beliefs and appetites of the invading spirit; even one's physical appearance might begin to change. If I was harbouring homeless entities, had my appearance changed? I checked in the mirror on a toilet trip and couldn't be sure. Epilepsy had brought mood swings and violent headaches that might have altered, subtly, the way I held my face. My loss of faith had made me vulnerable, angry, cynical, bitter and anxious. When I allowed it to, my confusion and disillusionment showed in my careworn frown, I'm sure. But that's what faces do, isn't it? I needed more than the assertion of an ordinary young woman – no older than myself, however inspirational and calming – to convince me that my present woes were down to a gang of parasitic and malicious spirits. I hoped that my new-found cynicism wouldn't negate the therapeutic potential of the day's activities, and that I could open my mind to Zoë's version of events, as I would have done in the past. To all you budding witches: be careful what you wish for.

There are two main approaches to spirit release or exorcism. Firstly, and most significantly, a 'psychic' practitioner may be able to see and communicate with any spiritual presence directly. The second approach is open to all. 'The Baldwin Model' is a structured, clinical approach that can be learned by any would-be practitioner, regardless of their extra-sensory talents. This was Zoë's method.

After a chat about how I had found myself in this position and what I hoped to achieve, Zoë began the process of hypnosis. An effort, she said, to alter my consciousness and focus my mind inwards. Also, she explained, by subduing my own personality, she could communicate with the spirit or spirits.

I had never been hypnotized before and, like so many mesmerized subjects before me, would happily have asserted that it wasn't working at all as I slipped slowly but surely into a strange, semi-conscious trance. I was aware of my actions and could acknowledge the sound of my own rational voice when I heard it, but the words didn't seem to be coming from me. Zoë placed my hands on a book – *The Complete Works of Shakespeare* – and commanded me to raise one finger from the cover in an exercise designed to establish whether she was communicating with my conscious or unconscious mind. I vaguely remember my finger twitching at her instruction – quite involuntarily – while deep inside myself, I remained convinced that the process wasn't working at all.

Once Zoë was satisfied that I was in a relaxed trance, and that she was dealing with my unconscious mind, she painted for me an image of a beautiful landscape; violet lakes, rolling green hills and impossibly blue skies. In this place I felt instantly safe and calm, protected and guided by her omni-present voice.

'You are standing at the top of a beautiful, multicoloured spiral staircase,' continued Zoë in smooth, velvet tones. 'Every time I say the word "deeper" you will take one step down the stairs.'

Her voice sounded clear but distant.

'Deeper.'

I felt myself sink.

'Deeper.'

Lower and lower.

'Deeper.'

I reached the foot of the imagined spiral staircase and, under Zoë's gentle guidance, found myself at the base of a huge oak tree, with its roots lodged at the very centre of the earth and leaf-heavy braches reaching high into the sky above.

'Next to the tree is a full-length mirror,' Zoë said, and I turned my head to see it. 'Look into it and tell me if you can see what has attached itself to you.'

My palms felt sweaty and my fingers slipped over the cover of the heavy book on my lap. My heart was hammering. I stood before the massive gilt-edged mirror and stared at my reflection.

'What can you see?' prompted Zoë after a long silence.

'Nothing. Nothing at all. I can't see anything,' I replied, crestfallen. 'Just me.'

'Concentrate on your aura,' said Zoë, and a haze slowly began to form around my reflection. 'What colour is it?' she asked.

I squeezed my eyes shut, focusing hard, and a wave of sudden terror washed over me. A bubble of dirty congealing crimson blood enveloped my reflected form, constricting me. I felt my breathing quicken as fear rose within me, but Zoë's constant, soothing voice provided an unbreakable link to the calm and safety of the real world.

'I'm covered in blood,' I heard myself whimper. 'It's horrible.'

Zoë moved closer, sitting next to me on her battered couch, reassuring me in soft lullaby words. 'I won't let you leave until you're clear,' she promised.

I could feel her at my shoulder, and in my reverie, sweeping away the image that haunted me from the mirror's surface.

'Now,' she said, as the gory aura dissipated, 'we're going to see if there's anything else with you in there.'

I shivered with apprehension. Something scuttled behind my reflection and stayed there hiding.

'There's something in the bushes.' I felt confused. 'It's, it's ... I don't know what it is.' Another shape, dark and ill-defined, across my line of vision. And another. 'There's something ... there are other things,' I mumbled nervously.

'Go on,' Zoë encouraged. 'Focus.'

In a flash of pain and panic, I realized the mirror scene anew. My own terrified reflection stared out at me, surrounded and buffeted by countless twisting, grotesque figures, humans and animals and things in between. I tensed and gripped the book balanced on my knees.

'Don't worry. I'll ask healing spirits from the light to take them all away.'

Zoë voice again proved calming. In a series of winds and beaming light, the spirits that danced around me malevolently were whisked away one by one. I felt their departure like the gradual lightening of a load I had not known I carried.

'Do you feel better?' Zoë asked. 'Does it feel like they are all gone?'

Despite my lonely reflection, I still felt as if someone was watching me. I shook my head slowly.

'It's OK,' said Zoë, 'no one can hurt you, I promise. You won't leave here until everything has been cleared,' she repeated.

'He's hiding,' I replied in a tiny childlike voice that didn't sound or feel like me. Emotion welled up, burning at my chest, and I felt an overwhelming sense of misery. I started crying and trembling uncontrollably. I forced myself to look back at my reflection in the magic mirror and found a pale, malicious face staring back at me. Cold eyes met mine. You're not rid of me that easily, they seemed to say, I'm sticking around girl.

'Oh God,' I cried out in alarm. 'He won't go.'

Zoë edged closer still, placing a cool, reassuring hand on my shoulder. 'We'll get rid of him in a different way,' she told me. 'Sometimes a presence may feel itself necessary to its host in some way, maybe out to harm, but we can deal with that. It might not even see the light. We can deal with that, too. If you've made a pact unknowingly, the spirit might expect to stay. It's time to call in a helping hand.'

I heard what sounded like a large book being slid from tightly packed shelves, and the thumbing of thin pages.

'We're going to do this verbally,' Zoë said, breathing deeply and rhythmically. 'Repeat what I say. We'll do this three times. OK?'

'OK.'

'Good. Repeat after me . . .'

*

After the call and answer of Zoë's banishing ritual, I felt immediately better. The haggard, haunting face faded with each repetition until it was gone. Zoë asked for healing spirits 'from the light' to remove any lingering residue from the foreign spirits filling the spaces left behind. Then she carried out some 'protection work', a Sealing Light Meditation apparently: 'Imagine your entire body is filled with golden-white light, which extends like a protective bubble about an arm's length around your body.' She led me gently into another vision. 'We'll make sure that nothing can get back in to Sara.'

And that was it. I felt strange afterwards, thirsty, tearful, shaky, drained. It was as if I had just experienced a painful break-up with a long-term boyfriend. However destructive the relationship, I couldn't help feel a sense of loss at its end. I felt guilty, too, like I'd cheated on a diet. In a way, my 'exorcism' felt like an intellectual step backwards after a year of debunking myths and trying to ground my beliefs in something less . . . well . . . less hippy. I could not deny, though, the cathartic benefits of my strange experience. Whether spiritual or purely psychological, something had shifted inside me.

'It's completely normal to feel weird at this point,' Zoë reassured me. 'You've just undergone the spiritual equivalent of a major operation. Lots of attachments were released.'

I rubbed my eyes and blinked a couple of times. 'Is it normal to have so many? There seemed to be quite a crowd in there.'

She nodded. 'Oh yes, people can have hundreds.'

'Blimey. What about this break-up feeling, then? I feel really sad. Shouldn't I feel better now they're gone?'

'Don't worry. You're bound to feel peculiar when spirits are detached from you. A loss is a loss after all, even if it's for best,' she replied. 'Now that the process is over it's up to you to deal with the emotional vulnerability that first allowed the spiritual attachment to take place. Try meditation. Get back in touch with yourself, minus all those visitors jostling for influence. I generally advise a few follow-up sessions just to make sure everything's fine. But in the meantime, look after yourself. Remember the Sealing Light Meditation, it's a good one to do. I'll email it to you. Take baths with sea-salt, have early nights, be positive and I'll send you some remote healing. OK?'

When I left Zoë's house it was like leaving a friend. She waved me down the street, calling out her promise to be just a call away if I ever needed to talk again. As a strictly NHS girl, I've got to say, it was the greatest patient aftercare I had ever been offered.

Had it worked? Had there been anything to 'work' on? Objectively I have to say yes. Once the trauma of the day had subsided, I found myself in spring-clean mode. I wanted to go through everything – house, files, drawers, friendships. I felt positive, confident and free to make my own choices. And choice number one took no time at all. I wanted – I needed – to work things out with Toby. I just hoped he felt the same way.

For most people spirit release is an archaic concept. But strip away the spiritual vocab from the act of exorcising, rename the spirits 'syndromes' and what is left looks a lot like modern psychotherapy.

Spirit release therapy gets results. Log on to the web and look at the case studies. There are no drugs used, no endlessly drawn out treatment courses. It might well be just be short, sharp shock-therapy based on suggestion through hypnotherapy – although Zoë did suggest follow-up sessions – but for many people it truly works. I read that Dr Sanderson believes that, despite not having 'factual status', the concept of spiritual release is at least worth investigating. And considering the benefits for those who embrace his line of treatment, and the effect it had on me, I tend to agree.

I'm still not quite sure what happened to me along the Caledonian Road. Something odd occurred that affected me on every level. There was an ignition spark, a sense of relief. For me, the angry apostate pining for her lost Lord, the process of surrendering to a hypnotic trance, was at least half the appeal of exorcism as a spiritual cleansing exercise. In a suggestible dreamlike state, the brain stops bothering with logic and reality. It just soaks up the ambience and spits back ideas like an automatic tennis ball server. Under the soothing influence of Zoë's voice, and closed to the world beyond my own personal space, I was briefly able to believe again. But I'd never be able to find out whether or not it was truly real; I just had to accept that something had happened that felt beneficial.

I left Zoë's place and staggered to the tube on autopilot. I was going home, back to Toby. My mind was made up. I wanted to be in love again. I wanted us to go back to planning our wedding, our future, as quickly as possible. I didn't know for sure he'd be there waiting for me, though, and the uncertainty was boiling my innards. And if he was there, would I tell him what I'd just done? No doubt he'd find it foolish. But I needed to believe it, for me, and if Toby couldn't respect that, well ... we'd be back to square one.

EX'S INTERRUPTION

Toby

She'd done it. I couldn't believe she'd actually done it. She'd 'gone home to Mother' – albeit only for the weekend – leaving me to stew in my own juices like a 70s sitcom cliché.

Sara and I never go to bed on an argument. It's an unspoken rule that works well for our passionate temperaments. The understanding that everything will be fine by bedtime sets a time limit on our rows, although it does mean the occasional very late night when neither of us is prepared to give ground, however attractive the prospect of sleep. This time, though, Sara had really gone. I considered the prospect of bachelorhood temporarily regained. Not that I was about to hit the meat markets, but a weekend of snack foods, kung-fu movies and sleeping had its charms.

Not for the first time, I cursed the God I didn't believe in for providing the fly in the ointment of an otherwise trouble-free relationship. Sara's search for spiritual significance had led her to a darker place than either of us imagined it would. My clumsy announcement that I was 'past caring' and would marry her however and wherever she wanted had come too late. Without her faith, Sara was losing interest in marriage altogether, just as I was realizing how important it had become to me.

The problem, I decided, was my own lack of empathy. With no experience of hereditary faith, my sense of the spiritual was limited to a sort of vague affinity with nature. I couldn't hope to know what Sara had lost. Indeed, I wore my ignorance of God like an atheist's badge of honour. No wonder Sara wanted to escape for a while. As she struggled with her loss of faith, all I could offer was impatient cynicism. Whether it helped or not, at least at home with her mum and dad, Sara would know that she was in somebody's prayers.

I cursed my lack of empathy as I paced our empty flat. Short of developing temporal lobe epilepsy, I wished desperately for a taste of Sara's visionary experience. Something I could share with her, an inkling of what it meant to believe.

In an article in *New Scientist*, I had read about a Canadian neurologist, Dr Michael Persinger, who developed a helmet that uses electro-magnetic waves to stimulate various sensual responses in the wearer. Every human emotion from lust to grief, he claims, can be aroused at the touch of a button for the wearer of his 'Korin Helmet'. But there's another, more remarkable feature of Persinger's magic hat. By tickling just the right spot with the right kind of electro-magnetic pulse, he has found that he can conjure up God. Just like that.

Hundreds of volunteers have slipped on the Korin Helmet and met their maker. The overwhelming majority of test subjects report a feeling of euphoric calm, coupled with the sense of a benign presence. The sensation is interpreted in different ways. Some subjects claim to have felt the nearness of lost loved ones. Others limit their description of the experience to the physical symptoms: a flood of warmth and a feeling of release from care. For the faithful, though, the experience seems easier to describe. Jesus, they have asserted confidently – or Allah or Yaweh or Mary – was with me. Right here, in the room.

Persinger's theory is that somewhere in the cross-wiring of the brain, where language meets our sense of the self, things have become tangled. The task of contemplating one's consciousness, he reasons, is literally mind-boggling. So the brain has evolved a neat little trick to distract us from the path of self-deconstruction. Dig too deeply into the nature of existence and up pops 'God', hovering in the back of our minds, mentally patting us on the back and telling us not to worry about such things. Of course, the faithful have got a terrific comeback, as usual. Dr Persinger's toy, they argue, cleverly replicates the serene euphoria of a religious experience but, like own-brand cola, it's not the real thing.

Electro-magnetism is present in nature, of course, so the hardened atheist might in turn argue that exposure to natural waves has led to a sort of low-level Korin effect, promoting myth-making and religious devotion in human culture. It's a curious coincidence that southern California, the undisputed capital of New Age America, is bathed with electro-magnetism, thanks to the region's constantly shifting geology. Perhaps it's not the sun that's frying the brains of La-La Land's Scientologists and rainbow-worshippers after all.

At one time, I had hoped to make the trek north and try Persinger's helmet for myself. It seemed a neat solution to my lack of spiritual empathy. An opportunity to see, however briefly, how the other half lived. The long silences that followed my repeated appeals to Dr Peringer, however, suggested that he might have had his fill of writers. Several had joined the ranks of the doctor's test subjects; not all had been respectful or generous to the doctor's scientific endeavour. One waggish webhead had written him off as little more than Uri Geller in a labcoat. Unsurprisingly, the offending journalist had been among the minority of subjects whose third eye failed to open, despite the persistent prising of his third eyelid.

I didn't blame Dr Persinger for wanting to keep a low profile, all things considered. However, as I contemplated dinner alone, I wished I had a Korin Helmet I could test-drive at home to get me back on Sara's wavelength. I plodded through the quiet hallway and into the kitchen, wishing we had a cat.

In the kitchen, I slid one chop under the grill and chucked a pathetic handful of french beans into our smallest saucepan. No potatoes. There were mushrooms in the fridge, though. Big, frilly posh ones from the reduced items shelf at Sainsbury's. I rinsed a handful under the cold tap, chopped garlic and threw the lot in a frying pan with a glug of olive oil. They sizzled and shrank satisfyingly, filling the tiny kitchen with their rich aroma. I stirred the beans, turned my chop and grabbed a mushy from the pan. As a kid I hated mushrooms. Even when chopped down to a subatomic level and hidden in my Mum's bolognaise, the merest suggestion of a mushroom would literally turn my stomach.

'Funny how your tastes change,' I muttered aloud, accustomed to having Sara's ear. 'Mushrooms are magic . . .'

My words trailed off as a plan formed in my mind. Had I stumbled on a shortcut to spiritual salvation?

'All right, God,' I dared, glancing upwards involuntarily. 'Come and get me.'

*

I spent a lonely night in our king-sized bed, tossing and turning under a duvet that seemed unmanageably large without Sara to anchor her half to the mattress. At nine the next morning, I made a no-nonsense dash to London on the Gatwick Express, arriving at Oxford Circus by tube one hour later.

By midday, London's busiest shopping street would be teeming with weekenders, but at this time, pedestrian traffic was still mercifully light. Oxford Street provides the northern border to my London stomping ground these days. Since escaping from the Kilburn/West Hampstead border, my movements in town had been limited to the off-off-Oxford Street office where I wrote the gravelly-voiced voice-overs for movie trailers. I have always loved working in W1. As pretentious as it sounds, there really is a hidden sense of community among the beer-swilling, pavement hounds of Soho and Noho. On a summer afternoon, when the work's dried up, the sun's come out and the streets are packed with drinkers perching their pints on pub window-sills, there's really nowhere I would rather be. On the weekends, though, the city is stuffed to the sky with casual visitors who dawdle along like lakeland ramblers and block your every move with designer carrier bags. I avoid London like nits on Saturdays, but I was here on a mission and hoped to be home in Sussex before the bulk of the shoppers and sightseers descended.

I wove my way up Oxford Street through the gathering crowd, stopping at one of the slightly shabby no-name boutiques that pepper the unfashionable end of the thorough-fare. The shop's stock was mostly cheap designer gear, but set aside from the Ben Sherman shirts and Tommy Hilfiger boxer shorts was a long glass counter containing an incongruous collection of tacky London souvenirs and the kind of smoking paraphernalia that has absolutely nothing to do with humidors or pipe-cleaners.

I was admiring an elaborate, three-headed bong when a spotty teenager wearing the world's last active Hypercolor T-shirt appeared behind the counter and looked me up and down with dewy, bloodshot eyes.

'Help you?' he mumbled, rubbing a hash-blackened thumb against his bottom teeth. I pointed at a sign on the counter, hand-drawn in multicoloured felt-tipped pens: 'FRESH MAGIC MUSHROOMS. TOTAL HEAD F*CK. ORNA-MENTAL OR RESEARCH PURPOSES ONLY.'

'Right,' mumbled Spotty, turning to open the door of a small fridge. 'Mexican. Psilocybe Cubensis. Thirty grams for a tenner.' He popped the lid of a Tupperware pot and displayed the contents; a handful of broad-stalked fungi, three inches or so in length, topped with little orangey balls of psychoactive goodness.

'They're very pretty,' I said, sniffing the shrooms and nodding like an expert. Spotty looked blank. I pointed at the sign. 'Ornamental purposes.'

'Yeah. Whatever,' said Spotty, snapping shut the lid of his pot, lest the magic get loose. 'Tenner.'

I handed over a note and Spotty weighed out my Mexican mushrooms before handing them over in a brown paper bag.

'Thank you. What should I expect?' I asked, waggling my bag. 'If, for example, I was examining my ornamental mushrooms and they fell into my mouth unexpectedly . . .'

'Giggly,' said Spotty, succinctly.

'Oh,' I answered, a little crestfallen. I was looking for a win-dow on Heaven, not a giggling fit. 'Well . . .' I turned to leave.

'Wait,' called Spotty. I turned back. 'You doing the whole lot yourself?'

I felt the weight of the little brown bag in my cupped hand and shrugged, nonchalantly.

'Yeah,' I said. Spotty's moist, pink eyes widened dramatically. 'What?' I asked. Spotty pushed out his bottom lip and nodded slowly, obviously impressed.

'Nice one.'

'And?' I blinked emphatically.

'Very fucking giggly,' said Spotty. 'At first.'

From Oxford Street, I rode the tube south to Victoria and the airport express back to Gatwick, where I coughed up a fiver to collect the car. I stuck to the speed limit all the way home, pondering the precise legal status of the powerful hallucinogens tucked in my glove box. As I understood things, the possession of magic mushrooms was legal in Britain, provided they were living or left untreated. Their consumption was a grey area that I had left uninvestigated, reasoning that ignorance, even wilful ignorance, was a better defence than no defence at all. I'd set my mind on a mushroom dinner, and the law be hanged. But behind the wheel of a car, guilt and paranoia nudged at my conscience. The psychoactive ingredient in Psilocybe Cubensis is comparable in effect to the synthetic hallucinogen LSD. You can get a five-year stretch for possession of acid. I just didn't feel comfortable with an ounce of the herbal alternative banging about next to my travel sweets.

I made it home unchecked, however, and immediately shook the contents of my little brown bag into a cereal bowl. In the hour or so since they had left the fridge in the head shop/clothes shop on Oxford Street, the white stalks of the fungi had acquired a mouldy, blue tinge that added to the impression of chemical potency. I poured myself a glass of water and carried my psychotropic snack through to the bedroom. Then I drew the curtains, unplugged the phone and tucked in.

Psilocybe Cubensis was the religious catalyst of choice for the Olmecs, Toltecs and Aztecs of pre-Hispanic Meoamerica. Its Aztec name, *teonanacatl*, means 'flesh of the gods'. For the record, God has an unremarkable, mild mushroomy flavour, and He's a bit stringy in the stalk.

With my Mexican mind-benders down and staying down, I booted up the laptop and logged on to a backgammon server. When the worldwide web's your oyster, there's always someone who'll come out to play and I was soon engaged in battle with a reckless but lucky American player calling himself Teflon Terry. He was three points up in a five-point match when my psychotropic supper made its presence felt. In fact, it was Terry who tipped me off in the in-game chat window, some time after the opening roll of game four:

Teflon_Terry says: Psst! U roll.

The message appeared with a gentle ping. I read and replied.

Starby says: Soz. Didn't realize.
Teflon_Terry says: Been 5 mins!

I read that one twice and checked the clock in the corner of the screen. I hadn't known the time five minutes ago so I had no way of knowing if now was really now or five minutes later. The chat window pinged again.

Teflon_Terry says: R U THERE? Havnt got all nite!

I frowned at my opponent's rudeness and glanced at the clock again. Doubletakes are like cold sweats. You assume they're just figures of speech until you experience them first-hand. I'd had my first cold sweat the night before my nuts were screened for mercifully non-existent tumours a couple of years earlier. And now I did my very first double-take. The clock had jumped from 2.10 to 2.14 in what I took to be the space of a few seconds. I rubbed my eyes – another cartoon gesture – and when I opened them again, everything had changed.

I could witter on about colours and contrast and texture, but it wouldn't begin to describe the shift in my perception when the mushrooms took hold. The world around me felt like a copy of the real one, precise in every detail, but built from entirely different materials. I became transfixed by every surface my eyes fell upon: the grain of the wooden bedstead; the neat weave of the cotton sheets. I scanned the room, slowly, drinking in the rich, warm colours that bled out of our deep red curtains on to the walls and ceiling. When I turned back to the laptop's luminescent screen, it was almost impossible to make sense of the images on screen. I was acutely aware of the thousands of pixels that made up the liquid crystal display and instead of well-defined images, I saw tiny, swirling, random points of colour. If I turned away and looked back quickly, or glanced out the corner of my eye, I could make out the familiar lay-out of my virtual backgammon board. But if I tried to focus on it directly for more than a moment, the illusion of solidity collapsed.

Covering the screen with my hands, I parted my fingers over the area I knew the chat window to be, and concentrated hard on the black and white text box. With less in the way of colours and shapes to distract me, I was able slowly to make sense of Teflon Terry's latest messages. I hadn't even heard the pings:

Teflon_Terry says: Well?
Teflon _Terry says: R U stoopid??
Teflon_Terry says: Fuck you then.
Teflon_Terry logs out.

Oops. Major backgammon faux pas. I resolved to apologize if I came across Terry on the server again.

As the latest wave of perceptual jiggery-pokery subsided, I got it together long enough to shut down the laptop, and fell back on the bed, breathing heavily and grinning like a chimp with his lips cut off. There were moments when I felt almost normal. They were vaguely anticlimactic, like the aftermath of a roller-coaster ride. They were short-lived, too. Eventually – I have no idea of the time-scale involved – my fleeting glimpses of sobriety were swallowed by a rising tide of euphoria and spectacle. Each wave of unreality was stronger than the last. I knelt on the bed, pouring over the intricate stitching on our Goan bedspread, like a twelve-year-old with the latest Potter novel. As I traced the gold thread across orange and pink silks that exploded with colour, I became aware of a pattern beneath – or perhaps beyond – the stitching itself; a pattern of impossible complexity that shifted and changed if I tried to get a fix on it.

I wriggled backwards on my knees, following the runaway pattern until I ran out of bed. Standing up, I was seized by the notion that a glass of water would be nice, and turned to make for the kitchen. To my amazement, the pattern that had defied close examination on my bedspread now covered the bedroom walls completely. The lining paper looked as if every available inch had been embossed, or watermarked, or both. I spun on the spot like a New York newbie in an MGM musical. Everything – the whole world – had been tattooed with one spectacularly detailed, cosmically significant design. At times, the pattern looked like Paisley, at others like the blackboard workings of a master mathematician. For a while, I saw floating fractals; the infinitely repeating shell-like designs that represent abstract numbers. There were aboriginal swirls and tessellating polygons; celtic knots and hieroglyphs. There was more than a flavour of the spiralling, animal-packed artworks that the mushroom-growing Mesoamericans were so fond of carving into their temples and tombs.

I never got my glass of water. The more I chased the ever-changing design over walls and ceiling, the more I thought I saw a logic to its elaborate flights of fancy. I stood in front of a favourite painting and looked beyond the soppy, pastoral watercolour to the very blueprints of creation. The pattern pulled me inwards to the horizon of the Shropshire scene. Trees swayed and the blue wash of the sky drifted around as if blown on a breeze. A voice, visible as bouncing, luminescent pearls, danced in the wake of the retreating pattern. 'This way,' it seemed to say. 'Deeper, and all will be revealed.'

For the first time, I was reminded of the purpose of my trip. This was business, not pleasure. I'd come looking for God, and if He hadn't turned up in person at least he'd had the good manners to leave a note.

For a moment, sanity reasserted itself. The tantalizing

sensation of having been on the brink of some enormous discovery was swept away. I took advantage of my moment of sobriety to take stock of the journey so far.

'Fuck,' I said aloud.

I hadn't really thought this through. Hadn't really considered the potential consequences of surrendering my ego to a psychotropic drug, with no one around to keep check on any mushroom-fuelled impulse to try public nudity or unpowered flight. I wished that Sara was around to make sure I didn't do anything silly.

'Fuck.'

A wave of prickly warmth spread up my body from my toes. My knees buckled as the wave washed over them.

'Woah.'

I could feel my mind slipping out of gear again. Time stretched and contracted unpredictably. I needed to ride this out somewhere safe. Somewhere comfy. What would Brian Wilson do?

I wobbled to the food cupboard, grabbed a bag of pretzels and bottle of R. Whites, wobbled back to the bedroom, gathered up the duvet and huddled in its feathery folds, grinning from ear to ear like a kid on a camping trip. And that's when thing's got really weird. I closed my eyes, and when I opened them again, I was not alone.

The air – no, that's not quite right – the *substance* of the physical world – every object in the room and every inch of space between – had been sliced, vertically, into a series of fine, freestanding, crystal sheets. The universe, I calmly observed, existed on a million different, overlapping planes, like a gigantic toy theatre. And gliding between the scenery, formless but beautiful nonetheless, were angels. This is what they told me:

Human beings are creatures of light. Our essence is eternal and unchanging. The physical world is inconsequential. It is merely an aspect of reality that we have learned to exploit for our own diversion, the pleasures of physical existence being judged to outweigh the myriad short-term pitfalls. Our time in the physical realm is short and, as such, should be cherished. We should dance in the light of the physical realm, feel the warmth of the sun on our skin. Give comfort to those in pain and friendship to those in need. Rejoice in the nearness of other souls. And, above all else, love.

I endured a fitful night of stomach cramps and mental realignment. The sense of anticlimax was crushing. Perhaps the strangest thing about the use of external stimuli for the purpose of mind expansion is that the very moment the stimulus wears off, the mind shrinks.

That's if you're lucky. Those who spend too long inside their heads occasionally find it impossible to find their way out. My come-down was sprinkled with mildly scary experiences. Faces on the TV seemed either beatifically beautiful, or impishly ugly. My inner dialogue – a noisy blend of rational thoughts and disjointed gibberish – was an impassable obstacle to sleep. I lay on my front with my face in the pillow, waiting for my discomfort to subside. At one point, I lay on my hands, frightened that if I freed them, I might scratch at my dry eyes and leave them bloody and torn. Take heed, would-be psychonauts, and save the mushrooms for 'ornamental purposes'. A taste of madness is much worse than none at all.

At dawn, as I peed out the last of my mind-bending,

Mexican mushies in a stream of Penguin paperback orange, my glimpse of the 'truth' seemed dull and silly. In my deepest reverie, I had accepted, without question, every dream my drug-addled brain had conjured. In the harshness of sobriety, with my intellect raggedly restored, the evidence no longer stood up. I mean, who was I going to believe? Some shroomed-up hippy who's frightened of the telly, or my own, mercifully restored self?

In retrospect, the vision I experienced was suspiciously appropriate to my established sensibilities. The Mesoamerican Indians apparently met fiery, wrathful gods who demanded human sacrifice – something that, had I considered it before, might have kept me away from my mushroom supper altogether. I met a bunch of charming but aimless astral travellers who basically told me to chill out and enjoy myself. The vision allowed me to feel good about the vaguery of my spiritual position.

As I stared at a soggy bowl of uneaten Cornflakes, I wondered whether my dalliance with the Timothy Leary school of enlightenment had been of any lasting benefit. Even under the cloud of my morning come-down, I couldn't help taking a guilty pride in my night of hallucinogenic excess. It was all very rock star. I would certainly remember my vision, even if I could not find it in myself to trust its substance. Was that all I was taking away? A dinner party anecdote and a newfound empathy with the schizophrenic?

I tipped my Cornflakes into the sink and pulled up Sara's Southend number on my mobile. I told myself that I hadn't decided whether or not to tell her about my somewhat irresponsible actions the night before. She would probably think I'd been stupid. She would probably be right. Inevitably,

I would confess; I knew that, of course. I would face the music and try to explain myself later. In the meantime, I just wanted her home.

As I hovered over the dial button on my ancient Motorola, I wondered how Sara had spent our weekend apart. Had time and distance healed the rift between us, or had I chipped away too long at my love's defences, opening an unbridgeable gulf? With cold-hearted pomposity, I had dismissed Sara's loss of faith as an unfortunate side-effect of her intellectual progress. Not progress towards the truth, I now realized, or towards God. Just progress towards agreeing with me. I thought I had been playing devil's advocate. In truth, I had been a sneering bully.

Suddenly, I realized the lasting lesson of my nocturnal dalliance with Psilocybe Cubensis. For one night only, in the company of angels, I truly believed. What I believed, precisely, is already obscure and fractured, but the feeling remains. The feeling of *faith*.

It was nice, for a moment, to let go of uncertainty, to surrender myself to the seductive simplicity of unquestionable truth. As I stood in our poky kitchen, staring at Sara's name on the tiny green screen of my phone, I missed her with all of my heart. Somewhere else, somewhere deeper, another ache was throbbing faintly. I covered my eyes and sobbed, suddenly and from the depths of my body, for my absent love, and my lost faith.

My mobile buzzed in my hand. I jumped and answered without checking the screen.

'Toby Starbuck.'

'Toby Starbuck,' said the caller, 'it's Sara Hulse, I'm . . .' She sighed heavily.

'I'm sorry,' I blurted, 'I really love you. Please come home.' There was a long pause and – what – a sob? 'What's wrong?' I asked, hoping with all my heart that Sara wasn't warming up to a big speech. The kind that starts with *it's not you* and ends with *friends*.

'Maybe nothing,' said Sara, 'maybe something. I don't know. I've . . . I've found a lump.'

'You've . . .' My voice trailed away.

Sara came back, chirpier but not convincingly. 'I'm sure it's nothing to worry about,' she squeaked. Her voice sounded as if the back of her throat had been glued shut. 'It's probably a cyst or something. I'd better have it checked out when I get home, though.'

'You are coming home?' I asked

'Of course I am,' said Sara.

'And you'll go to the doctor as soon as you get here, darling, won't you? I know you hate going, but don't fuck about. Come back now, OK? Promise.'

'I promise.'

'Because you know . . .' I trailed off again, my voice caught in my throat.

'I know,' said Sara.

One in three people will develop a form of cancer during their lives. And about one in four will feel compelled to write about it. The Cancer Confidential has become a literary genre in its own right, with the reading public regularly assailed by tales of triumphant recovery and tragic loss. I would not presume to add anything significant to the literary canon on the subject of one of Britain's biggest killers except to reiterate an oft-stated and commonly held opinion: cancer is a bitch.

I don't remember anything significant about the first time my mother got breast cancer. In part, this is because my parents chose to lighten the load of my final college year by playing down the severity of Mum's condition. At some point during her four years of remission, following a rather obvious mastectomy and follow-up radiotherapy, the full story came out. She had found a lump and visited Elizabeth Jennings, our family GP, that day. Elizabeth moved quickly and called the local hospital, who squeezed Mum in for immediate tests. By five o'clock the following afternoon, my parents knew that Mum had a malignant tumour that, left unchecked, might kill her before she reached fifty. Mum told the story of her brush with death with chirpy triumphalism. She had beaten cancer; of course she had. My mother, despite her slender frame, was a woman for whom the word formidable was coined. At the school where she taught, she was feared, loved and respected in equal measure by the children in her class. At home, she was the trouser-wearing, friend-scaring scourge of the badly behaved. I listened to her story with shock and relief, extracting a promise that should any further family health issues arise, I would be informed immediately. Mum kissed me on the cheek and that was that. We had four good years.

Mum and I had come on a long way since we bumped heads on a daily basis back in the eighties. When I was growing up, she was probably less strict than outsiders would have guessed. She was, however, noisily reproachful, which is not quite the same thing as authoritarian, but which undoubtedly led to friction when my sister and I hit our teens. My mother and I did nothing to ease each other's passage through puberty and menopause, respectively. We fought like cat and dog for several years. The fact that I can no longer recall the substance of a single argument – aside from a shamefully memorable teenage tantrum following the disposal of my old cub camp soap dish – leads me to believe that our protracted and painful conflict was nothing but mutual, hormonal bluff and bluster. In retrospect, I never once doubted my mother's love. And, while we did not share secrets or socialize in the manner to which parents of teenage children inevitably, and pointlessly, aspire, I always knew my mum and dad would come through for me. Nevertheless, when I left home for university, via a gap year in the States, the sense of release and freedom was, I'm sure, entirely mutual.

Time and distance healed any lingering adolescent sores. By my mid-twenties, my mother and I enjoyed a closeness that would have been unthinkable to me a decade earlier. The news that her cancer had returned hit me hard.

True to her promise, Mum pulled no punches when she summoned me to her aunt's Kingston home to pass on the awful truth. Following minor chest pains, which she initially dismissed as a cracked rib, she had been X-rayed at the Princess Royal Hospital in Telford. The images revealed advanced secondary cancers in her ribs and lungs. The odds of her surviving the next six months were given as ten to one. It was March and, she told me, she bloody well intended to be around for Christmas.

In the end, my formidable mother had another two and a half years and three whole Christmases. The last one was a traumatic affair. Physically able, if considerably weakened, for much of her fight, Mum slid suddenly into leaden immobility. At her cousin Jackie's seaside home, we spent a pleasant Christmas Eve, glossing over the obvious gravity of her sudden and shocking decline. On Christmas Day, though, she was gone entirely.

She hadn't died. (That wouldn't happen until 30 January at 1.30 p.m., while I sat in silence with my sister on the delayed 10.45 a.m. from Euston to Shrewsbury.) But from breakfast to the Queen's speech, Mum was entirely absent.

We sat in the living room, opening presents, but her face was fixed in a disturbing mask of childish curiosity. Not a trace of recognition as a succession of gifts were unwrapped and passed under her nose. Later, she sat staring at the ceiling with a look of distant reverie and total calm. At lunch, she picked at her food carelessly. A pair of tiny, plastic scissors – from one of the Christmas crackers – had to be wrested from her mouth after a few tentative chews failed to convince her that they were not food.

'What you doin', Pen?' asked Dad, gently, taking the scissors away and guiding her back towards the sprouts. I let out a burst of nervous laughter and got an angry glare from my father. Mum's detachment and loss of self were symptomatic of temporal lobe swelling. The cancer, which had reached her brain, had moved into a new phase. I'd read enough Oliver Sachs to recognize the symptoms for myself. And I'd borrowed the book off Dad. My laughter was a hysterical response to the dawning of an awful truth. My mum really was going to die.

On Boxing Day, she rallied round. She seemed calm, although she was probably terrified, when we filled her in on the previous day's events, going easy on the disturbing details. Her Christmas presents were re-presented and gratefully received. We watched a movie, *Play Misty For Me*, and listened to John Martin's mournful, melodic folk music on my cousin Angus's stereo. In the afternoon, Mum napped, while we went for a tramp along the ragged Selsey shoreline. I walked arm in arm with Sara, wondering how long we had Mum for, and what would happen when the holiday ended. From my infrequent childhood visits to Jackie, Rod and their three boys, I remembered a road, running along the beach, wide enough for two cars to pass. It had gone now, washed into the sea by twenty years of high tides and high winds. A handful of weather-worn houses at the edge of the land looked likely to follow.

'It'll be all right,' said Sara. 'Sorry. I mean, I know it won't, but I'm here for you. I love you.'

I pulled her close and strode into the wind.

Mum's will to live had never been in question, so far as I was concerned. Her drive to beat the odds, so starkly presented, was typical of a lifelong doggedness and unquenchable optimism. Only when the morphine – drip-fed into her weightless arm at the Shropshire hospice where she died – dulled her wits and quieted her voice, did my mother's defiance of her disease fail. Nevertheless, the gravity of her situation was something the whole family had to come to terms with extremely quickly. The notion that 'positivity' of the touchy-feely, green veg and grilled chicken, crystal-wearing, soul-bearing, Californian variety, might somehow overturn a diagnosis of terminal cancer was given short shrift in the Starbuck household. It's great when somebody confounds the considered opinions of the specialists who treat them, to beat back advanced cancer. But 'positivity' is an asset overrated by those who live to tell the tale, perhaps because the belief that they were in large part responsible for their own survival eases fears of a future relapse. In any such survival story, have no doubt, the plot turns on the toss of a coin. And my mother's luck had run out.

Losing a parent changes your life in ways you do not expect. Forewarning of a parent's death forces you to consider the implications of their absence from your life before that actually happens. It had been at least ten years since I relied on Mum for clean shirts and nutritious meals. Longer – being of an independent bent from a relatively early age – since I had honestly felt that I 'needed' her, in the 'rub it all better' sense. But to acknowledge that soon – in no time at all – we would lose her made me reconsider dreams and plans that were only half-conscious. Children, a family of my own, had always been a vaguely held ambition. Now, I realized, I was mourning as much for my children's grandmother as for my own mother. With her untimely death, my cosy conjured visions of future family life were meaningless. Their Norman Rockwell symmetry – Gramps, Grammy, Ma, Pa 'n' the twins – would have to be replaced with something else. Something different. Something worse. How could it not be? My mother would be dead.

The wind whipped Sara's long hair across my cheek. We stopped, facing each other, and I stroked it down as she gazed up at me, concerned. I wished that I had met her five years earlier. We might be further down the line. Mum might have got to know her grandchildren. She would certainly have had a wedding to go to. Even that, I acknowledged painfully, looked a remote possibility now.

Sara squeezed my waist and opened her mouth to say something, then sighed and shrugged, hopelessly. I wanted to marry her more than ever at that moment. I wanted to wake the local vicar and marry her on the beach, with my mother as witness. Then we could adopt a couple of kids and all go back to Jackie's for tea and mince pies.

*

Although Sara and I got engaged after I learned about my mother's terminal illness, I told myself that my decision to ask for her hand was in no way influenced by my mother's plight. In fact, I repressed the urge to pop the question for months while I decided for myself whether marriage plans and mourning, pre-emptive or otherwise, were compatible. In Sara, I knew I had found the woman I wanted to spend the rest of my life with. She was perfect combination of brains and beauty, warmth and humour, talent, sexiness, energy and oomph. Ultimately, I couldn't wait any longer. The hope that Mum might make it to the wedding was there, of course, and perhaps it was a factor in the timing of my proposal. There were plenty of compelling reasons to ask for Sara's hand in marriage, and none of them were about Mum. Waiting for my mother's death to confirm my heart's desire, I reasoned, was perverse and self-destructive. It had a touch of fairy tale about it. The scary, violent, German woodcut kind of fairy tale that always ends badly.

As we warmed up from our walk in Jackie's familiar family living room, the mood was superficially light. Mum, fresh from forty winks, pored over the Christmas *Radio Times* as leftovers appeared on trays. Traditionally, the purchase of a TV guide had been always been restricted to the holiday season in my mother's house. This was just one of many amusingly nonsensical TV-related snobberies that Mum entertained. She also maintained, at various times, an adamant objection to breakfast television, *Tiswas*, *Grange Hill*, *The A-Team*, *Neighbours* – which she rarely missed – and that arch enemy of culture, decorum and society in general, Sky 1.

I watched her as she channel-hopped and chewed a nail,

absent-mindedly. The pitiful disorientation of the day before was hard to picture. She seemed fine. Sara picked up on my thoughts and squeezed my hand gently, shuffling closer on the sofa. We scanned the room together, sharing and storing the picture of a family Christmas that we could not hope to repeat. Sara shuddered and hugged me tightly, stifling a sigh. I held her close, smiling as Mum caught my eye. She beamed back, glancing from me to Sara's curled form, and winked naughtily. That was the moment I knew for sure I had made the right decision with Sara. It was the moment that my dreams suddenly advanced beyond carving T + S 4 EVA into the registry office desk, and into the realms of children and families and Christmases of our own in our happy hypothetical home.

And now? I perched on the edge of our bed – the first we'd bought together – feeling like a jumper on a window ledge. Changing the sheets, I had uncovered a misplaced pair of Sara's woolly winter mittens underneath the mattress. Sara's hands are so small that she can wear one-size-fits-all gloves without stretching them out of their factory shape. She's small all over, something I love about her, though even I couldn't help but find the difference in our heights vaguely comical at the outset. Ah well, better to have loved a short woman than never to have loved a tall . . .

I knew that the lump might be nothing significant; might be nothing at all. But I couldn't suppress the wave of terror that swept over me as I considered the worst case scenario. Sara and I had vowed to spend the rest of our lives together. Did life have other plans?

LIGHTS GO GREEN

A few weeks after I found the lump in my breast, I visited the day-long, one-stop breast clinic at Crawley Hospital for further tests. Toby came with me, arming himself with a paperback novel and plenty of change for the vending machines. We settled in silence, and waited. Luckily for me, it was good news.

I knew just how fortunate I was when I was finally able to leave the hospital, but I was uncomfortably aware there were others present who would be less lucky. I'd shared a long day of prodding and poking, reading worn magazines and staring into space with a group of women I didn't know and hadn't even spoken to, but whose familiarity, however faint, was a comfort in the long day. A silent bond had been established with the nods we shared as we passed in the corridors and queued with our forms. And now, at the end of the day, we were to be called into the doctor's office one by one to find out whether or not we had cancer. It seemed surreal and cruel, like a life or death redundancy consultation. It was shift change for the hospital staff. A buzz of activity, crisp uniforms and rested smiles clashed against the weary, ashen silence of our waiting group. The only sound was the flimsy crackle of pages being turned from the pile of dog-eared *Bella*s and *Best*s.

The doctor didn't smile when he told us that the lump in my breast was benign. No doubt he felt the need to distance himself emotively from the many revelations and reactions his evening would hold. But his sternness unsettled me and I didn't quite register the happy result.

Toby picked up on my confusion, reaching out to steady me as the colour drained from my face: 'Benign, babe. Everything's fine.'

I waited a moment, breathing deeply, in case my mind was playing tricks on me, but the good news was real. I thanked the doctor, fighting the urge to cry, and hurried out, past the waiting room, feeling guilty and suddenly out of place. The woman who got her results before me was pacing the corridor with a worried-looking nurse, sobbing uncontrollably.

We sat in the car in silence. We were relieved, of course we were, but bewildered and emotional too. Since I found the lump, time had stopped and so many worries had become irrelevant. Over the weeks that I'd waited to find out what, if anything, was wrong, I hadn't realized that everything else in my life had taken a back seat. I had been entirely occupied with suppressing the rising tide of denial, terror, shock, anger, panic and utter helplessness inside. The world had lurched beneath me, leaving me shaken and unsure about everything. Toby remained strong and supportive, but I could see the fear lurking and felt guilty for putting him through this. It hadn't been that long since his mum died. Since then any diagnosis of cancer sounded like a death sentence to Toby.

My brush with breast cancer gave me my first glimpse of what it might mean to have a terminal illness. The strength and courage needed to cope with such a shitty hand are staggering. However solid your support, you're always alone when you face death. I thought a lot about these everyday heroes; my own mum, Penny, my wonderful friend Vandana. One winner, one loser, one beautiful girl fighting hard, determined to beat it. While all of us know that death is inevitable, some have to live with that reality every waking moment. I really knew now how lucky I was.

A while after the ordeal had passed I realized that it was the first time I hadn't leaned on religion in a crisis, although my mum probably had contacts at the Vatican doing circuits round the rosary for me. Before Toby and I set out on my naive expedition to locate the divine creator, analyse love, seek out inner peace and find the perfect wedding, I would have assumed that illness was part of God's inexplicable plan. I would have sent prayers and accusations hurtling into the ether, then more prayers apologizing for the accusations. I would have lit candles, cried in empty churches and wondered what I had done to deserve it all. But the status of my faith felt a little like the bloodied hollow of butchered self-dentistry and I couldn't turn to the mess I'd made for support. I tried to pray, even finding myself kneeling in a sparse hospital chapel, desperate for comfort. And while I admit there was a part of me that took comfort from simply being there, I ended up feeling even more confused, inconsolable and alone, worried even, that my problems were revenge from a wrathful God. So instead I turned to my family, Toby and friends, and found what I needed. If God does exist, wouldn't he enlist corporeal helpers anyway? In truth, I missed the inner dialogue and the comfort of prayer. While you're praying at least you're acting on something and somehow this gives you hope. When faced with the possibility of death I admit that I wanted my faith back because I wanted to believe in Heaven. Maybe one day I'll have that again. In the meantime the support I felt this time was tangible, not hidden in the lofty arches of an empty church or dependent on a divine plan that I wasn't privy to.

After leaving the hospital that day, Toby and I had hugged in silence in the car park. In the car, the silence gave way to tears for both of us, then more hugs and kisses. Neither of us said anything about my 'all clear' – there weren't enough words. The relief and the love were palpable. I found my voice.

'I need a drink.'

Toby nodded and pulled out of the hospital car park in search of liquor.

Crawley is a bit of an ugly, over-developed town, littered with car parks and faddish commercial architecture. It's the sort of place that looks as though it might have sustained massive bomb damage during the Second World War. It didn't, mind you; the good people of Crawley – the planners and the pen-pushers – did this to themselves. The town offers handy access to metropolitan mod cons like cinemas and department stores, when the lowing of the cattle outside our window gets too much for Toby and I in our rural love nest.

Toby and I sat in the window of a wine bar in Crawley's one unmolested street, watching an argument develop between a pair of pubescent parents across the way. The young father, who was suffering from fatigue brought on by a double armful of alcopops and bottled lager, was debating the propriety of offloading his burden into the baby's pram, in increasingly fruity terms. His lady companion, in matching baseball cap and moustache, felt that there might be some risk to the said baby, were he forced to share his carriage with twenty-four loose, heavy glass objects. Her beau pointed out that there would be considerable risk to both her and baby – at an unspecified future point – if she attempted to prevent his chosen course of action. With violence seemingly imminent, a last-minute compromise was reached and the wailing infant was wrenched from his snuggery to make way for the booze. The family's journey continued; doting daddy pushing his pram of grog, with mother and her babe-in-arms bringing up the rear.

'This is better than *Hollyoaks*,' I said, nursing a large vodka and tonic. 'Why isn't there a soap set in Crawley?'

'Would you leave a van full of filming equipment around here?'

'Point. Nevertheless . . .'

My musing was cut short by a tap on the shoulder. Toby glanced up to see who wanted me and flinched involuntarily. The smiling woman at my side was breathtaking in a way that would never lead to modelling contracts or marriage to a millionaire. And the sincerity of her smile was unknowable, because her lips – like her nose, ears and all but a tiny fringe of fine, black hair – had been burned away entirely.

Toby forced a smile, but was obviously reeling from the shock of the unfortunate young woman's disfigurement. I, looking up over my shoulder, smiled too, but I could feel my breathing quicken. Hers was the kind of scarring you can't ignore. The kind you pretend to, because there's nothing in the world you can say that's appropriate, or helpful, or remotely meaningful. Nobody would ever ask this girl how she came by her scars, the way you might tease a shark bite story out of a surfer, or bar brawl memories from a bouncer. It was immediately obvious what had befallen this poor soul. The horror of the scene – her trial by fire – was written in the tight creases of her stretched cheeks and crumpled scalp.

'I wondered ith you were interested in a crayer neeting.'

'What?' I shook myself. 'Sorry?'

'On Thriday ethening,' said the woman, in a pleasant voice that placed her in her late teens/early twenties. 'A gactist neeting at the—'

I had to say something, quickly. 'Oh, hang on,' I interrupted as politely as possible, 'look, I'm really sorry, but we're just not interested.' I turned to Toby. 'Right?'

'Right,' he answered, smiling apologetically at the wounded missionary.

It was completely obvious my firmness was a revelation to him. I am usually a soft touch for the soul scouts. Toby is the one who sends them packing.

'Gut,' said the lipless missionary, 'it's inthortant to nake your kiece with God vethore the end.'

'Thank you, but really, we're not interested.' I felt terrible.

The missionary's unclosing eyes surveyed us in turn. I held her gaze with a polite but firm smile. Toby took the coward's option, raising his eyebrows and shrugging in silent conspiracy with the jilted Baptist. The shiny, poreless skin around her mouth stretched back to reveal an extra pair of pearly whites at each side of her smile.

'OK,' she said, with a resigned nod of the head. 'Think agout it, though. You could get hit gy a gus tonorrow.'

'Or rolled in burning tar,' Toby murmured as she targeted a couple at the back of the room. 'Poor thing.'

The sympathy that we could not voice face to ravaged face poured out of us once we were left alone. We vented our horror and guilt with broad exclamations of admiration ('isn't she brave?') and self-diminution ('I couldn't live like that'). Then, when the shock of our encounter had subsided, my hard line rose to the surface once again.

'Bit of a cheap trick, mind you,' I smiled into the remnants of my drink, 'sending someone you can't just tell to fuck off.'

'That's more or less what you did, and very effectively.'

'Well, I decided the right thing to do was to treat her like anybody else. She's a person in her own right, not just the victim of a horrible accident. And I'm not in the mood to be saved. Not twice in one day.'

'It sounds like you've come to some kind of decision,' Toby said. 'A year ago you would have invited her home for tea.'

'You know what?' I asked, straightening in my seat. 'I think I have. This whole cancer thing. Do you realize neither of us has said the 'c' word for a fortnight? Well, it shook me pretty badly.'

'You and me both, babe.'

'I know. But it was a first for me. A bona fide brush with my own mortality. And the first time I've faced a personal crisis without my faith to fall back on.'

'And?'

'And it was all right, you know? I mean, it was shitty – completely shitty – but I came through. After everything I've seen this year it's difficult to believe that five minutes of bedside kneeling a day would have made much of a difference, although it might have made me *feel* better because I was actually trying to do something about it. We've met priests and brahmin, atheists and apostates and all manner of believers, and the only thing you can really say with any certainty is that not one of them knows any better than all the rest. We might well be on our own in this life and we have to find our own path. That can include a belief in God, if you want, but it's pointless and destructive to try to foist your version of an unknowable truth on other people.'

'You sound like a proper radical,' Toby teased, clearly impressed by the calm conviction in my statement. 'Are you telling me we can put an end to all this rainbow-chasing?'

'Do you want to?' I asked.

'Don't get me wrong,' he covered my hand with his across the table, 'I've enjoyed it, in part at least. I mean, we got about, didn't we?'

'New York,' I sighed.

'Old York.'

'India.'

'Oh God, India. Given six months in a sari, I could have been a Hindu, you know. I really respect their beliefs.'

'The way you were feeling when we got there, two weeks and a turban would've turned you Sikh. The point is, I've enjoyed most of it, haven't you? But we've also fought more than I thought possible, we're no closer to any great "truth" than we were when we started, and – unless you've forgotten – soul-searching nearly scuppered our relationship. You left me, Sara, albeit briefly.'

I covered my ears, melodramatically. 'Don't say it out loud.' I grinned like the Cheshire Cat.

Again the apologies about the huge argument that almost ended us came thick and fast from both sides. Toby was sorry for having been dogmatic and dismissive. I was sorry for jumping to conclusions. He was sorry for jumping down my throat. I was sorry for not talking things over rationally. He was sorry for being a patronizing arsehole. I was sorry for running off. He was sorry for chasing me away. Essentially, then, everybody was really, really sorry.

'You know what,' Toby said suddenly. 'I've got an idea to get you and me properly back on track.'

'You want me to Feng Shui the house?'

'No, I think we can do a little better.' He grinned. 'What we need, my love, is a little romance.'

WE'LL ALWAYS HAVE PARIS

I waited for Toby's breathing to relax, then grinned at the letter he was holding.

'What's up?'

'Bloody speed camera on the M1.'

'Well, you won't have to worry about speed cameras for this journey,' I announced, zipping up our suitcase. 'We'll be whizzing through the French countryside at 125 miles per hour in a state-of-the-art—'

'Have you been reading the back of the tickets again?' he asked.

'Sorry,' I apologized, hopping up and down as I clambered into my warm coat. 'I'm just so excited. I've never been to Paris before. And for Valentine's Day. It's so *romantic*.'

Toby left the speeding fine on the kitchen counter, determined to forget about it over the weekend.

'That's the idea,' he said. 'Come on. We've got a train to catch.'

*

At Waterloo, we joined the British contingent from the thousands of extra tourists who swarm into Paris every Valentine's Day. France's elegant heart is the self-proclaimed capital of romance. But is the claim justified? Romeo and Juliet were from Verona, after all. Cupid was Greek. And the Little Mermaid, who loved the prince so much that she gave up swimming, even though she was really, really good at it, washed up in Copenhagen, not on the banks of the silvery Seine.

Waiting for the ten o'clock shuttle to Gare du Nord, Toby admitted that he hoped that the city would live up to his teenage nostalgia. His last visit had been at the end of a gruelling thirteen-hour hitchhike in aid of a student charity. Apparently, despite the sleepless November night he had spent 'down and out' in the shadow of the Tour Eiffel, the trip had been 'magical'. It had opened his bleary, bloodshot eyes to the joys of Montmartre and the Latin quarter, the galleries and the Rive Gauche. And he wanted me to buy into beautiful, beret-wearing Paris. He knew better than anyone that I was still drowning in a sea of spiritual uncertainty, no matter what I said, and hated the fact that in my quest to find something to believe in, I seemed to have skipped scepticism and gone straight to cynicism. He told me that he missed the hippy Sara who thought every living thing was connected (and every passing jet was a flying saucer), and was determined to show me that whatever else I'd let go of, the love we had was real. My boy was planning to give me the most romantic weekend of my life, or die trying.

Later that evening, Toby and I stood on the highest level of the Eiffel Tower, staring out on the dusky city. The red sun hung low over the horizon like a glowing cigarette butt, casting a salmon-pink glow over the stretching scramble of buildings.

'We made it, then,' Toby said, gazing out on the incandescent panorama. 'Sorry to drag you up here straight off the train, but I wanted you to see all of Paris tonight.'

He snaked an arm around my waist and kissed my head. We'd dumped our bags in the hotel and raced straight round the corner to the pointy heart of Paris. Just as Toby had hoped, I'd fallen immediately and unabashedly in love with the city the moment we hopped off the Metro and I got a whiff of my first pastry. I reached for his free hand.

'And we made it for sunset too, my favourite time of the day. You can't get much more romantic than that,' I cooed. 'I'm glad you didn't let me stop and look at the mini Eiffel Towers now.'

Toby had dragged me through the clusters of grubby-looking men selling tacky memorabilia and refused to let me stop. He rolled his eyes and shook his head at me now.

'Why in God's name would you want one of those tourist trophies anyway? You know it will end up in the loft with your African carving collection, abundance of Thai statues and Indian fisherman trousers you never wear.'

I shrugged and squinted into the distance. 'Memories. Of course.'

'Most of your memories ended up in Oxfam after our last move.'

'I like to share.'

We paused to watch the sun disappear as the tower's strobing illuminations popped around us like paparazzi flashbulbs. The moon, impossibly ripe and bright, seemed fingertips away. I caught my breath.

'It's almost too beautiful. What a perfect place to propose.'

Toby turned to face me and grinned. 'Do you think so?'

I nodded enthusiastically. 'This must be one of the most romantic sites in the world. And just look at that sunset.'

'If you don't mind sharing,' Toby whispered, pointing discreetly. 'Look at them. And them, over there.'

There were couples everywhere, five in total, one German, judging by the sandals and spectacles, the other four all Japanese. Sweaty-fingered grooms-to-be grasped their rings tightly over the grilled floor of the observation deck.

'Oh no, look.' Toby pointed.

As he kneeled before his lover, one unfortunate suitor had been sent sprawling by a poorly timed stumble from a fat tourist. Fatso didn't even notice. I shook my head with dismay.

'Point taken. Romantic setting, but over-used.'

'Lazy. Romance by numbers,' Toby added, pulling the camera out and aiming it into the distance.

'It's all subjective though, isn't it,' I replied. I peeked bravely down over the side of the iron railings then stepped back immediately. 'Some people don't need original thinking, just authentic sentiment.' I threw my arms back. 'Your first proposal was perfect. You could do it again right here, right now, and it would be perfect all over again because it's you. Proposals, weddings, they're not about how are they. They're about who.'

'Oh, well then,' said Toby. He dropped to one knee.

'What's this?' I whispered in a thin voice, my hands suddenly shaky.

'Marry me, darling. Shall I rephrase that as more of a question?'

'No!' I exclaimed. 'No. It's yes. Yes.'

I grabbed at the leather-bound ring box in excitement, but

Toby kept it out of reach, pointing down towards the metal grill of the floor.

'I'm not having you lose another one. Allow me.'

He flipped open the box to reveal a pretty platinum ring with three princess-cut diamonds, identical to the one that slipped from my finger on Cissbury Ring.

'Insurance money came though,' he explained, sliding the sparkling ring on to my finger. 'The jewellers we bought it from still had the details of the last one, but I had it made half a size smaller.'

'All right, all right. I'm not going to lose it. I promise,' I said, hugging Toby tightly. We stood apart with our hands clasped between us and stared down at my newly redecorated ring finger. It looked right. In fact, I realized *I* felt right again. The replacement ring felt like a fitting symbol of a fresh start. I flung my arms back around my fiancé and squeezed the life out of him.

We stayed there for a while taking in the view, oblivious to the queue of ring-proffering Tokyo Romeos amassing behind us in what was undoubtedly the best spot in Paris to watch the sunset.

'Come on,' I said at last. 'Let's take the stairs down. I'm feeling frisky.'

'Paris getting to you?' asked Toby.

Paris *had* got to me. It was impossible to ignore its battered Gallic charm, the city equivalent of Serge Gainsbourg.

It was bitterly cold, as we clanked down the spiral staircase, and my face itched as the wind slapped at us from all directions, but I didn't mind, especially when I glanced down at my engagement ring every now and again ... and again. Paris had me under its spell. I was falling in love with the city, but more importantly, I felt like I was falling in love with love again. Perhaps it was because the French celebrate it all so shamelessly. Love and sex are out there like scarlet knickers dangling from a washing line in your front yard. In France they have an annual literary award, the Prix St-Valentin, for the most emotionally told love story of the year. *Libération* publishes a yearly supplement every Valentine's Day featuring funny lovers' declarations. And romance is truly alive and kicking in a small French village in the Berry region. St Valentin, made famous by romance novelist George Sand, has been hosting a three-day festival open to lovers from around the world. Every 14 February thousands of visitors travel to the village to celebrate the occasion – by having sex.

'It's beautiful.' I sighed, staring up at the glorious imperial purple of the West Rose window at Notre Dame, the next big stop on Toby's tour. Light filtered a rainbow on to the pale brick column beside me, and a wave of frankincense had me sniffing like a Bisto kid. 'I'm going to light a candle for everyone.'

'OK.' Toby nodded with a knowing grin. 'See you in a minute.' He wandered off to examine a row of impish angels carved into an arch of marble.

'Lovely here, isn't it?'

I looked away from the candles and smiled at the middle-aged woman grinning at me expectantly.

'Yes, it's spectacular.' I stood up with a crack of my knees. 'The windows are amazing.'

She held out her hand and smiled. A clump of grey-blond hair fell across her eyes; she blew it away with an irritated puff. I shook her cool, dry hand.

'I need a haircut,' she said in a rolling German accent. 'I'm Heidi, by the way. From Vienna.'

Austrian, then. I never claimed to be an expert.

'Sara. Pleasure to meet you.'

Heidi shoved a battered tourist guide in her bag.

'I just read that we're at the symbolic heart of the city here,' she told me. 'Outside, by the west door, is a point marked by a bronze star – *kilomètre zéro*. All the main road distances in France are calculated from there.'

'Oh,' I said. At the risk of revealing my prejudices, I couldn't help but feel that singling out the traffic facts in a cathedral guidebook was a peculiarly Germanic thing to do.

We strolled a few metres.

'Isn't that fine?' She pointed to intricate carving in a portal, of Mary being crowned by Jesus.

'Incredibly detailed,' I agreed.

'And so clean,' said Heidi.

We paused to watch a choir shuffle into their seats for an early evening mass. I looked around for Toby so we could leave before my Catholic guilt got the better of me and I felt obliged to stay.

'It's only because of Victor Hugo that it looks like it does,' said Heidi.

'*The Hunchback of Notre Dame* writer?' I asked.

She nodded enthusiastically. 'Him. It was 1820 and the walls were so dirty and horrid they were covered with cloths. Hangings. But Victor drew up a petition to clean the walls. Now they are very clean.' Heidi surveyed the stone appreciatively. I covered a wine stain on my combats with one hand.

Heidi waved over at another woman. 'Betsy. Hey, Betsy.'

Betsy grinned and strode towards us. They both towered above me in lofty Aryan splendour.

'Betina,' said Betsy, holding out her hand.

'Sara,' I replied holding out mine.

Betsy turned to Heidi. 'I am finished. Have you also?' Sweet of her to keep up the English for my benefit, I thought.

'Yes,' said Heidi. 'Good to meet you, Sara.'

As I lifted my hand to wave them off, Heidi zoomed in, hawk-like, on my wine-stained strides. They scurried off like church mice.

Right on cue, Toby arrived.

'Had your candle and a cry?'

I nodded. 'Can you remember exactly what happened in the Hunchback story? You know,' I waved my arm about theatrically, 'babies swapped at birth, doomed love and so forth?' I paused as the choir struck up. 'Shall we go?' I whispered.

We cut through the crowds and headed over the Seine to the Left Bank. As we walked, Toby dredged his memory for French Lit 101.

'Quasimodo was a deformed outcast adopted by a young priest, Frollo, at birth,' he began.

'That was nice of him,' I said. ' I thought Frollo was a baddie.'

'He is. Was,' said Toby. 'He was forced to shoulder Quasimodo – pun intended – because he caused the death of his gypsy mother. Quasimodo grew up to become Notre Dame's mysterious bell-ringer, unseen by anyone but Frollo, and forbidden to leave the cathedral.'

'Much more baddy-like behaviour,' I said. 'Where does Esmerelda come in?'

'At the annual Feast of Fools, Quasimodo finds the courage

to join the celebration below, where he meets a beautiful gypsy dancer, Esmeralda, as well as the heroic new Captain of the Guards, Phoebus.'

'Then what?' I asked.

Toby lit up one of his 'party fags', a filterless Gitane. 'Quasi gets crowned King of Fools, but it all backfires when the crowd realize he's not wearing a mask, that he's just genuinely minging. Esmeralda dives in and rescues Quasimodo from the jeering crowd, but Phoebus is ordered to arrest her. On the run, Esmeralda finds sanctuary with Quasimodo in the bell tower. He helps her escape. Frollo orders Phoebus to give chase—'

'Evil Frollo,' I interrupted. 'I know the next bit. Esmerelda falls for Hunch and gets strung up by the Parisian mob.'

'Bingo. Well, that's Victor's version. Disney had other ideas. Less death, more merchandisable character properties.'

'*Bien sûr*,' I said.

'Get you,' said Tobe, 'Edith bleedin' Piaf.'

'Why *are* all the really satisfying love stories tragic?' I asked Toby later.

We strolled by the banks of the River Seine, every now and again catching a glimpse of the Eiffel Tower sparkling between gaps in the skyline like a Brobdingnagian Christmas tree.

'They're not,' he replied.

'Well, the best ones are: Romeo and Juliet, Harold and Maude, Orpheus and Eurydice, Lancelot and Guinevere, Cathy and Heathcliff—'

'Pongo and Mrs Pongo,' interrupted Toby. '*101 Dalmatians* ends happily.'

'Fair point,' I agreed, 'but do you see mine?'

'Of course I do! Maybe it's because we all want what we

can't have? Things always become worth more when they're tricky to get, don't they?'

Hence inappropriate crushes that turn obsessive and forbidden love that grows out of control. As soon as my mum forbade me to see some spotty fuck-up when I was a teenager I was instantly in love with them, crawling out of my bedroom window at midnight for forbidden night-time trysts and cheap cigarettes. It's the yearning and the missing someone that makes it all so intoxicating and romantic. Reality doesn't come into it. It's like the good time sequence in rom-coms played on a loop; all that kissing in the rain, dry-humping on shorelines and walking barefoot in the city. It's a romantic, impetuous and deliciously crazy phase, but it can't last; it shouldn't last. When we fall in love, levels of the neurotransmitter serotonin, which generally has a calming effect, drops below normal in the same way as it does in people with obsessive compulsive disorders. Love-crazy and just plain crazy aren't the same thing at all.

'I think you need to be a bit mental to fall in love, though,' I said to Toby, bringing us to a halt next to a stall selling posters of cats and French things. 'When the blinkers are down you can't see the problems. You need to be crazy to springboard yourself into a new phase with someone. Otherwise you'd analyse yourself the hell out of there.'

Toby leaned against the river's wall to steady himself as he took a photograph; the water gurgled and swirled below us. He paused and frowned.

'There's a lot of bunny boilers out there, Sara.'

'That's conditional, non-reciprocal love, surely?' I argued. 'Rejection can drive people loopy.'

'People get loopy about love without rejection. You just have to look at all the teen-star stalkers out there to see that. '

'I know that grand passion doesn't last,' I replied. 'I learned about the stages of body chemical love from Mark Lythgoe, remember? But maybe it's rejection that sustains it.'

Studies by psychologists and social biologists seem to indicate that this intense passionate phase lasts from between six months to three years – no doubt ensuring our ancestors all shagged around, safeguarding the survival of their precious genes. But if couples aren't allowed to see one another and have to sneak around meeting sporadically, privately, they can't leave the intensity of that phase. And if you stay there too long the line between love and obsession becomes very faint indeed.

If lovers *can* only share stolen moments or know that they only have a short time together, they can fool themselves into believing that their love is impervious to all the normal, boring problems that couples have. It would be easy to believe that theirs was a divine love, more powerful than anything. Hence Romeo and Juliet topping themselves. The whole notion of passionate, impossible love is sexy and abandoned, whereas hitting the comfort zone with the same person and pack of shouty kids is, well, less than glam. It means you're a grown-up, with responsibilities and a mortgage. And even though it's nice to have all that security, danger and freedom are exciting. Fact. They're the defining qualities of youth. Stories about love reflect that time of limitless, unbridled promise and passion, even when the protagonists are proper grown-ups. These days, all that unrequited love just gives me a headache; bring on the comfort zone and shouty kids. It's not your occasional shag-buddy who fights your corner when things get tough. No, once you've got the real thing it's pointless jeopardizing it. But I'm happy to watch or read about everyone

SARA HULSE & TOBY STARBUCK

else's ordeals of the heart. Maybe that's the point. The best love stories – the tragic ones – give us a flavour of romantic love while a fictional someone takes all the risks and deals with the consequences.

Toby and I both stared down at a little red plastic welly boot bobbing up and down on the Seine.

'I remember the first grown-up weepie I read,' I reminisced. 'It was my mum's copy of *Love Story*. I was way too young. Cried for days. I think that was the moment I suddenly became aware that love doesn't necessarily last for ever, whether you want it to or not. That book crushed me. No more than *ET*, mind, but it hurt.'

'Sara, you cried at *Home Alone*,' said Toby. 'You cry at everything.' He waggled a finger at me. 'Beee goood,' he croaked.

I gave him a shove and surreptitiously stifled a sigh, then closed my eyes and breathed in the cold night air.

'Paris is the perfect backdrop for a love story.' I opened my eyes and stared out at the city across the river. 'It's so inspirational and rich in history. I bet there have been tragedies galore here.'

'Abelard and Heloise.' Toby replied. 'They were here, in Paris. They might have even copped off where we're standing now. In front of everyone. Now that's romantic.'

Abelard and Heloise fell in love in 1115 Paris and their story has been preserved in an array of passionate love letters. Abelard was a gifted Parisian philosopher, Heloise his student. For two years they wrote daily missives declaring the depth of their mutual passion. Their illicit meetings in churches, their heated love-making, a secret marriage and the birth of their child, are all chronicled in the record of their love. Later, the letters reveal the couple's discovery. Heloise's family were furious at their relationship and arranged for Abelard to be attacked and castrated. Even this horrific act, however, could not part the passionate pair permanently, although it did for their sex life in the short term.

The couple fled to separate monasteries where Abelard continued with his philosophy and Heloise became the Abbess of her convent. After some years passed the letters began again, with Heloise desperate to let go of the tragedy and to reclaim the love she had lost. A decade or so minus his nuts had done nothing to cool poor Abelard, either.

The pair were never able to get their relationship properly out of the pack, so their love remained shiny and new. It was them against the world, a single, star-crossed, symbiotic whole. Had they lived today things may have been very different. Given time, and untroubled by society, their passion might have cooled. Instead, preserved by tragedy, their love is fossilized and unchallenged, like mosquitos shagging in amber.

That evening, Toby and I decided on an intimate supper under the gas-fire umbrellas of a street-side café. I praised Toby's long-dormant A-level French as we posed with our Gitanes, waiting for food and wine to appear.

'*J'ai besoin de pratiquer*,' he said, showing off.

'That gendarme on Boulevard St-Germain thought you were Canadian,' I told him.

'Is that a good thing or a bad thing?'

'Good thing, probably.'

'I dunno, babe,' he said as the waiter arrived with our wine. 'They're awfully close to America. Easily mistaken until you hear them speak French. And there's no love lost on that side of Niagra, is there?' He tasted the Bordeaux and smiled his approval to the waiter. '*Pardonnez-moi. Qu'est-ce que vous pensez des Canadiens?*' he asked in hushed tones, lest there were maple-munchers nearby.

'*Les Canadiens?*' said the waiter with a shrug. '*Ils ne sont pas Americains.*' And with a clatter from his tip-filled apron pockets, he vanished into the café's candle-lit interior.

'I think I got the gist of that,' I said, grinning.

We sipped red wine and watched the pedestrian traffic until two giant *crocques madames* arrived. A period of silent gluttony followed, after which we refilled our wine glasses, ordered coffee and resumed our sidewalk voyeurism.

Nowhere beats Paris for people-watching. Of course, there are plenty of cities that pull in the international crowd, but for the fashion crowd it has to be Paris. We whiled away time guessing the nationalities of passers-by. Rich Spaniards are easily spotted in their English country colours; Burberry and tweed. West Coast Americans flap along like sunburned parrots in Versace and bling. Londoners try hard, but even the best-dressed have a touch of their home town's unshakeable scruffiness about them. New Yorkers, though the locals would be loathe to admit it, do the best impression of the Parisians themselves, impeccable in muted greys and classic black. Only their gift shop berets betray them.

'What about him?' I asked, pointing to a gangly, middle-aged man in skin-tight black jeans, brocaded red leather jacket and winkle-pickers.

'Russian,' Toby asserted confidently. 'The soft-rock mullet, the boots. It's 2004, right? Accounting for communism, that's 1985 on the Glasnostian calendar. A lot of Russians still look like they're not used to being out and about, which is understandable. Fifteen years ago, he'd've sold his granny for a pack of Wrigley's and a pair of 501s. Now he's got a pocket full of euros, a big can of hairspray, a brand-new pair of leg-warmers, and Paris at his pointy feet.'

As I giggled into my wine, a short, round woman wove through the crowd towards our table, her layered rags in stark contrast to the international fashion show that surrounded her. Her dirty white hair fluffed upwards and outwards from her spherical head in all directions. She accessorized her look with a pair of wide, blue eyes. The general impression was bewildered – possibly injured – owl.

'*C'est une bonne soirée, non?*' said the owl lady, smiling warmly.

'*Vraiment belle,*' Toby replied.

'*C'est toujours possible à passer une bonne soirée quand on est amoureux, n'est-ce pas?*' She lifted her bushy eyebrows at me, and I nodded and smiled. The owl lady blew a kiss at each of us in turn and backed into the crowd, vanishing in an instant.

'What did she say?' I asked immediately.

'She said it's always possible to have a good evening when one is in love,' he told me. I swallowed the last of my wine and shot him a smile as broad as the Champs-Elysées.

'Amelie-tastic,' I grinned. 'I bloody love this city.'

Toby did a quick once over for wallet and watch and, finding both in place, surrendered to the moment. He watched me with satisfaction as I sipped steaming espresso from a tiny, white cup, and wallowed in the unpredictable joie de vivre of the city.

'When even your tramps wax lyrical about love, you know you're winning the race,' he said. 'So here's to Paris: the all-out, hands-down, red-knickers-on-the-washing-line romance capital of the world.'

Toby scrutinized his dog-eared guidebook and scratched his head.

'This map's rubbish,' he grumbled.

The following morning we were taking a break from city life with a taste of city death in the cemetery Père-Lachaise.

'Edith Piaf's right here ... somewhere.' Toby looked up from the guide and frowned. He darted left and squatted to read the inscription on a pink marble tomb. A sparrow hopped along the weather-worn roof. It struck a pose: head cocked, feathers fluttering slightly in the breeze.

'Maybe she is here after all,' I said pointing at the bird.

Toby spun around. 'What? Where?'

I nodded at the sparrow. It hopped twice and launched skywards with a puff of powdered tomb.

Toby rolled his eyes. 'Got it. You're being a hippy again.'

A couple approached slowly, their heads bowed over another unhelpful map.

'*Bonjour*,' the man said, glancing up from his navigating. He slid his glasses purposefully up the ridge of his nose and smiled.

'*Bonjour*,' Toby and I replied together.

The stranger held up his map and tapped it with a finger. '*Où sont*, um, the grave, *pas* grave, *le* ... um ... *mausoleum de ... du ...*'

'English?' Toby interrupted.

'*Oui*,' replied his travelling companion. '*Nous sommes Anglais.*'

'So *sommes nous*,' said Toby. 'Hello.'

The woman sighed with relief. 'Thank God for that. Our French doesn't get us much further than two beers and which way to the beach, does it, Graham? Paris is proving a chore.'

Graham stuck out his chin defiantly. 'Ruth's French is rubbish; I get by. Have you got a better map?' he asked, oblivious to Ruth's fierce frown. 'We can't find anyone who's anyone.'

'Anyone who *was* anyone,' corrected Toby.

'I've never been surrounded by so many celebrities,' Ruth piped up. 'I know they're dead 'n' all but I'd like to be able to say I've been near one. Jim Morrison preferably.'

'Edif Piath is meant to be on this row somewhere,' I said.

'Edith Pee 'oo?' asked Ruth.

'All we've found is the war stuff,' Graham moaned. 'And that's just depressing.'

'Tombs we want,' said Ruth, waving at the family memorials on every side, 'for celebrities. There weren't no celebrities in the war. Not dead ones.'

The 'war stuff' that put a downer on Ruth's day are actually a series of memorials to the victims of the Nazi death camps. Located, for those of you with a more helpful map, in the cemetery's ninety-seventh Division, each stone statue marks a different camp – Dachau, Buchenwald, Sachsenhausen, Auschwitz, Bergen-Belsen and Mauthausen. Jews, French communists and Resistance fighters are all remembered. It's a moving experience, a visible indication of never-ending love beyond the grave. Their message dwarfs the grief represented by the neighbouring family graves. But while the scale of the tragedy is unmatched in all of history, the motivation behind these monuments to the Holocaust is the very same that keeps fresh flowers on the family graves at Père-Lachaise. When someone dies, we feel the loss. Grief is the flipside of love, and it can be as all-consuming as a burgeoning passion. Later, we feel the need to remember, so we erect gravestones and monuments where others can see the extent of our love for the departed; a place to focus our lingering grief. The Holocaust monuments are a twisted version of the family tombs, though. This is because, firstly, the events to which they allude were so obscene, and so obviously the fault of Hitler and his Nazi party, that unlike the cemetery's other memorials, these condemn the perpetrators of crimes against humanity as much as they remember the victims. This is reflected in the stark, stone images of emaciated prisoners, forced to collaborate with their captors and killers. And secondly, unlike even the most pretty or poetic personal memorials, the scale of the tragedy in Europe's concentration camps has the power to move even the most jaded among us. Faced with the sheer numbers involved we cannot help but empathize, our own sorrows stretched to very limits of our darkest imaginations. Such suffering echoes down the years. And how is it that we can share and therefore want to ease another's suffering? Well, that'll be love again; the emotion that forces us to put others first. Let's be honest, when we hear about the little old lady beaten in her home by teenage burglars, we're as likely to think 'imagine it was *my* gran' as we are to pity the actual victim. The end result is the same. Everyone agrees that granny-bashing is a bad thing, and that we should work together to stop it happening again. Love your fellow man is a message that pops up in every great faith. It's a pretty sound starting point if we are to avoid the need ever to erect such chilling memorials again.

'*Au reservoir* then, you two,' Graham said, nodding like a back-shelf bulldog. 'We're going to bugger off and try to find

Mr Mojo Rising.' He snorted and nudged Ruth, who chuckled on cue. 'You haven't see him, have you?'

We shook our heads. 'He's so famous he's got a twenty-four hour police guard,' Ruth whispered excitedly.

'That's to stop people leaving joints,' Toby said.

'No,' replied Graham patiently. 'I think he was a vegetarian. Come on, Ruth.'

He dragged her down the cobbles, whistling 'Light my Fire'.

Père-Lachaise feels like a ghost town, in its truest sense, with its labyrinth of streets, private chapels and grand mausoleums which sit like row upon row of tiny houses in different states of disrepair.

'It's as if the Pied Piper came over from Hamlyn and took the adults as well as the kids,' Toby joked as we walked. 'Eerie.'

'It's sad,' I said. 'You can tell which family lines have died off by the state their mausoleums are in. So many people have been utterly forgotten. Look.'

I pointed to a small chapel. The stained-glass windows sat in shards on the floor of a doorless, crumbling edifice about the size of a sentry box. The unmistakable smell of urine wafted out from its cobwebbed interior.

We strolled on through the city of the dead, coming to a halt by a large pillared monument. In its centre were carvings of a man and woman lying in rest, side by side.

'Who's here?' I wondered. 'Pissaro, Wilde, Piaf, Morrison. Who else?'

Toby scanned the list. 'Sarah Bernhardt, Chopin, Proust, Molière. Loads.'

I walked around the monument in front of us. 'This one's gorgeous.' I saw the inscription and gasped. 'Toby, can you believe it, we've accidentally found someone who I've heard of.'

He appeared, still squinting over the guidebook. 'It's not Piaf, is it? They haven't moved her.'

'No,' I replied excitedly. 'What star-crossed lovers did we mention earlier?'

'Pongo and Mrs Pongo?'

'No you twit. It's Abelard and Heloise. The Paris sweethearts.' My mind was racing. 'So they *were* reunited.'

'Unfortunately at death,' Toby replied. 'Not the greatest ending.'

We both stood staring at the grand monument to love in silence, the faint sound of cars swishing by in the distance. Toby finally held out a hand.

'Come on, let's find Oscar.'

Toby and I stood admiring an elaborate art deco grave.

'It was designed by Jacob Epstein and paid for by an anonymous female admirer,' I read from the guidebook. 'Get this. Apparently the Pharonic winged messenger thing had a giant penis which was snapped off and pinched. It was last seen being used as a paperweight in the cemetery director's office. Where would that have been, then?'

Toby and I both leaned towards the crotch of the sweeping marble design.

'Oh, there!' I exclaimed.

'I'm sure Oscar Wilde would have approved of the new design,' Toby replied.

'Look, the base is covered in pink lipstick kisses,' I pointed out as we circled the tomb. 'It looks quite nice actually, for vandalism.'

'Yes,' Toby agreed, 'it sort of works, doesn't it?'

I carried on scanning the page. 'It says here that Oscar was read his last rites.'

'Don't tell me he was an eleventh-hour Catholic convert,' Toby groaned. 'Not after the life he led.'

'I'm afraid 'e was,' said a voice behind us.

I turned to see a camp young man in a spotless cream mac and a baby-blue mohair beret.

'*Bonjour*,' he said, holding out his hand to me. 'I'm Michel. *Enchanté*.'

Michel, it turned out, was a local artist who pitched his canvas on Montmartre.

'So did Wilde really go Catholic, then?' I asked.

'*Oui*.' Michael nodded, coughing as he inhaled his Gaulois Rouge. 'Despite 'is sexy reputation, 'e flirted more with the Church than with the boys, all of 'is life. Oscar, 'e came from a Protestant family, but 'e once said: "Of all religions Catholicism is the only one worth dying in" and that is exactly what 'e did. A priest give 'im the last rites the day before 'e died.'

'What a cop-out,' Toby groaned. 'What a coward.'

Michel shrugged and took a deep drag on his cigarette. I noticed his fingertips bloomed with a multicoloured stain from his paint pallet.

'Some people say it was a life-long faith, and that in the end 'e just came back to what 'e always truly believed.' He leaned in conspiringly and lowered his voice. 'But I agree with you, I say 'e was scared. The last rites can get you out of trouble if you 'ave been a bad boy. "Die now, pay later."'

'Oscar Wilde?' I asked.

'Woody Allen,' he replied.

Wilde has been described as a protomartyr for the cause of gay rights and celebrated as a sort of shiny model of new man, emerging from the murky swamp of hypocritical Victorian morals. In the course of pushing a homosexual love life he was prosecuted for 'acts of gross indecency' with his lover, Lord Alfred Douglas, and other men. He was sentenced to two years hard labour in 1895 and, upon his release, appealed to the Jesuits, begging for a six-month retreat at one of their London houses. He was broken and ill and in desperate need of help. But he was refused, as the Jesuits had reservations about accepting a man of Wilde's immoral reputation. So much for loving all mankind. With his conversion on hold, Wilde fled straight to France to be reunited with Alfred. Their romance had all the ingredients of tragedy: objections from the families, separation, exile, a brief reunion, and ultimately death. Their romance, however, was to end before the writer's early demise. Poverty and family threats forced them apart.

Upon Alfred's return to Britain, Wilde went into exile in Europe. In Rome he attended masses and papal audiences and received a blessing from Leo XIII which he even believed to have had a physically restorative effect on him. It was in Paris that an ear infection gradually spread to his brain. On 29 November 1900, as he lay dying with two leeches on his forehead to drain blood from his brain, a priest was summoned, an English Passionist, Father Dunne. Wilde was given conditional Baptism and anointed.

''e died a Catholic,' Michael informed us sadly. 'I think it's a shame.'

Toby nodded in agreement.

'Why?' I asked. 'Does it matter?'

Michel lit a cigarette from the burning butt of his last.

'All 'is life he stood up for "the love that dare not speak its name". I worry that 'e regretted his passions.'

'No!' I exclaimed quite loudly. Both Toby and Michel jumped a little. 'You can't think that. You can't think that he regretted love. It's impossible to, even if it all ends badly.'

Michel beamed at me. 'You are being a leetle French.'

'Um, thank you.' I blushed like a Brit. 'But Wilde's conversion was understandable,' I blustered. 'After prison his reputation must have taken a real battering. He was a hedonist in a repressed environment. Friends must have deserted him, publishers refused to touch his work and he became an outcast from his beloved society. The thing with religion is that they always want you. And Catholics can be ever so impressive with their transmogrification and the like. If it helped him to die in peace, it shouldn't matter.'

Michel nodded slowly, then froze and scrambled at his watch in terror. '*Merde*,' he cried. 'I have to go. I have to paint the daughter of a rich lady.' He scrunched up his face. 'She looks like this, a leetle pug. *Au revoir*.'

'*Au revoir*,' Toby and I chimed. Michel turned back to us.

'I leave you with some great words from my hero.' He cleared his throat: '"Life is far too an important thing to ever to talk seriously about."' He grinned, blew me a kiss and walked away, wiggling his little bottom.

'Woody Allen?' I asked.

'Wilde,' Toby replied.

If I do return to the flock, I want to know it's because of a sincere belief in God. Wilde flirted with Catholicism his whole life. Maybe he wanted to turn his back on his own lot, the Proddies – who would have been just as quick to condemn him for his nocturnal activities as the other lot – but couldn't see beyond Christianity. These days he'd have gone all Eastern, done a bit of yoga, moved to California. Back then, as strange as it sounds, the Catholics were probably his best bet. The Church of Rome has always had a nifty line in forgiveness. The whole confession thing keeps your sin tally down to a manageable level like a sort of spiritual cleaning service. And even really naughty Catholics can have this sentence changed from eternity in Hell to purgatory with parole, as long as their faith's strong and their repentance is sincere. Wilde was born and raised a Christian. The doctrine was at odds with his lifestyle and he chose the earthly path. By the time he was staring death in the face, lifestyle choices were academic; his sinning days were over, and he knew it. The Catholics appealed to his fashion sense – they were always a little bit more flash – and offered a one-stop conversion and absolution service that must have seemed pretty appealing to a dying man with a guilty conscience. He must have believed – although maybe it was more a case of returning to Christianity than converting to Catholicism – but I think it might have been guilt that got him there.

Toby and I left Père-Lachaise a couple of hours before we had to be at Gare du Nord for the train home, and installed ourselves in a roadside bar opposite the cemetery gates where we set about killing the time with yet another bottle of red wine.

'Thanks for bringing me here,' I said to Toby. 'My faith in

romance is fully restored and my need for faith is, well, under control.'

Toby opened his mouth to speak, but instead bit his lip.

'Go on,' I prompted, 'just say it.'

'OK, what I want to know,' Toby replied, 'is that you're not just enjoying a boost from this weekend, staving off another crisis with a brave face and a temporary high. Are you sure you're ready to face a life of permanent fence-sitting? That is, we can keep looking, if you still want answers, even if it means going around in circles. I want you happy long term.'

'Bless,' I said. 'And don't worry; I'm ready. There'll be no more Godly goose-chasing. I found what I was looking for.'

'Really? Where does that leave us?'

I laughed loud enough to startle a passing waitress. Her tray of empties clattered and I grimaced, dropping my voice to a hush.

'Silly boy.' I craned over the condiments to plant a kiss on his nose. 'I found you.'

'I'm flattered, really, but – and brace yourself – I'm not a God, sweetie. I am,' palms up, head bowed, 'but . . . a man.'

That earned him a playful but necessarily hard kick under the table.

'This is big stuff, Tobe. Journey's end. No jokes, eh? What I had with God was a relationship that lasted. An ever-present, endlessly loving life partner. And a good listener to boot. Whether or not my prayers were heard, as long as I believed He was there, nothing could harm me. Suffering was always temporary while God was on hand. The hardest thing for me to come to terms with, when I started to question the faith I was born into, was the idea that my constant partner might have been nothing but an illusion. The idea that for nearly thirty years I might have been wishing into the wind to a God who probably didn't exist, let alone favour me over the rest of creation, made me feel foolish and guilty.'

'Guilty? Your brand of benign Christianity has hardly brought harm to the world.'

'When good people want to help,' I explained, 'they pray. Now that's no bad thing, regardless of the results. If you feel hopeless to help, in the aftermath of a distant flood, for example, prayer can release the frustration of that hopelessness and, in the context of group prayer, give a voice to shared concerns.'

'I'm still not feeling your guilt,' he admitted.

'But sometimes,' I continued, ignoring the interruption, 'I think, prayer becomes a way of passing the buck to the highest level. It allows the faithful to defer any sense of responsibility they feel. It disguises apathy with a public but pointless show of sympathy. You see, nine times out of ten, when you're on your knees asking God to rescue the poor little Bangladeshi children, you could be off somewhere doing something practical that would be measurably more helpful. A clothes drive. A petition to the government. A bloody coffee morning, if you must. I spent the eighties praying to God to patch up the hole in the ozone layer, with my hair backcombed and sprayed in place with enough CFCs to turn Queensland into a halogen grill. I'm not blaming myself exclusively for the destruction of the planet. I'm just saying that, from now on, if I want to make a difference I'll find a way to do it myself.'

'Go Sara.'

'But the real point is,' I continued, 'that my relationship with God was the only one I could ever count on ... until I met you.' I slipped a foot out of my shoe and wriggled my toes against his ankle. 'Like I said, that whole cancer scare thing was shitty, but I never really felt completely lost or alone. I had my family and I had you.'

'And you always will,' he told me, sincerely. 'Is that enough?'

I smiled and leaned over to kiss him again. 'More than enough. I think I've finally come to terms with the idea that you're not going to run off and leave me.'

'I've been *trying* to tell you that.'

'I know it sounds crap, but a lot of other blokes would have bolted for the door at the first sign of trouble. Trust me on that one. In my experience, people are great at saying they'll be there for you, it's the actually being there part they trip up on.'

'So I'm not going anywhere, and the faith fishing is all done. What do we do now?'

'What we should have done a year ago,' I said. 'Let's have a wedding; our wedding. Right now. Soon as poss, I mean.'

Toby's eyes were sparkling. 'Really? And you don't mind missing out on a church wedding? The bells, the walk down the aisle, all that?'

'Bells schmells. And an aisle is just a gap between the chairs. I mean it, Tobe. Let's get married. And quickly. Who knows what tomorrow will bring?'

CLOSURE

I threw a blanket over the vast piles of research Toby and I had amassed during our travels. Out of sight out of mind, I reckoned, or hoped at least. After all, I finally had a wedding to plan and sets of leaflets and brochures on country house venues and spit-roast catering were arriving thick and fast.

Planning a wedding can be a wonderful experience, or a living nightmare. The process is as complicated and stressful as you allow it to be. If you want everything to be 'perfect', you've already failed and you're heading for a headache that could scupper your honeymoon and haunt you for ever. If, however, you manage to relax a little and stay the right side of rational, you're in for some serious fun. After all, who really cares if your napkins don't match the bridesmaid's knickers? Stress is inevitable when you're playing with a budget, and some things will certainly go wrong at some point. Once it's over, all you have are memories. You might as well make them happy ones.

If your budget is as tight as ours was, dump the tradition. This means buttonholes that will wilt before the speeches, sit-down meals that cost their weight in gold and a hundred other expenses that no one will miss for a moment, provided the wine flows and the music's loud.

If you're going the civil route, take advantage of the freedom that affords. Write your own vows. Pick a reading that really means something to you. Face the crowd during your service because it feels more intimate.

And when it comes to involving Mum – or whoever the dominant female presence in your life is – don't be too quick to push her away. Small compromises will allow you to get your own way in the end, even if it's Mum and Dad's money you're spending. It'll still be your show and, believe me, you'll want all the help you can get.

While Toby and I were in New York meeting Will at the Natural History Museum, I took time out to track down a different sort of authority on love – a wedding planner. Laurie Nicoletti, the sassy owner of a company called Ravishing Affairs, was excellent company over coffee in Manhattan. As we watched Lexington Avenue disappear under a sudden flurry of snow, she'd filled me in on every possible kind of New York wedding, from Apache blessings to the great post 9/11 wedding rush. Laurie had orchestrated all manner of marriages, from mixed faith ceremonies to Shakespeare boffs who made their vows in Central Park, and in iambic pentameter no less. In NYC, a typical wedding can easily run up a bill of $50,000, so if you've got the cash having someone like Laurie on hand to haggle and harass on your behalf is worth her 10 per cent. As I threw together the Starbuck/Hulse wedding with somewhat less to spend, I dug deep to recall Laurie's warnings about common planning pitfalls.

'Remember,' her voice came back to me, smooth and

soothing and ideal for brides at the end of their tether, 'every vendor and supplier will do their best to persuade you that whatever they are offering is the most important thing. It's a business to them, OK? Nothing else. Don't let them persuade you into things you don't want or need.'

For a girl who works on commission in the cultural capital of money-mad America, Laurie's advice was honest, unexpected and as solid as Liberty's plinth. At the time I'd just nodded vigorously, failing to appreciate the sense of her words. However, as I gradually became swept up in my own plans, I soon learned how easy it would be to blow a grand on elaborate table decorations, linen-backed place cards, or some other expensive frivolity.

'Weddings have become a bit of a show these days,' Laurie had told me. 'Instead of a buffet and dancing, you've got casinos, jazz bands, Elvis impersonators, firework displays, bouncy castles and laser light shows to arrange. Remember this: the more time you spend worrying about entertaining the guests, the less romantic the experience will be for you and your intended.'

I'd been looking forward to my laser light show, but Laurie's words rang true. And thanks to that one consultation with my New York wedding planner, I felt much more comfortable and reasonable, cutting costs at every corner, phoning around to get the cheapest deal without feeling I was being cheap, and begging favours.

'Don't let it become more about the day than the commitment.' Laurie's words echoed in my head. 'You don't have to please everyone else. Whatever you do someone is going to be upset,' she had warned, 'so please yourself.'

That last warning was my biggest problem and a serious

source of anxiety. When you're in the thick of planning a wedding there are times when it actually feels impossible to please yourself. When I first announced our firm intention to have a secular wedding my parents initially went eerily quiet. Then there were talks of a second wedding, a Catholic back-up service to keep the family happy. But the more I thought about doing things their way, the more it belittled my own wedding plans, and the whole arduous journey that had got me that far. It's an impossibly difficult and frustrating situation, experienced by many a bride before me, I'm sure. Our wedding plans faltered as the talks became heated for a little while. And then, out of the blue, my mum and dad seemed to take a step backwards. They stopped pushing. But I knew I'd hurt them. A lot depended on this wedding of ours. If it wasn't right – if it didn't feel right – it wouldn't just be Toby and I who would be let down. And while I really wanted to stop worrying about finding God and simply let Him find me, I knew deep down that any breezy declaration that I was through with soul-searching was all bravado. I kept doing that – making sweeping statements, announcing I was free from God at last. Then I'd doubt myself and crumble. Toby had been right about that in Paris. The fact was I *was* feeling more settled, but remained nervous to be flying solo. What I really needed now, more than ever, was to speak to someone who had lost their faith and come out all right.

But for the moment I threw myself into the business of planning a London wedding for 150 guests, setting myself a ten-week deadline and working minor miracles with our modest budget. Menus and table plans were passed perfunctorily under Toby's nose as I tried to manage the various threads of event-planning and parental diplomacy. For his part, he found a 'stonker of a suit' in the Harvey Nicks summer sale, and got to work on the crucial task of putting together a mix tape to play during the buffet. He said he would have been more hands on, but that he didn't want to interfere 'with a force of nature'. And kept teasing me with my dad's wise words when he had asked him if he could marry me.

'And you can handle her?' Dad had apparently asked, grinning. 'She's a proper little whirlwind, you know.'

As the wedding pile in the corner of our bedroom grew to knee-height, and the strain of endless calls to florists and dressmakers began to show in my tired eyes and short manner, Toby began to voice his concern that all my feverish energy was a cover for some deeper problem. My 'just do it' approach to wedding planning was certainly getting things done. Nonetheless, he still thought that we might have unfinished business on my spiritual search. He explained that after his own round of cancer tests, in his early twenties, he had joined a gym, eager to turn his mercifully tumour-free body into the temple it deserved to be. His conversion to the church of treadmills and Lycra had, inevitably, been shortlived and now he was wondering whether my decision to call a sudden halt to my soul-searching had been hastily made in the wake of my all-clear. My faith, not just in Christ but in all manner of supernatural phenomena, had been at the centre of my life for so long. And he worried how he, however supportive in a crisis, could ever take the place of an entire system of belief. What would happen the next time the shit hit the fan? He was also quietly unnerved by the longstanding connection between faith and love in my mind, which I still couldn't quite untangle. Would I maintain my new, sometimes nihilistic attitude, or relapse into a state of spiritual uncertainty, despite all the romance of Paris?

He tried to broach the subject whenever he had me cornered – in moving cars and elevators, for example – but each time he steered the conversation round to my state of mind, faith-wise, I was quick to wave him away.

'Religion's a pain in the arse, whichever side of the fence you're sitting on,' I declared, when the Westminster Registry Office sent us a letter detailing the limitations of a civil ceremony. 'Do you realize we're not allowed any music with religious lyrics?'

'No hymns, then,' he shrugged. 'Are you bothered?'

'It's worse than that, Tobe,' I said, shaking my head at the letter. 'No religious words at all. No angels, no God, no Heaven.'

'No Robbie Williams or Belinda Carlyle, then. Are you bothered?'

'No "God Only Knows" by the Beach Boys, Tobe. I would have loved to walk back up the aisle to that.

He prised the letter from my hands and hugged me hard. 'We'll find you something else. How about Kokomo? Not their best work, but you can walk to it, I suppose.'

I prised him off and went to file the letter on the bedroom floor, muttering through the walls. 'Bloody Christians and atheists and Beach Boys and all this ... bloody ... God. Aargh.'

Apparently, after retreating to the distant safety of the study, Toby quietly confirmed to himself that yes, there were definitely still some issues there. We had encountered a variety of people who had found their own spiritual peace, whether through scripture or self-discovery, and none of them exhibited my symptoms of angry frustration and vociferous iconoclasm. He thought that I reminded him of *him*, before he'd been carried along for the ride over the past year and plunged into cultures and communities which he never expected to encounter.

By reaching deep into our own thoughts and feelings about love, Toby and I had risked more than we anticipated. Love is more than a hormonal response thanks to the miraculous, enriching power of the human brain. In some ways, we had turned our brains against love by picking away at the mystery that makes it work. Toby knew he had survived the ride with his belief in romance intact, but he couldn't vouch for me.

He realized I was lacking closure. And that perhaps there was one more stop to make on our prenuptial pilgrimage, after all. From my floor file-pile, he dug out a name, scrawled on a New York napkin months earlier that year which had been lost under flotsam and jetsam in our cluttered study. With the wedding looming, and our joint account as dry as a Mormon roadhouse, he began scanning the Net for cheap flights to Edinburgh.

He hoped to end our odyssey with a visit to an outspoken champion of secular morality. What I had failed to find, for all my searching, was an authoritative voice who had done anything other than attempt to sell me their version of the truth. I had come a long way to establishing my own view of the world, but the childhood churchgoer in me needed a priest – albeit, in this case, a non-believing one – to ratify my new spiritual perspective, and perhaps reawaken my sense of wonder. He had just the man in mind.

POST-CHRISTIAN PEACE

When London sinks beneath the rising Thames, it would be nice to consider a move to the majestic and lofty city of Edinburgh. Viewed from the castle's high parade ground, or projected by the miracle of Victorian optics on to the wide viewing table of the city's remarkable camera obscura, there is scarcely a blot on the landscape from Waverley station to the glittering, distant sea.

Like most self-proclaimed Edinburghophiles from south of the border, Toby had never before set foot in the city outside of the festival month of August. I had never been at all. This was the first time Toby had flown up; he was used to arriving on a train packed with fringe fans, pouring out onto Princes Street to find their bearings, a bag of chips and a box office. He could hardly believe the difference between the short hop by air and eight hours on the floor of an overstuffed Intercity train. He was amazed too by how the city, stripped of its festival crowds, was a different animal to the swollen, sleepless creature he remembered. Our taxi took us through the broad, sparsely peopled streets to our hotel, in the shadow of the architecturally brave and awseomely expensive Scottish parliament building.

In 1872, after a fundraising drive by Sir Walter Scott and others, the foundation stone was laid for the National Monument on Calton Hill, a memorial to the Scots who fell in the Napoleonic wars. It was intended to be a replica of the famous Parthenon in Athens, but the money ran out just twelve columns into construction, leaving a monument that has been variously described as 'Edinburgh's Shame', 'Scotland's Disgrace' and, in typically florid and moralistic tones of Victorian observers, 'Scotland's Pride and Poverty'. The National Monument has weathered its first century on Calton Hill, and acquired a certain romantic charm. It stands unfinished in illustration of the best known words of the best loved Sottish poet, that 'the best laid schemes o' mice an' men, / Gang aft a-gley'. Even in the early days, though, when the handful of Doric columns served only to remind onlookers of planning incompetence, the locals could take comfort from the fact that it wasn't their money sitting up there looking silly.

The new contender for the title 'Edinburgh's Shame', the Scottish parliament building, has cost the taxpayer tens of millions more than originally budgeted. Catalan architect Enric Miralles' ambitious, organic extension to the local landscape has been dogged by delays and spiralling costs, sparking a public enquiry and charges of gross incompetence among those responsible for its construction. During our visit, vandals set fire to a pile of building materials against an outside wall, nudging up the cost of completion by another £20,000. According to the *Scotsman*, the building has cost every man, woman and child in the country over £80. The National Monument was a rich man's folly; the parliament building is costing everyone. That said, it's a fascinating edifice, surging out of the grey rock that inspired it like a volcanic deposit, and when the current generation's grandchildren have finished paying for it, it may yet earn a place in the hearts of the Scottish people.

Toby was staring out of our hotel window, contemplating the strange, upturned boat shapes of the parliament's windows, while I made a series of urgent, wedding-related phone calls that couldn't wait for our return home. Florists and caterers duly updated, I tossed my mobile on to the bed and shuffled up behind him, resting my forehead on his back.

'You talked me up here,' I sighed, tired now from this seemingly endless spiritual journey. 'What's the deal? Who's the guy? You better not have dragged me up north to meet some bloody cult leader. I've had it with all that crap.'

'We've got an appointment tomorrow morning,' he told me. 'And no, he's not another holy man, not exactly. Call me psychic, but I got it into my head that you'd stopped looking in that direction. In fact, that's sort of why we're here.'

'Well?' I urged, digging him in the ribs. 'Are you going to tell me, or am I going to have to tickle it out of you?'

Richard Holloway has described himself as a 'post-Christian'. One of the most popular figures in the modern church, he stood down from his position as Bishop of Edinburgh when his own brand of radical theology came into conflict with the faith he had vowed to promote. He still loves to shock his former flock with articulate, sonorous pronouncements on all manner of subjects, from gay marriage to the decline of Christianity, and is one of liberal Britain's most respected defenders.

We rolled up to the Holloways' grey stone townhouse after a night among the stag and hen revellers in the Grass Market.

Festival or no festival, Edinburgh knows how to party. As we waited on the doorstep for our knock to be answered, Toby hissed that he felt fuzzy-tongued and under-prepared. I, who had sensibly stuck to mineral water all night, looked chipper by contrast. When the door opened to reveal a lean, smiling man, struggling to contain a small, brown bundle of dog in his arms, I beamed back and offered our introductions. Richard greeted us warmly before leaving us in the company of Daisy, the Lakeland Terrier, while he nipped to the kitchen for refreshments.

It occurs to me that the common thread to almost every stop on our piecemeal pilgrimage has been the offering of food and drink. Pretty basic social behaviour, I'll grant you, but I like to think it's been indicative of a certain charitable bent that reflects the teachings of our hosts' faiths. Whether anything can be extrapolated about individual religions, I am far from sure. Coffee and tea from the Catholics; a Tetley infusion from the unflappable Chudrun, our Buddhist nun; wine from Tristan, the free-floating spiritualist; ice-cold mineral water from the warm Juliusz; marble cake from the Baha'is and, when suddenly snowbound in New York City, a full night's board and lodging from Darwinist Will.

Richard reappeared with a pot of fresh coffee and a cascade of apologies for the family pooch, who was wriggling ecstatically in my lap.

'She's everybody's best friend,' he told us. 'Bit of a slut, if the truth be told.'

Truth telling. This was a good start. I knew that Toby hoped our host could show me that sectarian disillusionment did not preclude me from taking a meaningful spiritual stance. As Daisy was, still wriggling, relegated to the floor, Toby asked Richard to explain what had caused a professional preacher to turn his back on the church that he served for over thirty years.

'My religious DNA wore out,' said Richard. 'I did it for so long. And the constant talking. In Christianity they're always talking at you. Always explaining things in all that God language.'

Toby and I exchanged a look of surprise. Was this really an ex-Episcopalian bishop talking?

'I think I was always a bit subversive,' he continued, possibly registering our amusement. 'I was happy to marry divorcees and gays – the Church's position never made sense to me on those issues – but I found ways to live with the doctrine in an unorthodox way.'

I had a vision of the rebel bishop, subtly subverting his congregation while the synod squirmed, like an evangelical *Dead Poets Society*.

'Of course, that kind of spiritual shift evolves. Maybe other stuff in my life and my philosophy was catching up with me, but I went into overdrive after the 1998 conference.'

Holloway has described the Anglican Communion's 1998 Lambeth Conference as 'a festival of hate' akin to the Nuremburg Rallies. It was here that the issue of homosexuality was discussed, and a policy formulated that would perpetuate the exclusion of gay and lesbian Christians from the clergy, and ratify the bigotry of God-fearing homophobes across the Protestant world. Massachusetts' Barbara Harris, the Anglican Communion's first woman bishop and no stranger to doctrinal sexism, is reported to have muttered from the pews, 'If assholes were airplanes, this conference would be an airport.' Holloway's own conclusion was that the Anglican Church was 'a very diseased thing'.

'I had always preached a lot about doubt,' he said now, 'how faith was not a certainty, it was living doubt. History has shown that the role of faith declines with the acquisition of knowledge. I had plenty of rhetoric to deal with that, a standard routine that I wheeled out. I used to argue that the last ditch of faith was committing oneself to the idea of a universe that meant something, as opposed to an absurd, meaningless universe. It was existential, romantic, soul-building stuff, but it was misguided.'

On reflection, Holloway believes that the last thing mankind needs is universal meaning: 'One man's meaning is another's weapon.' The universe, he asserts, has the meaning that you give it, and the most noble and productive meaning, from a human perspective, is love.

Freedom from the notion of a divine plan also annuls the age-old Christian dichotomy of free will versus predestination. Even at the bloody climax of the New Testament, these incompatible notions clatter noisily against each other. Consider the fate, and I use the word advisedly, of Judas Iscariot. Jesus, having foreseen his betrayal, is so confident in the inevitability of events that he happily shares his knowledge with the turncoat himself. Indeed, Judas has been marked from the start for the role of betrayer. He is crucial to God's plan; the cleansing sacrifice of His only begotten son. Judas's free will is effectively suspended during the period of his treachery. Greed was not the motive for Judas's crime. Instead, his destiny fulfilled, he is immediately wracked with guilt, choosing lonely suicide over the life of a Palestinian playboy. As the expiry date on Christian redemption is the day of one's death, Judas's reward for playing his predestined part is eternal damnation. This makes God, the ultimate architect of Christ's suffering, the most notorious agent provocateur in judicial history.

But Richard Holloway rejects the idea of predestination, a central tenet of his Calvinist upbringing, out of hand: 'The incontrovertible logic of the doctrine of predestination is that God knows, even before we are born, who will be saved and who damned. In the Bible, Paul talks about being predestined by God to do this and that. Theologians have taken his words and inflated them into great theological architectures. By anyone's standards, though, Calvin really hammered it. His doctrine of predestination induced enormous anxiety; how did you know whether you're saved or damned? It created a sort of psychological crisis in adolescence, which the church could jump on and sort out with the experience of conversion. Ease the minds of anxious teens and they're all too ready to believe that God has saved them.'

Our conversation, punctuated by short bouts of terrier wrestling, was as easy and relaxed as our avuncular host. Having listened intently to Richard's Episcopalian escape story, I had a few questions of my own. Buoyed by articulate debate, Toby had dominated our side of the room, somewhat. A fact that Richard had not failed to notice.

'You don't get to say much, do you?' he smiled at me. Toby zipped his lips and sat back, clearly reminding himself that we were here for my long-term spiritual health, and also resolving to pause for breath between sentences from time to time. I grinned back at Richard, raising one eyebrow at Toby in a way that unmistakably said, 'What have I been telling you?'

'So,' I began, 'where are you now? What's life like for you without faith at the centre of it?'

'I don't personify God any more,' Richard told me. 'I don't believe in "Him" in that sense now. But I won't describe myself as an atheist because that's also a fixed position.'

Toby sat on his hands as he fought the urge to interrupt. Holloway's carefully chosen seat on the fence was smack bang up against his own. If they had a name, they might even have started a movement. I was pondering the options when Richard settled the matter.

'I call myself an Atheisor,' he explained. 'Anything with an ist or an ism, you have to be wary of. Atheisor is a verbal noun; it's about what you do, not what you've chosen to believe.'

Richard believes that honest, free-thinking people must refuse to let anything become an absolute idol. The history of theology and philosophy is littered with abandoned Gods and redundant thinkers. Liberal Christians, for example, have effectively renounced the God that subordinated women and demanded that they stone to death homosexuals and other supposed transgressors. They have abandoned the myth of seven-day creation for the more plausible theories of astronomy and geology.

'The whole history of the concept of God,' says Richard, 'has been the smile on the face of the Cheshire Cat, slowly disappearing. To use God as an explanatory hypothesis is to gradually whittle him down to nothing, as we learn more about the universe for ourselves.'

'But how much of God can you abandon and still refuse to call yourself an atheist?' I asked, frowning as I listened intently to our host. 'If you take away the philosophy of judgement and reward, and remove the supernatural from our explanations of the physical universe, what's left?'

Richard nodded as if he'd asked himself the same questions. 'For me,' he continued, 'the idea of God is a way to express the ultimate mysteriousness of the universe. Why is there something, instead of nothing? We'll never know. That is the most profound mystery of all, and it's the one that keeps me from declaring myself an atheist. If scientists tell me that the universe just popped into existence, well, I can buy that. But why? Where? How?'

The faithful Christian, it has been said, should not fear atheism, but idolatry. It is the faithful who are prepared to fly themselves into tall buildings, or tear out the entrails of the unconverted, to save their eternal souls. Nevertheless, I believe that there is reason to fear a Godless universe. Atheism removes, once and for all, the divine supervision that has undoubtedly kept man on his best behaviour over the years. It opens the door to anarchic nihilism and so would require a sophisticated moral code – and possibly martial law – if it were ever to replace religious faith as the dominant intellectual position.

Perhaps in shutting the door on dogmatic faith, but leaving it on the latch just in case God pops round after all, Richard Holloway has found the only valid absolute position in all of human philosophy; absolute uncertainty. Holloway the apostate is a champion of virtue for virtue's sake, whose book *Godless Morality* argues for the preservation of much of the moral teaching that religion has bestowed. He asks much of his readers when he proposes the adoption of a universal, liberal morality, minus the carrot and stick of religion. After all, if good deeds were ten a penny, and encouragement and assistance instinctively offered to those in need, the tale of the Good Samaritan would have died with Deuteronomy.

Perhaps the shadow of God in Richard's 'atheising' outlook – the humble 'what if?' – lingers in order to provide moral motivation. If this is the case it neither belittles, nor necessarily influences, his carefully considered conclusions. Holloway has surrendered himself to uncertainty and shed the bonds of inherited faith. His goodness, honesty and empathy may be, in part, the legacy of a solid, Christian upbringing. But in claiming ownership of his virtues, rather than bending to the will of a Heavenly authority, Holloway exhibits a genuinely noble humanist morality.

Maybe, just maybe, buried deep in that first-class brain, is the sneaking suspicion that if he strays too far from the straight and narrow, someone up there will not be happy about it.

Taken on the basis of one sunny morning, sharing banter and beverages, Richard Holloway seemed to personify the point Toby wants us both to reach. Holloway is willing to live and let live, preferring to espouse his own morality rather than do battle with individual faiths. Only the practical consequences of bad beliefs – bigotry and persecution – concern him. He is iconoclastic without being scornful, radical without being angry. Even after his own faith failed him, he remains sympathetic to the cultural and moral richness of the religions he criticizes, arguing that we should read religious texts for their myth-bearing value and the enhancements they offer humanity.

While dogma and deity have no place in Richard's world view, he does keep a place for one concept that figured large in his Christian roots, at least in theory. This is the force – the idea, if you like – that I believe sits at the heart of his post-Christian morality. What keeps the ex-bishop righteous is not the shadow of a judgemental God but love.

'I don't want to analyse it,' Richard told us when I asked him for his feelings on the 'l' word. 'Love is better than hate. I don't think you need any rational justification for that; very few people would debate the fact. When you lose religion, you don't lose anything fundamental to do with goodness or morality. These things are elemental. It only gets tricky when there's no obvious common sense approach. 'Do you steal to save a starving child?' – that sort of thing. Generalization is the enemy of justice when it comes to those dilemmas. The truly loving approach would always be case by case, so leaving religion and going it alone certainly leaves you with a lot more personal moral decisions to make.'

A person with standards, Holloway asserts, is always going to make life difficult for themselves; the world they inhabit is full of less considerate souls. But passion, if it is allowed to develop into anger, can undermine personal happiness.

With a regular radio slot looming for our gracious host, we wrapped things up and reluctantly readied ourselves to leave the Holloways' happy home. As Richard waved us off into the sunny streets of the Scottish capital, his parting advice would not have sounded out of place if he'd had the saffron robes to match his shiny pate. 'Don't turn into a curmudgeon. Be happy,' he smiled at Toby, before turning to me: 'And don't be bullied ... Just let go.'

I stood with my arms wrapped tightly around myself on the highest accessible level of Edinburgh's towering gothic monument to Sir Walter Scott. A biting wind was buffeting me from all directions at once. After leaving Richard, Toby navigated us back through Edinburgh, displaying his usual knack for geography of strange places. I skipped alongside him, darting into every sunny patch I could, as he marched onwards, waving his arms in the direction of landmarks and old festival haunts. With time to kill, we traced a circling route around the castle down the Royal Mile and back over railway tracks to Princess Street and the Scott Monument. After 287 steps up the increasingly cramped and winding tower we emerged to spectacular views and that bracing wind. I stared out over the Firth of Forth – it was clear enough to see the awesome suspension bridge – and thought about Holloway's parting words: 'Just let go.'

It had been refreshing to meet a man so comfortable with apostasy, and so knowledgable of the faith he had left behind. In the course of our meeting, the avuncular ex-bishop had referenced several Christian Bible stories, including that of Noah and the Ark. Unbeknownst to him, of course, it was Toby's casual debunking of that very story that had triggered my own spiritual crisis and set me on the path of pilgrimage that, ultimately, brought me to his door.

'Bible stories are merely vehicles for existential human experience,' Richard had said. 'If you abandon the pretence of historical accuracy and instead see them as myths packed with meaning, you begin to see the truths that they communicate more clearly.'

So the story of the fall of Adam and Eve becomes a parable about the bliss of ignorance and the dangers of bursting your own bubble. Noah's Ark, to borrow Richard's frank turn of phrase, is about 'fucking up the planet'. Reduced to their symbolic essence, the Bible's legends can be used in a constructive, educational way, without muddying their message with dogma or dictate. Unfortunately the religious have a tendency to demand that myth is taken as fact, completely and literally. And that's where it all falls apart. The problem is that we've become too sophisticated, cynical and self-aware to accept spoon-fed platitudes and flawed history. So we're slowly but surely shredding the lot. After all, if barely anybody believed that David

Blaine could really survive in a box for a few weeks on fresh air and body fat, who's going to listen to some nutty old geezer boasting about his flood-proof floating menagerie?

I think religion might be slowly dying out because dogma is fixed. If the Catholic Church had been flexible enough to recognize that 'gospel' and 'truth' are not necessarily synonymous, I might still have made the meetings. In reality, it was all or nothing at all, and I chose the latter. It was a tough choice, and a traumatic time that followed, so it was immensely satisfying to see that, after years of devotion far greater than my own, Richard Holloway's succession from the Church had apparently worked out all right for him in the end.

'For years,' he had told us, 'I avoided the works of Freud, Marx, Nietzshe and others. I knew in my heart that the writing of these big thinkers would have a great effect on me, because I felt that I would be looking into the abyss. I sensed that I would be undone. And it was true, I was. But it was liberating when it finally happened.'

He had peered at me quite intensely then, for a moment. 'You may reach the stage where your fear of losing religion is overcome by your fascination in speculation. Where none of this bothers you too much any more.'

'I hope so,' I had murmured in response, but I had still felt beaten down by the weight of my previous beliefs. I think Richard noticed.

'One of the things I wonder about Richard Dawkins,' he had said, 'someone I greatly admire by the way, is why he can't just let people believe. Why waste your time trying to sort everybody out – trying to bring everyone round to your atheist perspective – when it's obvious that for a great many people, spirituality is more or less hard-wired. You mentioned your epilepsy, Sara,' he continued. 'Epileptics objectify. It's a mental process symptomatic of their condition, so perhaps you'll always think about spirituality in terms of God – a third person, an entity. If that's how your brain's software works, so be it. It's only the practical consequences of bad beliefs, the persecution and the tribalism, that bothers me.'

And now, as I paced back and forth, high above the Princess Street Gardens, Richard's comments seemed to quieten something within me. I felt a burden shifting, and suddenly started to cry. I think this was that moment when I realized that I was finally ready to give up my Holy Ghost chase.

Before Richard had waved us off at his doorstep, I remembered to ask him what he thought we should do about our wedding plans. After all, he'd been to a fair few over the years, and had enjoyed the view from both sides of the altar.

'Oh, write your own,' he had told us, leaping out of his armchair to ferret around in a cupboard. 'Look, here are some models for you to look at.' He had handed us a stack of sample services that he had conducted himself since stepping down from his post. 'Make it personal,' he counselled. 'Make it about the pair of you and no one else. Think about having a Humanist service that satisfies you both without compromising your principles. And remember above all, it's about your love for each other, so just enjoy it.'

Back in our hotel room at the Holyrood end of town, Toby and I were busy packing for the trip home. As he opened wardrobes and drawers to check for any misplaced items, Toby let out a sudden somewhat theatrical 'A-ha!' and turned to me with a big red Bible.

'Look what I've found,' he said, wiggling his eyebrows. 'Fancy finding out what the Good Book has to say after all this religious rejection? You know, in the name of balance and fairness and all that?'

'And how do we do that, then?' I asked.

'Easy,' said Toby. 'We pick a passage at random. Surrender ourselves to fate; allow the Lord to steer our path.'

'Don't take the piss,' I admonished. 'But all right. Go for it.'

'OK,' said Toby. 'One shot. Whatever it says, agreed?'

'Agreed.' I nodded.

Toby held the leatherette Bible in both hands and, turning his head away, allowed the book to fall open.

'Now, close your eyes and point,' he told me.

I followed his instructions. There was a moment's silence.

'Wow,' exclaimed Toby.

I opened my eyes to see him staring slack-jawed at the page. 'Ecclesiastes, verse two.'

I took the Bible from his hands and turned it round to read. I traced the words with my forefinger as I read aloud: 'Meaningless, meaningless. All is meaningless.'

There was a beat of silence as we exchanged a look of incredulity.

'You didn't . . .' I began.

'No,' said Toby, 'I swear.'

In this Ecclesiastes verse Solomon expresses that life without God is meaningless, and yet that day in the Hollyrood hotel, while it was out of context, I assumed it meant that to carry on my searching was futile. In retrospect I find that passage ever more ambiguous, but I realized then that it was time to stop looking for what I might never find.

JOURNEY'S END?

At the beginning of this journey, I truly believed that at some point along the way my faith would simply snap back into place again intact. Stronger even, because it would be drawn from my own experiences, not just drummed in at church and convent schooling. In retrospect, that sounds naive, even to me. The more I learned the less I came to believe and, in a funny way, doesn't that just about sum up the place of religion in the modern world? Faith thrives on insularity. Broaden your horizons and you start to see the flaws. That said, I wholly understand why people often choose to cling on to their religion, because the space faith leaves behind is so vast and lonely. But I've come to believe that faith alone is not enough to validate an entire belief system and way of life.

Faith overrides logic and can twist the truth. Take, for example, the Jehoash Stone. Discovered near the walls of the Islamic cemetery on Temple Mount, Jerusalem, in 2001, the Jehoash Stone was an archaeological find of incredible significance to the Christian and Jewish faiths. Its fifteen lines of carved Hebrew text appeared to corroborate verses in the Old

Testament that sited the Temple of Solomon and its mythical contents, the Ark of the Covenant, in just that spot. Now Solomon was the greatest of all biblical kings, but to the best of my knowledge no record remains of his ever having existed outside of the pages of scripture. The Jehoash Stone apparently turned myth into history, confirming that at least one key figure in the Old Testament was demonstrably real.

Sadly, for all who had pinned their hopes on the find, the stone was revealed as a forgery in 2003. More rigorous testing on the stone proved that, while carefully chosen by its forger, who knew more than a thing or two about Jerusalem BC, it could not have come from the Jerusalem area. Moreover, the carvings themselves, skilfully aged but linguistically flawed, were ultimately revealed as the work of a clever contemporary stone mason, according to scholars of ancient Hebrew.

Despite all evidence to the contrary, however, there are still plenty of people who maintain that the Jehoash Stone is authentic. Apparently the *Biblical Archaeology* magazine went so far as to offer a cash prize to anyone who could demonstrate the skills necessary to produce so impressive a fake. That they still have their money is probably down to the fact that the master faker, one Oded Golan, was locked up in an Israeli jail.

Golan played a cruel trick that brought misery and desperation to countless hopeful believers. When the hoax was discovered, those that were duped, and there were many, lost more than an archaeological marvel. The loss one feels is proportionate to the hope invested. Oded Golan, therefore, did far more than expose the arrogance of a few Middle Eastern museum curators.

When I think about the endless toing and froing between adherents of this faith and that faith and no faith at all, I find

SARA HULSE & TOBY STARBUCK

myself quickly tiring of the lot of them. And so, after all my searching, this is an open-ended book. I was foolish to think I could reach a satisfactory and absolute conclusion. But I have found a kind of peace. And the trick, I think, as Richard Holloway said, is not letting it matter. I've indulged my soul-searching self for long enough. Over the last year I've forced Toby and myself to spend far too much time thinking about unanswerable questions that most people – for bloody good reason – ignore from the cradle to the grave. Some would say that we've wasted our time, chasing rainbows, but I can't agree. We've dipped our toes in waters that might otherwise never have been breached, we've met some remarkable people and found new friendships along the way. So I'm no closer to Nirvana. So I'm an Apostate. So what?

A while back I'd all but given up on the spiritual realm. Any mention of faith or spirituality made me feel angry, cynical and lost. Worse, because my own ideas about faith and love were so intertwined, I even began to jeopardize my deepest and most important earthly relationship – with Toby. I realize now that a large part of the painful spiritual vacuum I experienced after abandoning my Catholic roots was down to the habit of personification. For me, faith meant faith in a God, a supreme being. That God, in turn, was the very personification of 'love'. So when I lost God, I lost, for a time, the capacity to imagine any kind of spirituality beyond the physical world. I lost, too, my belief in the transcendent, spiritual side of love. It was like losing language. Without God at the heart of my world, I lacked a structure within which to express my thoughts and feelings about life's big issues. If I have learned anything, it is to let go of the idea of 'knowing' God. Now, with Toby at my side, and hopefully a long, happy life ahead of us, I can acknowledge that spark of the divine that man has always felt, without always feeling the need to give it a name, a story or a long white beard.

As for other people's faith, I no longer feel either pity or envy; only admiration for the truly virtuous who embrace the moral teachings of their religion and live thoughtful and loving lives. Each of us sits at the centre of our own universe, alone with our thoughts, a tangled mess of hard-wired instinct, early socialization and personal experience. Each of us faces, eventually, some crisis of heart or health. If faith can help someone through dark times, keep them sane and grounded and hopeful while their world turns upside down, no one should deny them such comfort. Only when individual faith is twisted into a dangerously competitive team sport – with each team observing slightly different and non-compatible rules – does faith becomes a malign force. There are so many new religious franchises opening, each with their own colour scheme and super-size-me options, each claiming that they are the best. Instead of focusing on what sets us apart from one another we should celebrate what is the same. We should be aware of our differences, respect them and learn from one another. It's not rocket science, is it? If we are to believe the theory that all matter in the universe was created when the universe began, nothing goes anywhere; it just changes form. So we are all part of each other, a finite amount of atoms enchanted by sentient life. We share base emotions; we are each other.

There is nothing to recommend one religion over another in my mind, except force of numbers. And that's why I find myself on the outskirts of all of them. Yours is the one true faith? Says who? You? OK then, I'm the rightful Queen of New Zealand and I dare you to prove me otherwise.

The decision to stop looking for a Jesus substitute, and to tackle my thoughts about spirituality has liberated me. If God is love, as I was taught to believe, why would love require exclusive devotion or meet transgression with terrible punishment? If God is love, then when *we* love, we are close to God. It's a simple philosophy, but after negotiating a maze of different and conflicting beliefs, I've got to say, I like simple. I admit, it does do my head in slightly to think that I've spent an entire year running from pillar to post, bashing my head against a wall of confusion and guilt, only to find that the Beatles got there thirty years earlier, with no more than a handful of funny cigarettes and a catchy chorus. I'm all for the ordination of Pope John-Paul-George and Ringo, who said it so well: 'All you need is love.'

As for our wedding day, well, it was wonderful. It's funny, you worry yourself sick over something for months, then it's over in a blink of an eye, with nothing but snapshots and cake crumbs to show for it.

I shared my last night as a single girl with my parents, who'd splashed out on a suite at the Savoy. The three of us had padded around our opulent rooms in matching slippers, none of us quite believing that the much-debated day of my marriage was only hours away. Every now and then I'd catch my mum standing agog in front of my hanging bridal dress, gently stroking its delicate silk folds. Or I'd spot Dad nervously scanning the notes for his speech. Several times, I felt an overwhelming surge of love for them both. I'd put them through it with this journey of mine, and I know that a part of them will probably constantly worry for the sake of my eternal soul, but however far apart our thoughts on matters metaphysical drift, I know they'll always be there for me. In the run-up to the wedding I'd spent so much time feeling guilty that I was letting them down that I failed to notice just how excited and happy for me they actually were. They could have made things difficult for Toby and me. They might have turned their backs on their wayward child, and those empty chairs at my wedding breakfast would have haunted me for life. In the end, though, my parents – in fact all the believers in my family – set aside their own longstanding expectations out of love and respect. It was honourable and giving, and it meant we could have the wedding we truly wanted. That special day is now something that we will all share for always.

If most of my marriage whizzed by in a whirl of champagne and dancing, I do at least remember the service itself, in vivid photographic detail.

'Ready?' whispered my dad, squeezing my arm as we stood in the candlelit corridors of the Royal Society of Arts waiting for our musical cue.

'Ready.' I nodded.

I turned and winked at my bridesmaids just as the first chord rang out.

'This is it,' Tash hissed, fiddling with her posy of Michaelmas daisies.

'Remember to go slowly. OK,' Rachel added, grinning at Dee, 'none of us can walk in these heels.'

I nodded, and Dad led us between the flickering tea-lights that threatened our flowing hems, into the vault where Toby and the guests were waiting.

The first faces I saw were those of Van and Gav. They were beaming broadly. It was just a year since their they were married themselves. In those twelve months, Van had first beaten breast cancer, only to see it return as secondary cancer which then spread to her liver. Apparently she was back on chemo and battling the odds as bravely as ever. I had feared that the wedding would prove too much of a strain during her treatment, but here she was, as radiant and beautiful as ever, with Gav, as usual, by her side. I felt swollen with absolute love for them at that moment, so honoured and excited that they'd made it. I hadn't known quite how ill she was that day until a few months later.

And then I turned the corner. A mass of happy, expectant faces peered up at me, but I was only looking for one. Toby had never looked so handsome. Toby Starbuck: this was the man who had saved my life, who had stood by me through sickness, grief and confusion, though every dark and hopeless hour. I'd seen his own grief, too. Mornings when I woke to feel him sobbing in the bed beside me in the months following his mother's death. I'd felt then the strength of his love and the fortitude of his character, and I knew what a special man I had. As our eyes met across the room, I saw his mouth twitch slightly with barely contained emotion and his eyes glint with captive tears, and I wanted to run down the aisle to him. At that moment, all the whats, whens, wheres and hours of our protracted wedding plans seemed trivial and silly. There was the man I loved, and who loved me, waiting to share a promise that would carry us together across any obstacles life threw in our path. I had never been so sure of anything in my life.

There you have it. From now on, I'm going to try not to worry too much about the big stuff. Despite all that self-imposed pre-wedding torment, I didn't really miss the religious aspect to my marriage at all in the end. It was painful getting there, but the pay-off was spectacular.

As for faith, look, I'm a good person. Honestly I am. So if there is a God up there, cut me some slack, eh? I don't want to entertain the notion that He's some kind of tinpot dictator, sitting on high, chucking thunderbolts at transgressors. That would belittle His achievements – you know, creation and all that. OK, I've gone a bit quiet, prayer-wise, and I'm still not entirely sure what to call Him any more. But I take comfort in knowing that I do believe there's something beyond the profound miracle of this physical world. I just don't know what it is and guess what, I'm OK with that, at the moment.

My fascination with spirituality remains – my faith in the transcendent worth of the human soul – but along with much of the dogma of my childhood faith that no longer makes sense to me, I have finally shed the crushing need to belong. Reason won out on the subject of my apostasy and official 'damnation'. I have come to terms with my rebel status on the fringes of a church built on rebellion. I'll catch myself fingering a crucifix, or splashing Lourdes water around the corners of our rooms at home. These talismans still hold their power for me, but the focus of that power has shifted away from the literal belief in a specific saviour, and they have been joined in my personal fireplace shrine by new objects and idols; a statue of Ganesh, the elephant god given to me by Van, the incense and flowers of Hindu *puja*, prayer flags sent by Chudrun, my grandad's woven straw fedora. I embrace all of the wondrous possibilities of the spirit, without tying myself to one, narrow world view. The cynical atheist would accuse me of fence-sitting, and so be it. I'll still respect them, whatever their own beliefs.

I might go to church once in a while. Christianity is still my frame of reference. It gives me a vocabulary to talk about my personal faith and I still find comfort in the prayers that I have spoken ever since I was a child. But from now on, the church is just a special, pointy house where I can get some peace and quiet, a place to think about God in less specific terms than I used to. Is that OK? Can non-members use the facilities?

I've spent my life swallowing other people's lines on the divine. From now on if anyone asks what I believe in, I'll tell them this:

I believe in love.

Amen.

HUSBAND'S AFTERWORD

Toby

Women: something to consider before your wedding day; your husband will always try to get the last word ...

'Fnnf,' said the minicab driver through his nose as he swung his vomit-scented saloon into a tight, right-hand turn. 'Don't do it is my advice, mate.'

I'd had a lot of this crap in the fortnight leading up to my wedding. Mostly from pale, dishevelled and portly middle-aged men who seemed to think that, had they avoided the pitfall of marriage, they would still be fit, virile, irresistible to women, and twenty-five.

'When's the day, then?'

None of this conversation was my doing. Returning from a shopping trip and a last-minute trip to the tailor, I had stumbled into the cab of an amateur sleuth who deduced my 'predicament', as he called it, from the contrast between my thrift shop attire and the haul of upmarket clothing and accessories cluttering up his back seat.

'Friday.'

'Struth. Like waiting for your execution, isn't it?' growled the driver, warming to his subject. 'You've still got time to make a run for it,' he pointed out. 'Got days. You could get to

France, easy. I can drive you down to the coast, if you like. Find you safe passage.' He roared with laughter, which segued neatly into uncontrollable coughing. I grabbed the door handle as we snaked from side to side across the road.

'I don't want to make a run for it,' I protested, wincing as we slalomed between parked cars. 'I'm really happy to be getting married.'

'Good for you, mate. I daresay she's got hold of your passport already, anyway. Keeping it for the honeymoon, is she? And clipping your wings if you see sense before the big day.'

Sara *was* keeping hold of my passport, along with our E111s and the tickets to Amsterdam, but I wasn't going to give this cantankerous old fucker the satisfaction.

'I don't pretend to understand your personal misery, but I'm less than a week off marrying the woman of my dreams, and I'm pretty bloody excited about it. So if you haven't got anything nice or encouraging to say, can you please keep your opinions to yourself?'

'Sorry, mate,' said the surprised driver as he pulled up at the kerb outside my house. 'No offence meant. Best of luck and all that. Three-twenty.'

I paid in change and dragged my bags up the garden path. The cabbie's rasping voice followed me to the doorstep.

'Dead man walking!'

The obnoxious taxi driver was quickly forgotten as I unpacked my purchases and tried on my wedding outfit from top to toe for the first time. A simple, single-breasted suit, blue/black with a narrow pinstripe, powder-blue shirt with pearl buttons, powder-blue and white striped silk tie; dark tan brogues and my grandfather's cufflinks. I looked a million dollars, for only a fraction of the price. My mother would have wept at the sight, before begging me to shave and do something about my hair.

The crabby cabbie had been way off with his talk of executions. I think it's a fairly safe bet that if that's your state of mind in the week before your wedding, you're on the verge a monumental mistake. For my part, I felt like a kid waiting for Christmas; it couldn't come fast enough. My only worry was that I might roll over on my wedding night only to find that my beautiful new wife was really just my dad in a cotton wool beard.

Children, once school has broken for the holidays, spend the run-up to 25 December staring blankly at *A Raccoon Christmas* on TV. Now, even the under-tens can recognize these endlessly repeated, annual, animated schmaltz fests for the unwatchable shite that they are. When kids sit in front of these saccharine seasonal offerings, they're not really watching at all. They're deep in a hypnotic trance, brains ticking over in neutral; just killing time until the fat guy turns up with their stuff.

In the same way, as the day of our union approached, Sara and I several times discovered each other simply staring into space, willing the hours to pass. On one occasion, Sara accosted me in the corner of our bedroom, where I had been examining the buttons of my suit intently for over twenty minutes.

'What are you doing?' she asked, snapping me out of my daze with a soft hand on my cheek.

'Waiting for Saturday,' I answered, honestly. It was Wednesday.

*

The day came. I slept lightly on the eve of my wedding, and woke at the Battersea home of my old bachelor pad-mate, Andrew, and his wife, Natalie, heavily pregnant with their first child. After seeing Natalie off to her prenatal Pilates class, Andrew and I shared bacon sarnies and our astonishment at how adult life had caught up with us, in his beautifully equipped, but woefully under-used, kitchen. At midday, my best man, Alex, turned up, immaculately dressed in a pair of charcoal Burberry trousers that were cutting off all the blood below his evidently expanding waist. We took the piss for five minutes, then left for the pub round the corner, with Alex in a pair of borrowed strides generous enough to give his circulatory system room to recover before showtime.

At three the cab arrived to carry us over the river to Westminster. By four, I was standing at the north end of the RSA's magnificent red-brick vaults, waiting for Sara to make her entrance.

To be honest, a first-hand account of my wedding would be sketchy at best. From the moment Sara floated into the candlelit basement, to the early-morning stroll, arm in arm, down the Strand to our hotel, I was entranced. The day swept by so fast that I can recall it only as a series of Kodak moments. Still, that's what wedding videos are for, and with a broadcast-quality DVC on loan from the office, and more than one family handycam in the crowd, I can reliably relate the following:

Sara and I had the best wedding in the history of weddings since wedding one.

In 2003, the cost of the average UK wedding had topped £14,000. In London, a city that sucks the money out of your pockets like Rambo sucking venom from a snake-bite, the sky's the limit. Miraculously, through a combination of discreet corner-cutting and major favour-pulling, Sara and I kept our wedding the sane side of £10,000. I know its insanely blokey to begin an account of one's marriage with a financial summary, but believe me, a wedding will max out your credit cards and run up your overdraft, so coming in under budget is a massive bonus on the morning after.

As for the night before ... Well, my most resonant 'spiritual' experiences in my life have been musical. There's R.E.M. at Glastonbury, the Polyphonic Spree at the Union Chapel in Islington (an unwieldy, cassock-wearing improv pop orchestra who play like a Baptist revival choir and made a believer of me for one night in 2002), Handel's *Messiah* at the Proms, and now, our wedding.

Months earlier, we had persuaded my usher, Ed, baby bro of best man Alex, and a pianist of some note, to play Sara down the aisle. As it turned out, our wedding fell neatly between an all-day video shoot and the launch date of his third album. Ed had been touring for months, and hauling his piano from station to studio on a gruelling publicity schedule. Nevertheless, he later admitted to my sister, that those ninety seconds of Wagner for Sara's glide down the aisle rattled his nerves more than any other gig for years.

Ed's hands, which have tickled the ivories for festival crowds in the tens of thousands, were shaking more than mine when the cue came from the far side of the vault, but he played the Hell out of that tune. The plod was gone; it was pure poetry. As Sara entered the room, her dazzling beauty – I mean, she's gorgeous on a daily basis, but *really* – heralded by Ed's divinely delicate playing, produced an audible gasp from the assembled guests. Sara held my gaze as she floated towards me in a strapless gown of white silk and, if you look closely at the footage from Ushercam 1, I swear you can see my knees buckle.

A civil ceremony, however secular, covers much the same ground as the traditional C of E wedding service, and is at times strongly reminiscent of its religious forebear. Bride and groom are called upon to exchange vows of commitment and unity, rings are exchanged, readings read, though not from the Bible, of course. For our wedding, Sara chose a passage by Laurie Lee extolling the virtues of lifelong love, with reading duties taken by another nervous friend, Sarah Ballard, selected for her sonorous tones. In a departure from the path of many church weddings, we did get to enjoy a wonderfully soppy 'you may kiss the bride' moment. This is a modern addition to the marriage ceremony, made popular by Hollywood and absent from the traditional Christian service. It's often incorporated by your trendier vicar, but in my experience, even the Dibley variety find it impossible to allow without letting everyone know that 'this isn't really part of the service, strictly speaking, but . . .'

There was another advantage to a Godless ceremony. Without an altar to face, or an idol to bow before, Sara and I were free to face our assembled guests throughout the ceremony. Now this could have been disastrous if one of us had been racked by last-minute doubts, or reduced to a blubbering wreck during the vows, but fortunately no such face-crumpling catastrophe occurred.

Perhaps it's just my way of looking at the world after writing one too many movie trailers, but to my mind the whole thing ran like a high-class rom-com finale, complete with soaring musical number as Ed came back to the piano to accompany his own beautiful bride-to-be, Gita, on violin. 'La Vie En Rose' had not sounded so magical since Paris's Little Sparrow flapped off to Père-Lachaise after one too many Gitanes.

Ed's big brother Alex, meanwhile, excelled in the best man department, bustling from room to room and being ludicrously nervous on my behalf until well after the buffet was wheeled out. His Equity credentials were put to great use with a speech that echoed around the cavernous cellar like whale song in the open ocean, and raised a laugh without resort to roasting.

'My mother was in the audience,' he later explained. 'I've got endless shit on you, but it's all either illegal or immoral, and most of it implicates me.'

I managed to get through my own speech on the right side of teary-eyed, despite the lengthy roll-call of departed loved ones. My suggestion of eight minutes silence seemed to lift the room, once they realized they had permission to laugh again.

If I'm honest, the biggest gap in the room – the one where my mother should have been – didn't upset me on the day as much as I thought it would. When Mum died, all sorts of subconscious future family scenarios played out in my head. Losing Mum meant rejigging every half-acknowledged daydream: we wouldn't have to worry about her ticket for Junior's graduation; she couldn't be called on for babysitting duties; she wasn't going to see me married . . .

I have become accustomed to my mother's permanent absence and though I still feel it painfully from time to time, those moments of rekindled anguish are never predictable. I'm not the type to look at the calendar and think, it's Mum's birthday on Saturday. I'll be sad. I'm far more likely to get sideswiped by grief when I pass a particular perfume counter,

SARA HULSE & TOBY STARBUCK

or find an old postcard in the bottom of my chaotic sock drawer. At the wedding, there were plenty of tears shed for Mum – by her sister, her cousin, and her closest friends – but I didn't join in. Not because of some stoical sense of propriety, but because I simply didn't feel sad right then.

I don't go in much for communing with the spirit world, as I think we've established. But if I am to articulate my thoughts on Mum and the marriage fully, I'm going to have to borrow some vocab from beyond the veil. In a very real sense, you see, I felt my mother's presence throughout our wedding day.

Sometimes, an absence can be so keenly felt that it becomes a sort of presence. And there were so many people who loved and missed my mother present for the celebrations; so many hand-me-down jewels and trinkets worn in her memory around the room. Everyone who was there, and knew her, could imagine the unadulterated joy that Mum would have taken in seeing Sara enter the Starbuck fold. For those of us, myself included, who have come to terms with the injustice of her early death, and the cruelty of the illness that took her, it was impossible to think of my mum on that most happy day, without picturing the whopping great grin that would have been plastered all over her face like cake mix on a kindergarten cook. Wherever I looked, she was dancing in the shadows, as family and friends laughed and remembered all around her. Her memory was tangible; her influence inestimable. I was reminded again of the inscription on a marble plate, above a rose bed in a Shropshire garden: 'All that remains of us is love.'

My wife. My beautiful wife. Sara Starbuck. Wow.

It's got quite a ring to it, you know, on the morning after, when it means something. I sat, propped up on about a dozen generously stuffed feather pillows, in the swanky suite where Sara and I had shagged and talked until dawn, before passing out in our cosy hotel robes. Room service had been and gone, delivering lattes and freshly squeezed orange juice at an hour that seemed preposterously ambitious in retrospect. Nevertheless, we had arranged to meet parents and brand-new in-laws for breakfast in Covent Garden, so the caffeine and Vitamin C was a welcome substitute for sleep. I listened to Sara splashing about in our Philippe Starke bathroom, and stared in disbelief at the Westminster wedding certificate in my shaky hands. I could feel the weight of the shiny band on my newly initiated ring finger. It tugged at me, tickled the corner of my mouth into a smile. 'You're married,' it said. 'That's your wife next door. In the bath. In the nuddy, I shouldn't wonder.'

For all of our planning and procrastination, Sara and I both admit that in the immediate aftermath of our wedding, we couldn't help feeling that we had done something incredibly rash. 'It's a big step,' people tell the betrothed, who nod and smile vacantly, while they wonder whether to opt for lilies or orchids in the bridal bouquet. Once you've signed the paperwork and swapped the metalwork, however, the 'bigness' of marriage really hits home.

I suspect that for those who truly marry in haste, this is the moment, in the quiet of the honeymoon suite, that the enormity of their error suddenly sinks in. And what a hangover to wake up with. Option A: resign yourself to making the best of it; maybe try a kid to bring you closer together; gradually bore of the effort involved; use kid as weapon against each other in unceasing domestic war of wills;

surrender to acrimonious divorce. Option B: look for a window to climb out of.

But if you *know* you're doing the right thing, then waking up on the morning after your wedding, next to the love of your life, is like dreaming about a fantastic meal, then waking up to find pudding on the bedside table. As I sat in bed, listening to my wife's happy humming through the hotel wall, I felt incredibly close to her. A deeply buried insecurity that I had not even acknowledged in myself – the fear of losing Sara – had vanished overnight. We'd sealed the deal. We were united now; man and wife. It was final and profound and made the cohabitation we had enjoyed for three years seem childish and half-hearted. We may already have built our happy home, but marriage was the retrospective planning permission that made everything legit. Nobody could come along and bulldoze us. We might even try for an extension.

From the bathroom came the noise of a plug being pulled. Sara rounded the corner with a towel in her hair, still humming to herself. 'La Vie En Rose.' I rose from the bed and padded across the deep carpet to fold her still-damp body in my arms. She smiled and sighed, resting her head on my chest.

Fade to black. Roll credits.

EPILOGUE

This is the bit that plays out while the credits are rolling. The bit that starts just after you've decided the film's definitely over and joined the queue to leave, so that you end up craning backwards over your shoulder to see what's going on, while you're shuffled forwards towards the exit by the people who are desperate to get out of the car park before the cinema empties.

We made it to breakfast al fresco in Covent Garden – me, Sara, two sets of parents and siblings and a handful of guests. Sara and I stared sleepily at each other as the others got down to some good old familial bonding, sharing memories of the night before and snapping photos up and down the table. At six o'clock, we'd be boarding a plane to Holland, then a train to Amsterdam, where the world's largest and most comfortable bed was waiting for us. Three nights in 'The Snug' – a warm, womb-like basement flat on the edge of the red light district – would give Sara and me the opportunity to do the newly-wed thing in spectacularly sleazy style. In the meantime, it was good to play host and hostess for one more meal, with our extended family around us.

At the foot of the table, sat my dad, pawing over a guidebook from the museum visit he had somehow already squeezed into the day. Beside him, his partner, Nadine, swapped frock tales with Sara's mother, Eileen. My father-in-law, Alex, waxed lyrical about his temporary home at the Savoy. Emily and bridesmaid Rachel nursed their epic hangovers with scrambled eggs and coffee. My brother-in-law, Jonathan, surprised everyone with the first set of speedily developed wedding snaps.

Dee and Lee, down from Yorkshire, completed the post-wedding breakfast party.

'So, how does it feel, then?' asked Dee, with a window-wiping motion that was either a gesticulative effort to express the idea of 'marriage', or a half-hearted Al Jolson impression. The diners fell silent, their eavesdropping shamelessly exposed. Sara and I scanned their expectant faces and smiled soppily at each other.

'I think that answers your question,' said Alex. 'Say cheese.'

We pulled faces and buried our heads like petulant celebrities. Our fixed smiles and interlacing fingers may have been answer enough for the crowd around the table, but they didn't go halfway to expressing how I felt about waking up as a married man. I wanted to tell Dee and Lee – unmarried but in it for the long haul – to stop worrying about the money, the time and the hassle of organizing a wedding, and just do it. Not because it's the 'right' thing to do. Not because it would get their neighbours off their backs, or reduce the threat of playground bullying for their sprogs. Not even for the sheer thrill of experiencing one day in your life when the world – your world, at least, and everyone in it – genuinely revolves around you. But because getting married is the biggest, boldest promise you will ever make, and it feels fantastic.

Lumbered with a lingering Victorian morality and a sense-less pride in the good old British stiff upper lip, there are still plenty of people out there so emotionally stifled that they utter the words 'I love you' only on very special occasions; spousal birthdays, for example. With marriage, love is a given. However devalued it may have been by the revision of divorce law and broader cultural change, it is still universally recognized as a profound and positive commitment. So profound, in fact, that even the most unfortunate unions face little criticism on the big day itself. Well, we reason, she's marrying him, so he can't be all that bad. However ill-advised our friends' and relatives' choice of partner, when there's nothing else nice to say, we can always fall back on love. 'They're so in love,' we say, as if that will somehow overcome his serial philandering and her smack habit. And you know what? If they really mean it, maybe it can. Because love is what marriage is all about, isn't it? A wedding is basically an opportunity for two people to stand in a big, echoey room and shout at the top of their lungs, 'I love this person! I really, really do!' Where it goes after that is their lookout. They're on their own. But they're on their own *together*.

Before long, we were swilling foam around the bottoms of our coffee cups and fiddling with the catches on our hand luggage, buoyed by the family's happy faces, but eager to be alone together again. There was a protracted round of cuddles and fare-thee-wells as we shouldered our bags and scanned the traffic for taxi lights. As Sara's mum and dad took turns trying to hug me two sizes smaller, I was overcome with a sense of belonging – of family – that had been all too rare since my mother's death.

Jonathan stepped into the road to hail a cab. Sara and I peeled ourselves away, then turned back to face the waving well-wishers. I panned across the smiling faces, from my dad and Nadine, arm in arm, to my warm and welcoming in-laws. We were so different, our two families. Catholics versus iconoclasts. CND vs C of R. And yet, despite their various reading habits and Sunday morning routines, I knew we'd get along just fine.

The common thread that binds our different families together is a deep sense of moral obligation. We have all grown up with very solid ideas of what constitutes responsible, sympathetic behaviour. Sara's family would no doubt see this as all part of being a good Christian. In my own family's case, the religious imperative for good behaviour has been erased over two generations without any apparent harm done to our innate sense of right and wrong. Either way, I know that whatever life throws at our now united family, every problem will be approached with respectful, responsible and loving motives.

'Family' means support, love, kindness and care – involuntary and unconditional – when it matters and whatever the circumstances. For the faithful, this is what God provides, too. But God, unlike our fragile families, is unaffected by the ravages of time. And perhaps this is His core role. God is a parent that won't go away.

Well, I don't need Him. I'm not rejecting God any more, in an active, angry sort of way. I simply don't feel the lack of love, from parent or partner, that would necessitate recourse to a 'higher love'. This is the real world, where things change and people grow old and die. I've learned that if you face the future with love, tolerance and hope, instead of regret, pessimism and self-righteous surety, spirituality becomes a tangible quality of your inner life. Religion can never fully express the 'soulfulness' of human existence, because of its reliance on formalized doctrine that is often at odds with common human experience. Individual faiths may capture elements of our spirit, but looking for God through any one faith is like pinning the tail on the donkey. Only with no donkey. Because I love and am loved, I am a good person. Sorry if that sounds like blowing my own trumpet, but I do believe it. I know right from wrong and I act accordingly because I want the world I live in to be a nice place. I take it on trust that other right-minded people, regardless of any particular religious beliefs, think similarly and will, on balance, behave themselves, too. I don't need God to feel loved, or to tell me what to do when a dilemma presents itself. Heaven help me if I ever do.

Sara and I hope to have children of our own. It's not an unusual ambition for newly-weds; personally, I think the 'ding' part of the word 'wedding' might have something to do with the sound timers make when your eggs are ready. The point being that I'm actually looking forward to bringing a child up in a comparatively diverse household, with a mother and grandparents who will open the door to the possibility of faith, where my own childhood pretty much nailed it shut. This is by no mean a reversal of my earlier position. I maintain that a child raised in a strong, single-faith environment is at a distinct intellectual disadvantage when it comes to making up their adult mind about matters metaphysical. But in the spirit of steadfast agnosticism, I must acknowledge that the kids who see both sides of the coin while growing up might be getting the best of both worlds. At the very least, my children will grow up with a real choice to make. And if I'm serious about a child's right to form their own opinions, rather than mirror my own, I will have to let my children hear voices other than my own. I will not encourage them to believe, for I cannot sincerely promote religion over reason, but I will encourage to them to follow their parents' example, whatever the outcome. Get out there and have a look around.

To my unborn children, the next big love of my life, a little premonitory paternal advice that you can chuck back in my face in the years to come: Find your own path – but go easy on the mushrooms.

Throughout our dear friend Vandana's illness, Sara had made visits to her Kilburn home, keeping in touch by phone in between trips. When the severity of Van's treatment put her out of action for a while, her husband Gav would fire off an email to keep everyone in the loop. It was a desperate situation, we all knew, but nobody doubted Van's determination to beat the disease. So of course, beat it she would; she was indomitable. Only, as it turned out, she wasn't.

Gav and Van had dropped off the radar for while when we got the call from one of Gavin's college friends. A few days later, we found ourselves standing in a flower-strewn hall in the grey, windy Midlands, surrounded by the same loving faces that had smiled and laughed with us at Van's wedding just a year earlier, this time streaked with tears.

Van's death was a terrible blow to everyone who knew her and especially to her devoted husband. Gavin dealt with grief the same way he had dealt with Van's illness; stoically, nobly, finding comfort in his friends and peace in his own nameless brand of spirituality.

As winter gave way to spring, Sara visited Gav at the home he and Van had shared in north London.

'You know, I really would do it all again,' he told her as they thumbed through old photograph albums. 'Even if I knew exactly how things would turn out. If I knew every last detail of what was in store for us, I wouldn't change a thing . . . I'd do it all again to spend one more second in the company of that beautiful, brilliant, incredible woman.'

This book is dedicated to that beautiful, brilliant, incredible woman, Vandana Andrews. With all our love.

ACKNOWLEDGEMENTS

Our family and friends, much neglected while writing this book; thank you for your patience.

Tif Loehnis and Toby Mundy, for kick-starting our adventure and having faith in us.

Louisa Joyner, for all of your hard work, enthusiasm and passion.

We are indebted to the following people for their time, hospitality and cooperation. Without them we'd still be chasing rainbows: Father Liam Griffin: the English language chaplain-coordinator of the Lourdes sanctuary, Peter and Jane Walmsley, Sameer and Parminder from Baga Beach, Father Mario Pires, Ani Chudrun, Ron Ford and Michael Alcorn, Tristan Morell (www.geocities.com/Athens/Rhodes/2922/tristan.htm, Juliusz Wodzianski, (www.JuliuszW.com), Dr Rebecca Earle from the University of Warwick, Will Harcourt-Smith, Amira Thoron, Dee Lunn and Lee Barker, Dr. Mark Lythgoe: endocrinologist: Ph.D, at Institute of Child Health, University College London (www.mlythgoe.com), Zoë the Spirit Release Therapist, Laurie Nicoletti from Ravishing Affairs and Richard Holloway.

Special thanks to Sara's blushing bride research group: Natasha Mountford, Siobhán McMurray, Natalie Turner, Sophie Laurimore, Jackie Campbell.